INFORMATION-BASED SYNTAX AND SEMANTICS

CSLI
Lecture Notes
Number 13

INFORMATION-BASED SYNTAX AND SEMANTICS

Volume 1
FUNDAMENTALS

Carl Pollard
and Ivan A. Sag

CSLI was founded early in 1983 by researchers from Stanford University, SRI International, and Xerox PARC to further research and development of integrated theories of language, information, and computation. CSLI headquarters and the publication offices are located at the Stanford site.

CSLI/SRI International
333 Ravenswood Avenue
Menlo Park, CA 94025

CSLI/Stanford
Ventura Hall
Stanford, CA 94305

CSLI/Xerox PARC
3333 Coyote Hill Road
Palo Alto, CA 94304

Library of Congress Cataloging-in-Publication Data

Pollard, Carl Jesse.
Information-based syntax and semantics.

(CSLI lecture notes ; no. 13)
Bibliography: v. 1, p.
Contents: v. 1. Fundamentals.

1. Grammar, Comparative and general–Syntax.
2. Semantics. 3. Phrase structure grammar. 4. Information theory.
I. Sag, Ivan A., 1949– II. Title. III. Series.
P291.P63 1987 415 87–71618
Library of Congress Catalog Card Number: 87–71618
ISBN 0–937073–24–5 (Paper)
ISBN 0–937073–23–7 (Cloth)

Printed in the United States

Preface

The work reported in this book, undertaken from fall 1984 through summer 1987, belongs to a long-term research program with the ambitious goal of establishing rigorous mathematical foundations for linguistic theory. Within this research program, two closely related subgoals are to be distinguished, one general and one specific. The general subgoal is to develop a class of mathematical structures suitable for modelling natural language phenomena, together with a logical formalism interpreted by these structures, in terms of which it is possible to formulate precise linguistic theories with determinate empirical consequences. The specific subgoal is to produce a series of such theories, by selectively drawing upon and synthesizing insights and results from a wide range of contemporary syntactic and semantic research communities.

In this book, which is intended primarily for an audience of graduate students and professional researchers in syntactic-semantic theory, we sketch the underlying mathematics in fairly nontechnical terms, and then use it to formulate a particular linguistic theory, head-driven phrase structure grammar (HPSG), which freely avails itself of ideas from categorial grammar, discourse representation theory, generalized phrase structure grammar, government-binding theory, lexical-functional grammar, and situation semantics. This is not to say that the theory is purely eclectic; our presentation includes numerous original ideas that should be judged on their own merit. But we believe that much of the theory's interest resides in the novel way in which it weaves into a common intellectual fabric materials from distinct traditions which have often viewed each other with indifference or hostility. By recasting ideas from different frameworks within a common formalism, it becomes possible to compare, modify, and combine them in a meaningful and mutually advantageous way.

With all due respect to the numerous predecessors and colleagues whose ideas we have appropriated or adapted, we believe the theory set forth here compares favorably with the ones we have cannibalized, in terms of degree of explicitness, precision of formalization, breadth of coverage, conceptual clarity, aesthetic elegance, equal attention to both syntactic and semantic matters, and conformity with the facts. At the same time, many critical issues remain to be explored. For this reason, we have left many questions unresolved in this book, pointing out wherever we can open problems and the potential advantages or disadvantages of particular directions of inquiry. The reader may find this unsatisfying at various points, but this is as it should be; no theory is ever complete. Our aim in adopting an eclectic, synthetic approach has been to take advantage of the perspectives of many different research traditions and at the same time to show that they can all be seen as parts of a single enterprise. We hope that the background provided by this book will provide a point of departure for the development of further, more adequate linguistic theories which draw both inspiration and substance from the successes of the whole field, without dogmatism or prejudice.

It would be impossible for us to pay the intellectual debt we have incurred to all the students and colleagues who have discussed with us the ideas presented here and who have helped us to weed out many of the infelicities and mistakes in earlier versions. Nonetheless, we shall try.

In the formative stages of our thinking, we were influenced primarily by discussions with members of the Winter 1985 Unification Seminar at Stanford's Center for the Study of Language and Information, especially Mark Johnson, Lauri Karttunen, Martin Kay, Fernando Pereira, Stuart Shieber, and Tom Wasow. As the main outlines of our project began to emerge, we profited greatly from ongoing discussions with many of these same people, as well as with Bob Borsley, Lew Creary, Dan Flickinger, Mark Gawron, Gerald Gazdar, Jeff Goldberg, Takao Gunji, Kris Halvorsen, Geoff Huck, Bob Kasper, Drew Moshier, John Nerbonne, Geoff Pullum, Bill Rounds, Mats Rooth, Peter Sells, Hans Uszkoreit, and Annie Zaenen.

Tom Hukari, John Nerbonne, Fernando Pereira, Bill Rounds, Peter Sells, and Tom Wasow were kind enough to provide valuable and detailed comments on early drafts. As the book neared its present form, the following people also helped us by noting errors of both form and substance and suggesting improvements: Alex Alsina, Chris Culy, Cheri Garcia, Kathryn Henniss, Evan Kirshenbaum, Bente Maegard, K. P. Mohanan, and Chris Tancredi. We are grateful, too, to the numerous students and colleagues whose work on concrete linguistic problems and computer implementations so often imposed much-needed reality checks on ill-considered or insufficiently precise preliminary formulations. They include Susan Brennan, Mary Dalrymple, Lyn Friedman, Dave Goddeau, Masayo Iida, Smita Joshi, Derek Proudian, Diana Roberts, and Simran Singh.

We owe a special debt of gratitude to Dikran Karagueuzian, editor and friend, without whose intelligence, humor, and sense of proportion the creation of this book would have been a far longer and far less pleasant task. Thanks are due as well to Tom Burke, Kaija Lewis, Emma Pease, Lucie Pollard, and Lynne Ruggles, who assisted in various stages of manuscript preparation. And we also take this opportunity to express appreciation to the agencies and institutions whose support has made the work that went into this book not merely plausible, but possible: to the National Science

Foundation, for the grants (BNS-8511687 to Stanford University and BNS-8718156 to Carnegie Mellon University) that supported our research; to the System Development Foundation, for a gift to the Center for the Study of Language and Information; and to the Hewlett-Packard Company, for access to the technical staff and computing facilities of its laboratories in Palo Alto, and for an equipment grant to Stanford University. But our deepest thanks go to the members of our families: Claire, Becca, Lucie, and Penny, for loving us and for enduring the all too numerous interruptions of family life that writing this book has caused. They have made all the difference.

Contents

1 Introduction

What kind of thing is a human language? What is the connection between the sound of a word or phrase, its grammatical structure, and its message or content? What kinds of things are language sounds, grammatical structures, and the pieces of information that linguistic utterances convey? What is it to know a language, and what is it about a language that makes it possible for people who know it to exchange information? The purpose of this book is to present a certain set of concepts, tools, and methods for seeking answers to questions like these. More specifically, we will try to introduce and develop an *information-based* approach to the study of natural language syntax and semantics, an approach that considers the objects that make up a human language as bearers of information within the community of people who know how to use them.

Information-based linguistics has its roots in a number of distinct research traditions within linguistics and neighboring disciplines such as philosophy, logic, and computer science. Thus we will be drawing upon and attempting to synthesize insights and perspectives from several families of contemporary syntactic theories (such as categorial grammar, lexical-functional grammar (LFG), phrase structure grammar, and government-binding (GB) theory); but many of the key ideas arise from semantic theories such as situation semantics and discourse representation structure (DRS) theory, and from computational work in such areas as knowledge representation, data type theory, and unification-based formalisms. There will be ample time to explore such connections in the chapters to come; but to get started, we would do well to consider what sorts of things the objects are that linguistic theory studies.

1.1 Conceptualism and Realism

What sort of thing is a natural language object, say, the English common noun *cookie*? Is it a mental object, something which only exists in the minds of English speakers? Or is it a part of the real world, external to minds? This is one of the fundamental questions in the philosophy of language, and it is a question that is hotly debated today, not only by philosophers, but by syntacticians, semanticists, and cognitive scientists.

On the one hand, it is obvious that a token utterance of the word *cookie* is a real-world event which includes an articulation of speech sounds, a transmission of sound waves, an act of auditory perception, etc. It is equally obvious that the word *cookie* is used to talk about cookies—or, more generally, situations which involve cookies—and that cookies too are something in the real world. It is possible, then, to view a natural language as a system of correspondences between certain kinds of events (utterances) and the kinds of objects or situations in the world that the utterances are about; users of the language exploit those correspondences in order to communicate. This is the essence of the perspective which has come to be known as *linguistic realism*. For the realist, the study of language is best limited to the classification and internal structure of things and events outside the language user. Realists do not deny that the mind exists, or even, necessarily, that language is mentally represented; but according to the realist, the mind and mental representations are not what linguistics is about.

On the other hand, it seems clear that the users of a natural language could not communicate linguistically without *knowing* the correspondences between types of utterances and things in the world which the language embodies. We say of an English speaker that he *knows* English. *Linguistic conceptualism*, also called *mentalism*, *representationalism*, or *psychologism*, is the view according to which a natural language is a mental system learned and shared by the members of a communicating group of organisms. According to conceptualism, then, linguistics is about psychological objects which *represent* things in external reality, not about external reality itself. Of course conceptualism does not deny that utterance events—or the things in the world that utterances decribe—actually exist. But for conceptualists, such things are merely outward manifestations of language, not language itself.

One of the most influential proponents of linguistic conceptualism in this century was the Swiss philologist Ferdinand de Saussure, who is often credited with the creation of modern linguistics (i.e. the study of languages as synchronic systems in their own right, in contradistinction to the historical-comparative studies characteristic of most earlier linguistics). Saussure considered linguistics to be a part of social psychology. And language (*langue*) itself he described as a shared psychological system of things called *signs*. In Saussure's conception, a sign was a mental associative bond (*lien de l'association*) between two component mental objects called the *signifiant* (the signifier) and the *signifié* (the thing signified), as illustrated in (1). The *signifiant* here is what might nowadays be called a phonological representation, the psychological image of the sound of the word "cookie"; the *signifié* is what might be called a semantic representation, the psychological concept of cookiehood. For Saussure, the possibility of linguistic communication arose from the sharing of a sign system among the members of a community.

(1)

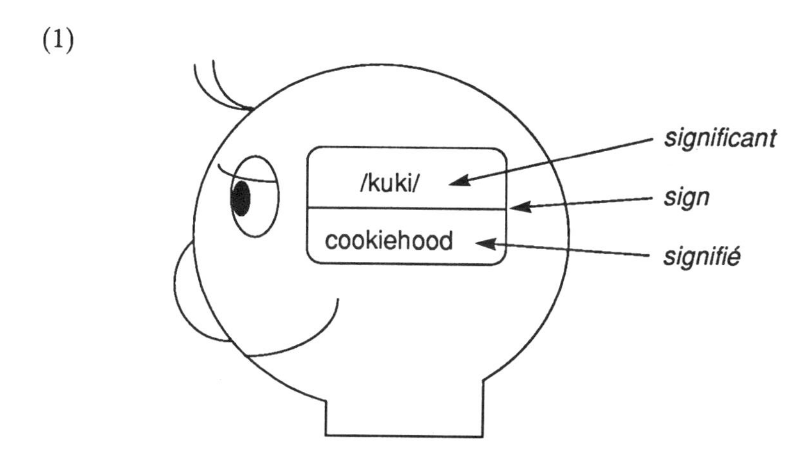

Mentalism, of course, fell into disrepute during the era of American linguistic structuralism, conventionally dated from the publication of Leonard Bloomfield's *Language* in 1933 to the appearance of Noam Chomsky's *Syntactic Structures* in 1957. Strongly influenced—at least in principle—by Bloomfield's logical-positivistic and behavioristic sympathies, the structuralists were little concerned with language use or with meaning (except as a diagnostic for nonidentity of linguistic forms); the bulk of linguistic activity consisted in the gathering and classification of data from the languages of the world. The chief theoretical constructs of American structural linguistics, such as the morpheme and the phoneme, were generally regarded not as psychological objects but as classes of physical events. Whatever went on in speaker's minds was considered to be inaccessible to empirical study, and therefore outside the realm of linguistic science.

It is not clear to what extent Bloomfield's essentially realist ideology really affected the everyday practices of structural linguists. It is clear, though, that within a few years after Chomsky's introduction of transformational generative syntax, mentalism had reasserted itself as the conventional view within the linguistic community; and few linguists nowadays, regardless of theoretical persuasion, doubt that the human mind, or some part of it, is their principal object of study. It is not hard to see why the reemergence of mentalism should coincide with the emergence of linguistic syntax as an object of study. Syntactic objects—phrases and sentences—are obviously infinite in number. Unlike phonemes or morphemes, we can never obtain an exhaustive characterization of them by-classifying data gathered in field studies. Instead, the principal technique has been to characterize syntax in terms of *finite systems of recursively applicable rules*, relying largely upon *judgments of grammaticality* by native speakers. Grammaticality judgments, though, are evidently based upon reflection on something internal to the speaker. And it is difficult to imagine just what in the outside world we might take a recursive rule system to be;

but it seems quite plausible that such rules might be embodied as systems of knowledge inside speakers' minds.

There is less uniformity of opinion among semanticists on the issue of conceptualism vs. realism. This may well be simply because there has not been enough time—or enough semanticists!—for a consensus to develop. Since the mid-1970's, the dominant paradigm for linguistic semantics has been that of Richard Montague. But Montague's approach was to characterize natural language meaning in terms of truth and entailment in abstract set-theoretic models, much in the same way that a mathematical logician would give a semantics for an artificial logical language; and there is no obvious sense in which Montague's *possible-worlds models* favor either a conceptualist or a realist interpretation. In recent years, semanticists who have concerned themselves with the issue have generally fallen into one camp or the other. Closer to the mainstream, but not clearly in the ascendancy, have been those who see the objects of linguistic semantics as conceptual representations or mental models, such as Jerry Fodor, Ray Jackendoff, and Hans Kamp. The principal challengers to this view have been Jon Barwise and John Perry, whose *situation semantics* seeks to replace both possible-worlds semantics and representationalism with a thoroughgoing realism.

According to situation semantics, the world is made up of such things as *individuals* (like Jon Barwise or the moon), *properties* (such as being a cookie or being a donkey), *relations* (such as seeing or kicking), as well as *situations*. Roughly, situations are limited parts of the world which consist of individuals having (or not having) properties, or being (or not being) in relations. An example of a situation is the particular event of Carl Pollard eating a certain orange in Office D-2 at Ventura Hall, Stanford University, at 9:42 p.m. PST, December 2, 1986. Individuals, relations, properties, and situations are real, but different groups of organisms are *attuned* to different ones in accordance with the exigencies of their ecology; as it is sometimes put, different communities of creatures "tear the universe apart along different seams."

What does this have to do with meaning? According to situation semantics, meaning arises from *constraints* that hold between different kinds of situations. For example, any situation that has smoke in it is part of a situation that has fire in it. We say smoke *means* fire; any organism that is attuned to this constraint can pick up from a smokey situation the information that there is fire. So it is with language, but in that case the constraints involved are not *natural* ones; rather, they are *conventional* linguistic constraints that can be exploited by the people who are attuned to them, as when an English speaker acquires from an utterance of "Here is a cookie" the information that there is a cookie. Linguistic meaning, then, is a relation that holds between types of utterance situations and the types of things in the world that utterances decribe. This view is called the *relational theory of meaning*. It is a realistic view because it locates meaning not in speakers' heads but in the world.

Adopting the relational theory of meaning, one might reinterpret the components of the Sausurean sign (1) in realistic terms as follows: the *signifiant* is a certain type of utterance situation, namely one where "cookie" is uttered; the *signifié* is a certain property of things in the world, namely the property of being a cookie. And the sign itself is not a psychological association, but rather the real-world linguistic-meaning relation (constraint) between the *signifiant* and the *signifié*. On this view, a natural language such as English is not a shared mental system but rather a type of linguistic-meaning situation in which certain conventional constraints are observed. The English "cookie" sign, then, is a subtype of English linguistic-meaning situation: the type of situation where "cookie" is used to mean cookie. This is illustrated in (2):

(2)

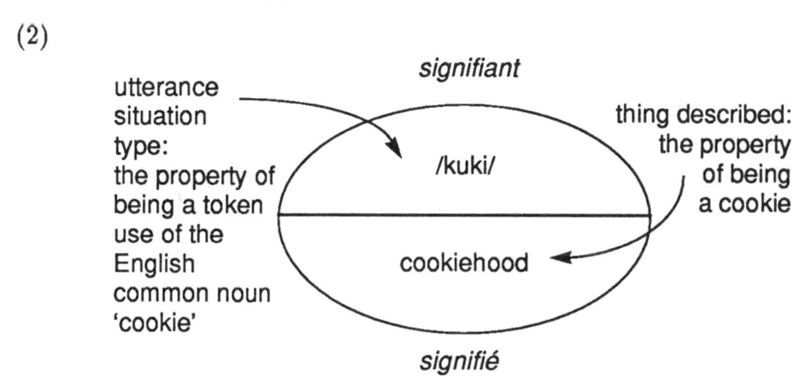

It is important to keep in mind that a sign such as (2) is a *type* of situation, not a situation itself. An actual language-use situation where "cookie" is uttered with the meaning cookie is an instance, or token, of that type. To avoid confusion, we shall sometimes speak of *sign tokens* when it is important to distinguish the occasions of use from the signs themselves.

In spite of the fact that the mentalistic and the realistic views of language have usually been held to be in an adversarial relationship, it is not clear that the two views are fundamentally incompatible. Meanings are meaningful only to those organisms who are attuned to the constraints that give rise to them; in the case of conventional constraints (including linguistic ones), this attunement consists of knowledge that is socially shared, culturally transmitted, and mentally encoded. It seems pointless to prolong the debate about whether the language is the system of situation types that conform to the conventions, or the system of shared knowledge by virtue of which the conventions can be used and transmitted. Given that the organisms and their minds are themselves constituents of linguistic-meaning situations in any case, the difference between the two may well be far less significant than recent debates have suggested. Fortunately, it does not seem necessary to settle this question in order to have a workable linguistic theory. Much as a physicist can go about his or her business without being clear about the philosophical status of theoretical constructs in quantum mechanics, so linguists can theorize about signs without knowing for sure whether they are the mind, out of the mind, or somewhere in between. At the same time, of course, we would do well to be on the alert for evidence that might help resolve the issue one way or the other.

1.2 Linguistic Information

In this book, we will try to walk a tightrope between conceptualism and realism. Instead of dealing directly with signs, we will consider a natural language in terms of the *information* that it makes available to the members of a certain community. We will be concerned primarily with hypotheses about how that information is structured so as to make communication possible; but we will set aside questions as to whether that structure arises from features of the organism, features of the environment, or both. To put it another way, we believe it would be premature to make particular claims about the relationship between the information structures that we posit and the structures of those mental objects that actually encode linguistic knowledge inside human brains. If indeed the hypotheses that we set forth about the nature of universal grammar can be correctly construed as being about mental phenomena, then they should be subjected to empirical verification on the basis of psycholinguistic experimentation. Of course, all linguistic theories are on an equal footing in this respect. Thus, we would argue, the theory set forth here—called *head-driven phrase structure grammar* (HPSG) on account of the central importance of the notion of *the head constituent of a phrase*—is of no less interest to those who seek an understanding of the psychology of language than other current linguistic theories, such as GB and LFG, which have advanced strong claims about the connection between their respective posited structures and mental representations. With such theories, HPSG shares a concern about such matters as modularity of design and the deduction of particular facts from the complex interaction of general principles; as will become clear in later chapters, the family resemblance is strong enough that we have had little difficulty in adapting significant chunks of other theories, e.g. LFG's lexical rules and GB's binding principles, and incorporating them (albeit not without significant modifications) into our own framework.

Although our rhetorical stance is more cautious than that taken by some advocates of other theories, we doubt that this fact reflects any important difference in the potential psychological significance of the theories in question. Indeed, HPSG shares with certain other current linguistic theories (including LFG, the LFG-related approach of Fenstad et al. (1985), as well as some recent variants of categorial grammar proposed by Karttunen (1986); Uszkoreit (1986a); and Zeevat et al. (1987)), and also with computational linguistic formalisms such as functional unification grammar (FUG)(Kay (1985)) and PATR-II (Shieber (1984); Shieber et al. (1983)), a number of design features that may well prove to be of relevance for understanding the relationship between linguistic information—including both the general information which consitutes the object of linguistic knowledge and specific information which a language-user has about a particular language-use situation—and the uses to which such information is put during actual human language processing. In all these theories and formalisms, linguistic objects are analyzed in terms of *partial information structures* (discussed in detail in Chapter 2) which mutually constrain possible collocations of phonological structure, syntactic structure, semantic content, and contextual factors in actual linguistic situations. Such objects are in essence data structures which specify values for attributes; their capability to bear information of non-trivial complexity arises from their potential for recursive embedding (the value of some attribute may be another information structure with internal structure of its own) and structure-sharing (one and the same structure may occur as the value of distinct attributes in a larger structure). Crucially, too, such structures can naturally be viewed as partially ordered according to their relative degree of informativeness: we say one structure is *subsumed* by a second in case it contains at least as much information as the second. In LFG, grammatical functions are described in terms of such objects; in GPSG, syntactic categories are. But in HPSG, following ideas due originally to Martin Kay, so are lexical entries, phrase structure trees, semantic contents, and even the rules and principles of grammar.

Thus HPSG exemplifies *par excellence* the family of grammatical theories which have come to be known as *unification-based* (see Shieber (1986) for an excellent introductory survey). The name arises from the algebra that governs partial information structures: the fundamental operation upon them is the *unification* operation, which yields from a set of compatible structures a structure which contains all the information present in the members of the set, but nothing else. Underlying all such theories is the assumption that in actual language-use situations, whatever the processing task at hand (e.g. interpretation, production, making judgments of acceptability, playing language games, translation, etc.), the specification of a token linguistic object comes about in a cumulative (or *monotonic*) fashion via the interaction of constraints arising from several sources, including lexical entries (which contain phonological, syntactic, and semantic information), the grammar rules that combine them, language-specific and language-universal principles of well-formedness, as well as the particular language-use situation itself (i.e. contextual factors); the final result is obtained by unifying the information from all these various sources. Yet the theories themselves are purely declarative (as opposed to procedural) in the sense that they characterize *what* constraints are brought to bear during language use independently of *what order* the constraints are applied in.[1] In addition, the theories themselves are unbiased as to the kind of processing task at hand; more specifically, they are *reversible* in the sense that they are neutral with respect to interpretation versus production. The "common pool of constraints" (as Fenstad et al. (1985) put it) is freely accessible to the full range of potentially quite distinct processing mechanisms that come into play during language use.

On a realistic reading, such theories accord well with the relational theory of meaning, holding as it does that linguistic meaning arises from conventional constraints between types of utterance situations and the types of things in the world that utterances describe. But at the same time, the monotonicity, declarativeness, and reversibility of theories based upon the unification of partial information structures (as opposed to derivational theories wherein totally specified linguistic structures are successively *transformed* into different structures according to a rigid ordering) dispose them well toward embedding their theoretical constructs into a model of language use which takes into account the obvious flexibility and portability of human linguistic processing.[2] Indeed, there is every reason to believe that in the course of language use, diverse kinds of information, including both linguistic (e.g. syntactic, lexical, semantic and phonological) information, often of a fragmentary nature, and contextual information, as well as general world knowledge, are *interleaved*, i.e. brought to bear in a complex, incremental, nondirectional (and in all likelihood highly parallel) fashion. Declarative, partial information which can be accumulated piecemeal without affecting the final result may be flexibly consulted in language processing; since there are no destructive operations, the partial information associated with a piece of an utterance remains true of that utterance, no matter how much additional information is acquired. Linguistic information of all kinds may thus be directly integrated with other kinds of knowledge on an as-needed basis, whatever the linguistic task at hand: the common information pool is equally accessible to one process that takes non-linguistic information as input and produces strings of words as output (a generator), and to another that takes word strings as input, producing semantic information as output (a parser). In actual use, both kinds of device (among others) are at work; yet both can be assumed to depend ultimately upon the same system of linguistic information. Grammars of the sort we present here should be regarded as models of that system.

---

[1] The advantages of monotonic and declarative constraints as opposed to the traditional generative view (wherein phonology and semantics are "interpretive" components driven off of a "generative" syntax component) are discussed at length in Fenstad et al. (1985), particularly with respect to the task of determining the semantic interpretation of an utterance.

[2] For further discussion of this point, see Sag et al. (1986).

One way to understand our notion of linguistic information is to consider the problem of language understanding. Suppose that Rebecca, an English speaker, has just been told "Your cookie is on the table". She is confronted with the problem of determining which type of English linguistic-meaning situation—which sign—she is participating in, e.g. the "Your cookie is on the table" type, the "Look out for the truck" type, etc. What does she have to go on? Of course she has perceptually derived information about the sound of the utterance and other surrounding circumstances. But as an English speaker, she is attuned to a whole system of signs; therefore she has the ability to recognize different parts of the situation that she is in as tokens of different English signs, much as she can recognize her sister Claire as a baby or the fussy yellow kitty from down the block as a cat.

For example, by recognizing part of the utterance as an instance of the sound [kUki], she can exploit her attunement to the English *lexical* sign which relates that sound type to the cookie property, thereby obtaining the information that a subpart of the linguistic-meaning situation at hand is an instance of that sign. That is, she uses the "cookie" sign in order to get partial information about the linguistic situation she is in, including the information that it has something to do with cookies.

Such lexical signs are the simplest signs. Rebecca gets further information from more complex signs called *grammar rules*. For example, simplifying somewhat, there is a type of English situation that we might call the "S → NP VP" type. Any situation of that type fits the following description. To begin with, just like a token of a lexical sign, it has a certain sound and describes a situation. That is, it has a phonology and a semantics. But unlike a lexical sign token, an S → NP VP situation has in addition a *constituent structure*. This constituent structure consists of two parts which are familiar from traditional grammar as the subject and the predicate; they themselves are sign tokens. Moreover, in any S → NP VP situation, certain conditions must obtain. The subject and predicate have to be tokens of certain types, called "NP" and "VP" respectively. The sound must be what you get by uttering the sounds of the subject and the predicate in rapid succession. And the situation described by the whole must be the same situation that the predicate describes, although the subject will provide some additional information about it. Finally, the whole situation is a token of a certain type called "S"; that will affect its possibilities for being a constituent of some still larger English situation (e.g. one of the type "I think that ..."). Of course, S → NP VP is only one of the English grammar rules. There are others, but not very many more, in fact far fewer than there are lexical signs. Between them, the English lexical signs and the English grammar rules exhaust the possibilities for English signs. Each time Rebecca uses her knowledge of a lexical sign or rule, she derives further information about the linguistic situation at hand.

In addition to such language-specific information, still more linguistic information arises from constraints which are not particular to a single rule of a single language, but which hold cross-linguistically of all language-use situations. Such constraints are called *universal principles*. For example, it is a universal principle—the *Head Feature Principle*—that certain features of a sign token (such as its case and inflectional form) are shared with a certain constituent (called the *head* constituent). If the communication was successful, Rebecca zeros in on the type of her linguistic situation by combining sensory data with pieces of linguistic information derived from lexical signs, grammar rules, and principles of universal grammar. The structure of such information will be our principal concern in this book.

1.3 HPSG: A Preview

One of the most significant contributions of unification-based linguistics has been the development of a common, mathematically precise formalism within which a wide range of distinct theories (and differing hypotheses about a given phenomenon in the context of a fixed theory) can be explicitly constructed and meaningfully compared. Inadequate formalization of some theories has often made it difficult or impossible to determine their empirical consequences (that is, strictly speaking, they were not quite theories!). In addition, notational differences have tended to make comparison of results across theories difficult, or to prevent work conducted within one "framework" from being duly appreciated by adherents of a different research tradition. In Chapter 2, we set forth in not overly technical terms the common formal foundations upon which unification-based linguistic theories are built: the subsumption ordering and unification operation on feature structures; other logical operations on feature structures (disjunction, implication, and negation); and the logical structure of linguistic theories. In addition, we present some tools for working with feature structures borrowed from current computational work on knowledge representation and data types, such as feature structure types and inheritance; list and set values; and functionally dependent values. These tools are of sufficient expressive power that very considerable portions of most current linguistic theories can be formalized through their use (at least to the extent that the theorists' intentions are sufficiently clear to admit formalization of any kind). Indeed, numerous variant theories from research traditions as diverse as categorial grammar, DRS theory, GPSG, LFG, situation semantics, systemic grammar, and—most recently—GB, have all been implemented within unification-based formalisms, both in principle and in running computer-based natural language processing systems.

A pleasant and important consequence of this highly favorable state of affairs is the rapid obsolescence of a certain authoritarianism in the sociology of the field, which has dictated that one's investigations are to be conducted in the "right" framework and that one's fruitful collegial interactions are to be confined to devotees of the "right" research tradition. Fortunately, the contemporary linguistic researcher need not be bound by the orthodoxies dictated by his or her teachers' and senior colleagues' doctrinal affiliations. With the development of an expressive and formally precise *lingua franca*, essentially the full range of current theories can be composed, decomposed, compared, recombined, and generally tinkered with, in a manner constrained only by the individual researcher's aesthetic sense, philosophical predispositions, and responsibility to get the facts right.

As we proceed, it will become evident to readers familiar with a range of contemporary syntactic and semantic theories of language that many of the constructs and hypotheses of HPSG—perhaps most of them—are borrowed or adapted from elsewhere. Thus, for example, the HPSG treatment of syntactic features and categories (Chapter 3) borrows freely from work in GPSG. Indeed, two of the proposed principles of universal grammar, the *Head Feature Principle* (HFP) and the *Binding Inheritance Principle* (BIP) are in essence reformulations of GPSG's Head Feature Convention (HFC) and Foot Feature Principle (FFP). Roughly speaking, the syntactic category of a sign is analyzed as an assemblage of attribute-value (or feature-value) specifications; and syntactic features are classified as *head* features, *binding* features, or the *subcategorization* feature, depending on which universal principle constrains their behavior. Head features, such as part of speech, the case of nouns, and the inflectional form of verbs, are subject to the HFP, which requires that the head features of a phrasal sign be shared with its head daughter; thus the case of an NP is determined by the case of its head noun and the inflectional form of a verb phrase (or of a sentence) is determined by its head verb. Binding features, which encode syntactic dependencies of signs that are essentially nonlocal in nature (i.e. not determined by the lexical head of the phrase) such as the presence of "gaps", relative pronouns, and interrogative elements, are subject to the BIP, which requires that information about such dependencies be transmitted upward through the consituent structure of signs until such a point is reached that the dependency in question can become "bound" or "discharged"; for example, by virtue of the BIP, information about the gap in the sentence *On whom does Kim believe we can rely __?* (e.g. that it must be "filled" by a PP headed by the preposition *on*) will be passed upward from the gap position, from daughter to mother, until the point in the constituent structure where the "gappy" S *does Kim believe we can rely* __ is combined with the interoggative PP *on whom*.

A third principle of universal grammar posited by HPSG, the *Subcategorization Principle*, is essentially a generalization of the "argument cancellation" employed in categorial grammar. The subcategorization (or valence, or combinatory potential) of an HPSG sign is decribed by a special feature called the *subcategorization* feature (usually abbreviated SUBCAT), whose value is simply a list of the kinds of signs with which the sign in question must combine in order to become *saturated* (e.g. in the case of a verb, in order to make a complete sentence). For example, simplifying slightly, the SUBCAT value of the past-tense intransitive verb *walked* is the list ⟨NP[NOM]⟩ since *walked* must combine with a single NP in nominative case (the subject) to become saturated; the past-tense transitive verb *liked* has the SUBCAT value ⟨NP[ACC], NP[NOM]⟩ since *liked* requires both an accusative-case NP (the direct object) and a nominative-case NP (the subject); and the past-tense verb *forced*, which requires an infinitival VP complement in addition to a direct object and a subject, has the SUBCAT value ⟨VP[INF], NP[ACC], NP[NOM]⟩. The Subcategorization Principle states that in any phrasal sign, each complement daughter must satisfy (or, more precisely, unify with) a member of the head daughter's SUBCAT list, and that the SUBCAT list of the mother must consist of those elements on the head daughter's SUBCAT list that remain to be satisfied; more succinctly, the subcategorization of a phrase equals the subcategorization of the head daughter less the requirements satisfied by the complement daughters. In Chapter 5, we argue that not only category selection of complements (loosely construed to include subjects and determiners as well as objects, verbal complements, sentential complements, etc.), but also a broad range of other local (i.e. lexically determined) syntactic and semantic dependencies, including case assignment, lexical government (e.g. of particular prepositions), semantic role assignment, and verb agreement, can all be accounted for on the basis of this simple principle.

A related, and centrally important, point of contact with categorial grammar is the definition of grammatical relations (subject, object, etc.) in terms of a "deep" grammatical order (as opposed to "surface" order, i.e. the temporal order in which the corresponding signs are phonologically realized): in HPSG the subject, direct object, and second object of a verb are defined to be those signs which satisfy (unify with) the last, second-last, and third-last elements, respectively, of the verb's SUBCAT list. Thus HPSG embodies a *hierarchical* theory of grammatical relations analogous to the one articulated within categorial grammar by Dowty (1982a, 1982b) and others. The chief difference is that in categorial grammar, this order has been taken to correpond with the order of arguments in a Montague-style predicate-argument structure. By contrast, we argue (Chapter 4) that the notion of semantic argument order is misguided, and should be replaced with an order-free notion of *semantic role* similar to the one employed in situation semantics. Thus the ordering of grammatical relations associated with the order of elements on the SUBCAT list of an HPSG sign corresponds not to argument order but rather to the traditional grammatical notion of *obliqueness*, with leftmost members of the list being most oblique. As we shall see below, the notion of the obliqueness hierarchy plays a key role in the HPSG account of numerous linguistic phenomena of very diverse sorts.

In HPSG, words (i.e. lexical signs) are highly structured and rich in information. In conjunction with universal principles like those mentioned above, which constrain the "flow" (more properly, sharing) of information between lexical signs and the phrasal signs which they head (i.e. their *projections*), they very largely determine the syntactic and semantic properties of phrases in general. (Roughly the same intuition lies behind the "Projection Principle" of GB theory; we would argue, however, that the HPSG principles responsible for the transmission of information from lexical heads to their projections are much more explicitly formulated, and therefore their empirical consequences are considerably clearer.) As a result, there is correspondingly less work left for language-specific rules of grammar. Thus, HPSG shares with categorial grammar (and also with GB) the elimination of category-specific phrase structure rules in favor of very partially specified combinatory schemata that constrain the relation of constituency among signs. For example, four highly schematic HPSG rules (presented in Chapter 6) account for a substantial fragment of English (viz. English signs whose consituents are all heads, complements, or adjuncts). One of these rules, informally written (3)

(3) [SUBCAT ⟨ ⟩] ⟶ H[LEX –], C

says that one of the possibilities for an English phrase is to be a saturated sign ([SUBCAT ⟨ ⟩]; here "⟨ ⟩" denotes the empty list) whose constituents are a phrasal head (H[LEX –]) and a single complement (C); this rule subsumes a number of conventional phrase structure rules, such as those shown in (4):

(4)
S ⟶ NP VP
NP ⟶ DET NOM
NP ⟶ NP's NOM

Another HPSG rule, informally expressed in (5)

(5) [SUBCAT ⟨[ ]⟩] ⟶ H[LEX +], C*

says that another option for English phrases is to be a sign which subcategorizes for exactly one complement ([SUBCAT ⟨[ ]⟩]; here "⟨[ ]⟩" stands for any list of length one) whose daughters are a lexical head (H[LEX +]) and any number of complement daughters (C*). This rule subsumes a vast array of conventional phrase structure rules, such as those in (6):

(6)
VP ⟶ V; VP ⟶ V S'; AP ⟶ A;
VP ⟶ V NP; AP ⟶ A PP; PP ⟶ P NP;
VP ⟶ V PP; VP ⟶ V VP; VP ⟶ V AP;
VP ⟶ V NP NP; VP ⟶ V NP PP; etc.

Note that the precise expansion of categories on the right-hand side need not be specified in the HPSG rule, since that information will be unified in from the SUBCAT list of the lexical head.

It is important to be aware that HPSG grammar rules such as those above determine constituency only, and do not make reference to the surface order in which the constituents are realized. Unlike theories such as GB, LFG, and "directional" versions of categorial grammar where rules determine relative order as well as consituency, HPSG follows the tradition of work in GPSG, wherein generalizations about the relative order of sister constituents is factored out of the phrase structure rules and expressed in independent language-specific *linear precedence* (LP) constraints (Chapter 7). That is, HPSG phrase structure rules are really *immediate dominance* (ID) rules. This is as it should be, for it is a well-known fact (though little acknowledged in most current syntactic theorization) that the linear order of sister constituents in a given language is not an idiosyncratic property of particular classes of phrases but rather is determined by general constraints which have force across the whole language. In HPSG (unlike GPSG), some LP constraints may refer not only to the syntactic categories of the sisters which they order, but also to their grammatical relations (i.e. their relative position in the obliqueness hierarchy). An example of such a *hierarchical* LP constraint is the one given in (7):

(7) COMPLEMENT[MAJ ¬V] ≪ COMPLEMENT

The intended interpretation of (7) is that in English any complement with major feature (roughly, part of speech) other than V (i.e. any complement whose head is not a verb, thereby excluding VP and S complements) must linearly precede its more oblique complement sisters. Among the numerous consequences of this constraint are the fact that direct objects precede second objects (so that, e.g. in American English, *Kim gave Sandy Fido* can never mean the same thing as *Kim gave Fido Sandy*, and the fact that in inverted ("subject-auxiliary inversion") structures the subject precedes the VP complement (e.g. *Did Kim leave?* but **Did leave Kim?*). A further consequence involving control (the interpretation of "understood" subjects) will be noted below.)

As we saw above, the relocation of subcategorization information from phrase structure rules to the lexicon *à la* categorial grammar results in a marked reduction of the number and complexity of phrase structure (ID) rules in HPSG. Additional "lexicalization" of linguistic information, and concomitant further simplification of the grammar, is achieved by the use of *lexical rules* (Chapter 8), similar to those employed in LFG, to handle "structure preserving" processes such as passivization, causativization, and extraposition with the expletive pronoun *it*. Lexical rules operate upon lexical signs of a given *input* class, systematically affecting their phonology, semantics, and syntax (including, crucially, their SUBCAT lists), to produce lexical signs of a certain *output* class. For example, English passivization is handled by the lexical rule stated informally in (8):

(8) ⟨ϕ, V[BSE, SUBCAT⟨..., NP, NP⟩]⟩ ⟼
⟨passive(ϕ), V[PAS, SUBCAT⟨(PP[BY],)..., NP⟩]⟩

Here the input word, a base-form verb (V[BSE]) with phonological form ϕ, that subcategorizes at least for a subject NP and a direct object NP

(SUBCAT⟨..., NP, NP⟩), is mapped to a passive-form verb (V[PAS]) with phonological form passive(ϕ), where passive is a morphological operation that systematically produces the regular passive morphology, unless an irregular passive morphology is specified by the input word. Note that the SUBCAT list of the passive form is obtained from that of the input verb by dropping off the least oblique (subject) NP specification and adding to the leftmost (most oblique) position a specification for an optional it by-PP (optionality is indicated here by parenthesization). The effect of (8) is illustrated in (9–11):

(9) a. ⟨admire, V[BSE, SUBCAT⟨NP, NP⟩]⟩
    b. ⟨admired, V[PAS, SUBCAT⟨(PP[BY]), NP⟩]⟩

(10) a. ⟨blame, V[BSE, SUBCAT⟨PP[ON], NP, NP⟩]⟩
    b. ⟨blamed, V[PAS, SUBCAT⟨(PP[BY]), PP[ON], NP⟩]⟩

(11) a. ⟨force, V[BSE, SUBCAT⟨VP[INF], NP, NP⟩]⟩
    b. ⟨forced, V[PAS, SUBCAT⟨(PP[BY]), VP[INF], NP⟩]⟩

Phrases headed by lexical signs like these (both active and passive forms) can now be produced from one and the same phrase structure rule (the one stated in (5) above), as indicated in (12–14):

(12) a.

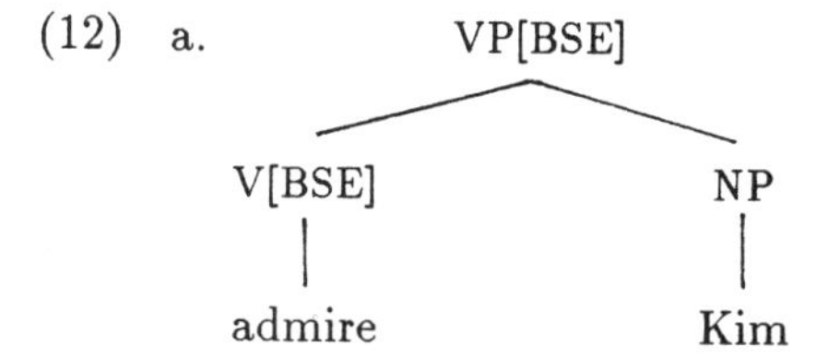

b.

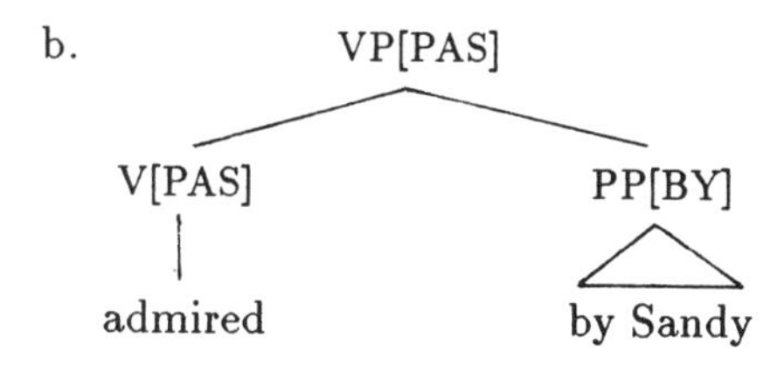

(13) a.

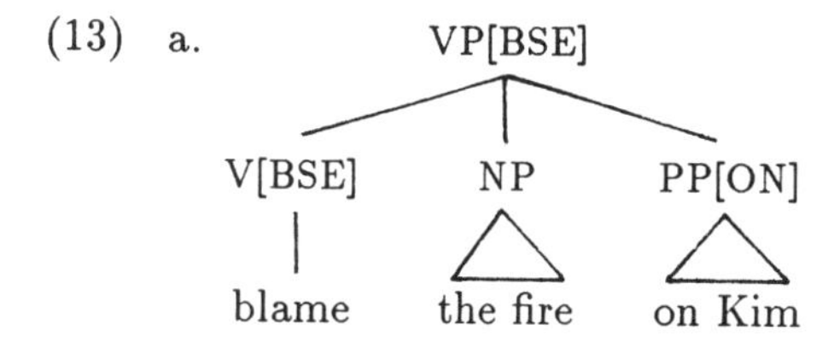

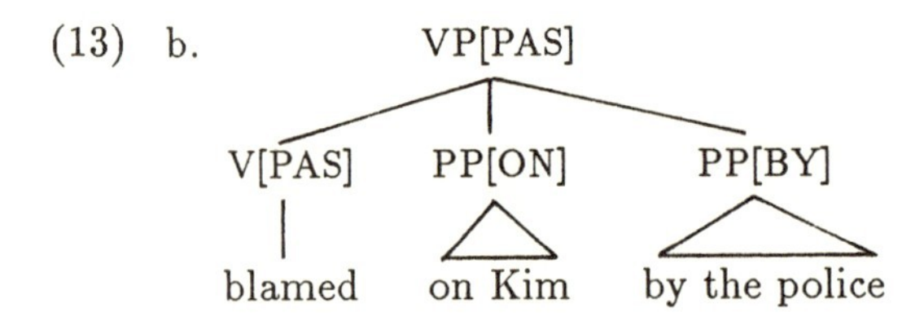

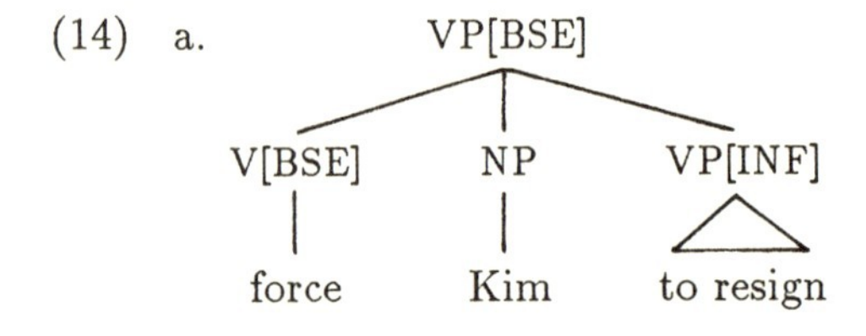

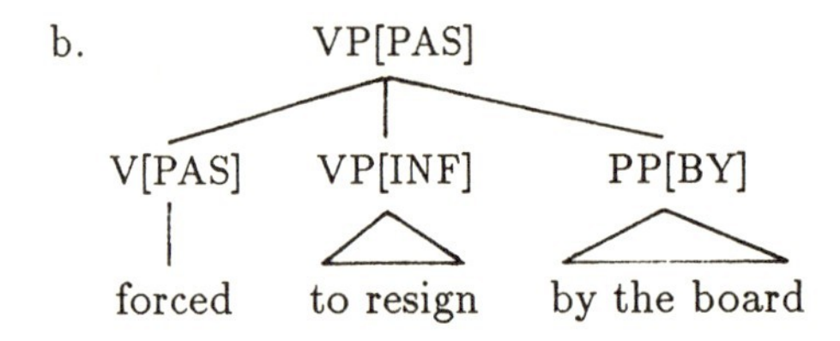

This is in contrast with GPSG's metarules, which operate upon lexical ID rules (i.e. ID rules which introduce a lexical head) to produce additional lexical ID rules (thereby enlarging the grammar), and in even sharper contrast with GB's transformational rule "Move α" which operates directly upon constituent structure trees to derive successive "levels of representation" (thereby complicating the overall architecture of the theory).

In one important respect, HPSG differs from all the syntactic theories which have influenced its development, for it is not at heart a theory of syntax. Rather, it is concerned with the interaction among all the forms of information that bear upon the linguistic meaning relation, including (inter alia) both the syntactic information borne by signs (roughly, their syntactic category and constituent structure) as well as their semantic content. This is not to say that linguistic theory has slighted semantics: it is surely a thriving subdiscipline in some quarters, if not quite in the mainstream of the field. But with a few significant exceptions, syntacticians and semanticists have tended to go their own ways. Workers within theories such as GB, GPSG, and LFG have concentrated upon syntax; on those infrequent occasions when they have touched upon semantic concerns, this has usually been as a kind of afterthought, typically by way of demonstrating that the syntactic theory in question can be equipped with a Montague-style system of model-theoretic interpretation (see, e.g. Halvorsen (1983) for LFG and Gazdar et al. (1985, chapters 10–11) for GPSG). On the other side of the fence, semanticists, far fewer in number, have for the most part cast their lot with Montague, who famously asserted (Montague 1974:223, fn.) that "I fail to see any great interest in syntax except as a preliminary to semantics", usually adopting as a syntactic underpinning, on a no-questions-asked basis, either the then-current version of transformation grammar or the categorial grammar inherited from Montague. This traditional division of labor is reflected in the structure of linguistics curricula, where semantics has customarily been taught in sequence after syntax, or else not at all. In HPSG, which is radically at odds with this tradition, syntactic and semantic aspects of grammatical theory are built up in an integrated way from the start, under the assumption that neither can be well understood in isolation from the other. In this respect, HPSG is much closer in spirit to work in situation semantics (e.g. Fenstad et al. (1985)) than it is to most current syntactic approaches.

The influence of situation semantics on HPSG is reflected not only in its general outlook, but more particularly in the choice of ontological categories in terms of which the semantic contents of signs are analyzed (Chapter 4): *individuals*, *relations*, *roles* (ways of participating in relations, a little like argument positions), *situations*, and *circumstances* (roughly, types of situations). To simplify somewhat, the semantic content of a simple declarative sentence is a circumstance, a situation-theoretic object composed of individuals playing roles in a relation. For example, the semantic content of the sentence *Kim admires Sandy* is the circumstance described in (15):

(15) $$\begin{bmatrix} \text{RELATION} & \text{ADMIRE} \\ \text{ADMIRER} & \text{KIM} \\ \text{ADMIREE} & \text{SANDY} \end{bmatrix}$$

Here the relation is ADMIRE; the individuals KIM and SANDY play the roles of ADMIRER and ADMIREE respectively. The semantic content of sentences, and of phrases in general, is determined by various pieces of syntactic and semantic information associated with their constituents, in conjunction with universal linguistic principles (and contextual factors). In the present case, KIM and SANDY are part of the semantic contents of the subject NP *Kim* and the direct object NP *Sandy*, respectively. The relation ADMIRE and the assignment of the ADMIRER and ADMIREE roles to the subject and direct object respectively come from the head verb *admires*, which has roughly the form indicated in (16):

(16) $$\langle \text{admires, V[SUBCAT}\langle \text{NP}_i,\ \text{NP}_j\rangle],\ \begin{bmatrix} \text{RELATION} & \text{ADMIRE} \\ \text{ADMIRER} & j \\ \text{ADMIREE} & i \end{bmatrix} \rangle$$

Note that the lexical sign consists of phonological, syntactic, and semantic information. The crucial assignment of semantic roles to grammatical relations is mediated by the SUBCAT feature; here i and j are variables (in the semantic sense of classical mathematical analysis, not in the syntactic sense of mathematical logic), parameters which make up part of the semantic content of NP's and which play a role in HPSG semantic accounts analogous to that played by reference markers in DRS theory. The specification "NP_i" calls for a noun phrase whose variable is to be identified (i.e. unified) with the filler of the ADMIRER role. By virtue of the Subcategorization Principle (which requires that the actual subject and direct object constituents be unified with the corresponding SUBCAT specifications on the head), the variables j and i must therefore be unified with KIM and SANDY respectively. That (16) is the semantic content of the whole sentence now follows from an additional universal *Semantics Principle*, a sort of "semantic HFP" which requires (roughly) that the semantic content of a phrase be unified with that of its head daughter. Unlike Montague semantics, the semantic content of a sentence is not determined by a syntax-directed process of model-theoretic interpretation; instead, it "falls out" from the semantic contents of its lexical constituents by virtue of general linguistic constraints which require that certain pieces of information associated with signs be unified with certain other pieces.

The reader familiar with GB theory can scarcely fail to note the analogy between the semantic roles and NP variables mentioned above and the GB notions of and "θ-role" and "syntactic index". Our perspective on these notions is fundamentally different, however. GB θ-roles and indices are unexplicated syntactic entities whose existence is required by the theory in order to account for syntactic well-formedness. In HPSG, by contrast, semantic roles and variables are straightforwardly treated as situation-theoretic objects (ways of participating in relations, and parameters introduced by NP tokens) which arise naturally as constituents of the semantic contents of signs. In practice, the two sets of concepts are exploited by the two theories to account for roughly the same phenomena, but we believe our semantic explication of the underlying notions provides a firmer conceptual foundation for their use in linguistic analysis.

In Volume 2, we build upon the foundations established in Volume 1 to provide explicit, formally precise, and—in many cases—highly novel accounts of a wide range of syntactic and semantic phenomena, for the most part concerning agreement, control, long-distance dependencies, and anaphora. Here we can only try to convey something of the flavor of these analyses.

Our theory of agreement begins with the unconventional hypothesis that agreement information such as person, number, and gender (including both formal gender and natural gender) are not syntactic features but rather attributes of NP variables. Agreement takes place between two signs whose semantic contents make reference to variables which are required to be unified, and it is overtly signalled in case at least one of the signs in question belongs to a class in which the agreement information of the variable in question is reflected by inflectional morphology. This hypothesis provides the basis for a principled and integrated account of verb agreement (with both subjects and objects), agreement of nouns with their determiners and adjectives, and interactions of agreement with control, relativization, and anaphora (broadly construed to include deictic pronouns). It also leads to straightforward explanations of numerous otherwise puzzling facts, including the following: pronouns and their antecedents cross-linguistically agree in person, number and gender, but not in case; coordinate structures cross-linguistically share with their conjunct daughters' inflectional features like verb form and case, but not agreement; a prepositional phrase appears to inherit the agreement of its object, even though the object is not the head of the phrase.

Variables and roles figure predominantly in the HPSG account of control, viz. the interpretation of "understood subjects", e.g. in "unsaturated" verbal or predicative complements such as those in (17):

(17) a. Kim seemed *to be optimistic.* (subject control)
b. Kim tried *to be optimistic.* (subject control)
c. Kim promised Sandy *to be optimistic* (subject control)

(18) a. Kim believed Sandy *to be optimistic.* (object control)
b. Kim persuaded Sandy *to be optimistic.* (object control)

In HPSG, such complements are analyzed not as clauses (as in GB theory) but simply as VP's (as in GPSG, LFG, and most categorial grammar analyses). In accordance with the Subcategorization Principle, VP's in turn are analyzed as V[SUBCAT ⟨NP⟩], i.e. they subcategorize for the "missing" subject NP. The distinction between subject and object control is then accounted for on the basis of lexical entries such as those in (19–20):

(19) ⟨promise, V[SUBCAT⟨V[SUBCAT⟨NP_j⟩], NP_i, NP_j⟩]⟩

(20) ⟨persuade, V[SUBCAT⟨V[SUBCAT⟨NP_i⟩], NP_i, NP_j⟩]⟩

That is, choice of controller depends on whether the variable of the "missing" (i.e. subcategorized-for but unrealized) subject of the VP complement is unified with the subject variable or the object variable of the main verb. At first blush, it would appear that we are claiming control is lexically specified; in fact, however, we argue that control is predictable on the basis of more general semantic constraints which apply to whole classes of unsaturated phrases (not only those which appear as complements). Such constraints explain why, e.g. *Kim* controls the VP[INF] in all the examples in (21), whereas in all the examples in (22) the controller is *Sandy*.

(21) a. Kim promised Sandy to be home early.
b. The promise that was made to Sandy by Kim, to be home early, was never kept.
c. Kim promised something to Sandy. It was to be home early.

(22) a. Kim appealed to Sandy to be home early.
b. Kim's appeal to Sandy to be home early went unnoticed.
c. Kim made an appeal to Sandy. It was to be home early.

The much-studied distinction between "raising" and "equi" control, reflected in the contrast between the (a) and (b) examples in (23–24), also admits a straightforward analysis:

(23) a. Kim believed there to be a unicorn in the garden.
b.*Kim persuaded there to be a unicorn in the garden.

(24) a. 1. Kim believed Sandy to have examined Chris.
2. Kim believed Chris to have been examined by Sandy.
(truth-conditionally equivalent)
b. 1. Kim persuaded Sandy to examine Chris.
2. Kim persuaded Chris to be examined by Sandy.
(not truth-conditionally equivalent)

The essence of the analysis is that equi verbs assign semantic roles to the controlling complement (in the present examples, the object), but raising verbs do not, as indicated by the following lexical signs:

(25) $\left\langle \text{believe, V[SUBCAT}\langle \text{VP[SUBCAT}\langle \text{NP}_i\rangle\text{], NP}_i\text{, NP}_j\rangle\text{]}, \begin{bmatrix} \text{RELATION} & \text{BELIEVE} \\ \text{BELIEVER} & j \\ \text{PROPOSITION} & \ldots \end{bmatrix} \right\rangle$

(26) $\left\langle \text{persuade, V[SUBCAT}\langle \text{VP[SUBCAT}\langle \text{NP}_i\rangle\text{], NP}_i\text{, NP}_j\rangle\text{]}, \begin{bmatrix} \text{RELATION} & \text{PERSUADE} \\ \text{PERSUADER} & j \\ \text{PERSUADEE} & i \\ \text{PROPOSITION} & \ldots \end{bmatrix} \right\rangle$

A more subtle difference, not indicated in the simplified lexical signs above, is that raising verbs require that the *entire* SUBCAT element (including its syntactic information) corresponding to the controller be unified with the subject SUBCAT element of the VP complement, while equi verbs only require that the (semantic!) variables of the elements in question be unified. The existence of a syntactic dependency associated with raising explains the otherwise mysterious fact that there are no raising verbs with PP controllers analogous to PP-controlled equi verbs like *appeal*, for no PP can unify with the NP subject SUBCAT element of the verbal complement:

(27) Kim appealed to Sandy *to be optimistic.* (PP object control)

The same syntactic dependency accounts for the well-known fact that in Icelandic sentences involving verbal complements whose head verb assigns "quirky" case to its subject, the quirky case will uniformly be borne by the controller if the matrix verb is a raising verb, but not if it is an equi verb:

(28) a. Honum mæltist vel í kirkjunni.
him(DAT) spoke well in the-church

'He spoke well in church.'

b. Honum virðist mælast vel í kirkjunni.
him(DAT) seems to-speak well in the-church

'He seems to speak well in church.'

c. Ég vonast til að mælast vel í kirkjunni.
I(NOM) hope to to to-speak well in the-church

'I hope to speak well in church.'

The obliqueness hierarchy also assumes a central role in the HPSG analysis of control, by virtue of a further universal principle, the *Principle of Lexical Control* (PLC), which requires that the subject SUBCAT element of an unsaturated complement be controlled by (i.e. have its variable unified with the variable of) some less oblique complement, provided such exists. In conjunction with the general semantic constraints cited above in connection with examples (29–30), the PLC accounts for the fact ("Visser's Generalization") that subject-control verbs do not passivize:

(29) a. Kim persuaded Sandy to leave.
b. Kim promised Sandy to leave.

(30) a. Sandy was persuaded to leave (by Kim).
b.*Kim was promised to leave (by Kim).

Another oft-noted contrast involving control, shown in (31–32), involves the verbs *appeal* and *appear*, both of which subcategorize for a VP[INF] and a PP[TO]:

(31) a. Kim appealed to Sandy to be optimistic.
b.*Kim appealed to be optimistic to Sandy.

(32) a. Kim appeared to Sandy to be optimistic.
b. Kim appeared to be optimistic to Sandy.

What about the obliqueness order of the complements? Since the PP[TO] controls in (30a), the PLC implies that the PP[TO] must be less oblique than the VP[INF], i.e. the subcategorization of *appeal* must be (33):

(33) ⟨VP[INF], PP[TO], NP⟩.

The ungrammaticality of (31b) is then predicted by the independently motivated LP rule (7) above. On the other hand, the grammaticality of (32a–b) shows that the subcategorization of *appear* must be (34), for otherwise (32b) would be ungrammatical:

(34) ⟨PP[TO], VP[INF], NP⟩.

The PLC therefore predicts that *appear* is subject-controlled, which of course is the case. This analysis of the contrast in (31–32) is further corroborated by the contrast (35)

(35) a. Kim was appealed to to be optimistic.
b.*Kim was appeared to to be optimistic.

under the reasonable assumption that a PP complement can be "pseudopassived" only if it is a "pseudo-direct object", i.e. the least oblique complement other than the subject.

We conclude this preview by sketching some highlights of the HPSG analysis of reflexive and nonreflexive pronouns. As with control, NP variables and obliqueness are central to our account. We begin with the assumption that the semantic content of a noun phrase[3] is an information structure of a certain type that we call an *indexed object*. The connection between these objects and the sorts of things that are usually taken to be the meanings of NP's (e.g. individuals and quantifiers) is explained in Chapter 4; for now the only important properties of indexed objects to be aware of are these: (i) the indexed object which is the semantic content of an NP has the variable of the NP as a subpart; (ii) distinct NP tokens have distinct indexed objects as their semantic contents, though the variables themselves may be identical (unified); and (iii) every indexed object has a *referential type*, either R-PRO (e.g. reflexive pronouns like *herself*, reciprocal *each other*), PRO (e.g. non-reflexive pronouns like *him*), or NON-PRO (e.g. nonpronominal NP's like *Kim*). The referential types of the semantic contents of NP tokens provides a classificatory scheme for NP tokens reminiscent of the GB classification of NP's into "anaphors", "pronominals", and "r-expressions"; however, the treatment of traces is quite different, and

[3] The following discussion is equally applicable to nonpredicative PP's (i.e. PP's in which the preposition has no semantic content but functions essentially like a case marking), which we assume to have the same semantic content as their prepositional objects.

we will argue that the HPSG scheme is preferable to that of GB in terms of conceptual clarity and conformity with the facts.

Facts about the distribution of different types of NP are then explained on the basis of a set of principles governing the "binding" (i.e. unification) of variables which parallel the principles of GB's binding theory. For ease of comparison, we name the HPSG binding principles after their GB counterparts:

Principle A. The variable of an R-PRO sign must be unified with the variable of a less oblique SUBCAT element, provided such exists.[4]

Principle B. The variable of a PRO sign must not be unified with the variable of a less oblique SUBCAT element.

Principle C. The variable of a NON-PRO sign must not be unified with the index of an *o*-commanding SUBCAT element.

Here ***o-command*** (obliqueness command), the HPSG counterpart of GB's "*c*-command", is a kind of transitive closure of the less-oblique-than relation, i.e. X *o*-commands Y iff X is a SUBCAT element of the same head that subcategorizes for a more oblique constituent that dominates Y. (Any constituent is considered to dominate itself, for the puposes of this definition.)

Thus Principle A entails that an English reflexive or reciprocal that is (or is contained in) a complement must have as its antecedent a less oblique complement if there is one:

(36) a. Kim_i introduced $Sandy_j$ to $himself_i$.
b. Kim_i introduced $Sandy_j$ to $himself_j$.
c. Kim_i introduced $himself_i$ to $Sandy_j$.
d.*Kim_i introduced $himself_j$ to $Sandy_j$.
e.*Kim_i knew $Sandy_j$ admired $himself_i$.

(37) a. The $girls_i$ introduced Kim_j to each $other_i$'s fathers.
b. Kim_i introduced the $girls_j$ to each $other_j$'s fathers.
c. The $girls_i$ introduced each $other_i$'s fathers to Kim_j.
d.*Kim_i introduced each $other_j$'s fathers to the $girls_j$.
e.*Kim_i's father admired $himself_i$.
f. The $girls_i$ knew each $other_i$'s fathers were wrong.

[4] This is a simplification; R-PRO variables are passed from daughter to mother until they reach a consitituent that *has* a less oblique SUBCAT element whose variable can unify with it; this accounts for the binding of reflexives or reciprocals that are or are contained in subjects or possessive phrases.

Likewise Principle B entails that a (non-reflexive and non-reciprocal) pronoun cannot have a less oblique complement as its antecedent:

(38) a.*Kim$_i$ introduced Sandy$_j$ to him$_i$.
b.*Kim$_i$ introduced Sandy$_j$ to him$_j$.
c.*Kim$_i$ introduced him$_i$ to Sandy$_j$.
d. Kim$_i$ knew Sandy$_j$ admired him$_i$.

(39) a. Kim$_i$ introduced his$_i$father to Sandy$_j$.
b. Kim$_i$ introduced his$_j$father to Sandy$_j$.
c. Kim$_i$'s father admired him$_i$.

And Principle C entails that no complement can be "coindexed" with (i.e. have its variable unified with the variable of) a non-pronoun that is (or is contained in) a more oblique complement:

(40) a.*Kim$_i$ introduced him$_j$ to Sandy$_j$.
b.*He$_i$ introduced Kim$_i$ to Sandy$_j$.
c.*He$_i$ introduced Kim$_j$ to Sandy$_i$.
d.*He$_i$ knew Kim$_i$ was wrong.
e. He$_i$ knew he$_i$ was wrong.
f. His$_i$ father admires Kim$_i$.

In addition, the HPSG binding principles predict the existence of the much-discussed configurations where *either* R-PRO or PRO NP's can occur:

(41) a. John$_i$ was delighted that a picture of him$_i$/himself$_i$ was featured in the newspaper.
b. The kids$_i$ wrecked their$_i$/each other's$_i$ cars.

In conjunction with the theories of agreement and control sketched above, the HPSG binding theory also accounts for interactions of control and anaphora such as the following:

(42) a. They$_i$ persuaded him$_j$ to shave himself$_j$.
b.*They$_i$ persuaded him$_j$ to shave him$_j$.
c. They$_i$ persuaded him$_j$ to shave them$_i$.
d.*They$_i$ persuaded him$_j$ to shave themselves$_i$.

(43) a.*They$_i$ promised him$_j$ to shave himself$_j$.
b. They$_i$ promised him$_j$ to shave him$_j$.

(43) c.*They$_i$ promised him$_j$ to shave them$_i$.

d. They$_i$ promised him$_j$ to shave themselves$_i$.

And together with HPSG's account of filler-gap relations, wherein the syntactic category and semantic content of a filler are unified with the syntactic category and semantic content, respectively, of the corresponding gap, the binding theory sketched above predicts a wide range of facts involving interactions between anaphora and unbounded dependency constructions which have proved problematic for other accounts, such as the following:

(44) a. It was HIMSELF$_i$ that Kim$_i$ adored e$_i$.

b. What Kim$_i$ really likes e$_i$ is HIMSELF$_i$.

c. John$_i$ thinks Mary$_j$ dislikes Kim$_k$, but HIM$_i$/HIMSELF$_i$, he$_i$ knows she adores e$_i$.

1.4 Suggestions for Further Reading

Three of the syntactic theories on which HPSG has drawn, GB, GPSG, and LFG, are summarized with exemplary lucidity by Sells (1985a); pointers to the current literature are provided at the end of each chapter. For more thorough treatments, standard sources are: (GB) Chomsky (1981, 1982); (LFG) Bresnan, ed. (1982); (GPSG) Gazdar et al. (1985). The more loosely organized linguistic tradition of categorial grammar lacks an official manifesto; among the more influential studies from the first half of this decade are Ades and Steedman (1982), Dowty (1982a, 1982b), Bach (1983), and Steedman (1985). A direct predecessor of HPSG, which constitutes something of a GPSG-categorial grammar hybrid, is the *head grammar* (HG) theory of Pollard (1984). The term "DRS theory" refers to two closely related treatments of quantification and anaphora proposed by Kamp (1981) and Heim (1982); for brief and readable synopses of the former, see Sells (1985b, Section 2) or Asher (1986, Section 2). For situation semantics, the standard source is Barwise and Perry (1983); since then, the theory has been in a period of flux, of which the interview with Barwise and Perry (Barwise and Perry (1985)) and the collection of commentaries on Barwise and Perry (1983) (published together as volume 8.1 of *Linguistics and Philosophy*) may be taken as early representatives.

The twin monuments of mentalism and antimentalism respectively in twentieth-century linguistics are Saussure (1915) and Bloomfield (1933). For the past 30 years the leading proponent of mentalism has been Chomsky, whose recent views on the matter are set forth in Chomsky (1986, Chapter 2); another representative mentalist work, primarily concerned with semantics, is Jackendoff (1985). The principal defenders of linguistic realism in recent years have been Barwise and Perry (1983); a lively introduction to some of the key issues dividing mentalism and realism is provided by the recent public debate between Barwise (1986a, 1987) and Jerry Fodor (1986a, 1986b). The general approach to language in terms of informational constraints is the result of a cross-fertilization of ideas from both situation semantics and from the community of unification-based formalisms (Chapter 2). The fruitful coming-together of the two lines of thought within linguistic theory originates with Fenstad et al. (1985); many of the same issues are discussed in less technical terms in Sag et al. (1986).

HPSG theory itself has undergone considerable evolution since its inception as an outgrowth of HG, which itself began as an attempt to place ideas from earlier GPSG work on a firm mathematical and computational foundation. Early versions of HPSG, which have a decidedly procedural flavor, closely resemble HG, except that the Montagovian semantic approach of the earlier theory yields to a version of situation semantics, and the earlier account of word-order in terms of nonconcatenative operations is replaced with an ID/LP approach. Representative papers from this period are Pollard (1985), which focuses on the elimination of metarules, and Pollard (in press), which compares HPSG with one of Steedman's variants of categorial grammar. Creary and Pollard (1985), Flickinger, Pollard, and Wasow (1985), and Proudian and Pollard (1985) are a set of closely related papers from the same period which describe the implementation of an experimental HPSG-based natural language processing system. More recently, under the influence of colleagues such as Martin Kay, Lauri Karttunen, Fernando Pereira, William Rounds, and Stuart Shieber, the theory has been reformulated in declarative terms in the light of insights from computational linguistics and theoretical computer science; an overview of the theory that reflects these influences is given in Sag and Pollard (1987).

2 Formal Foundations

The fundamental nature of linguistic information remains a mystery. We cannot look at a piece of linguistic information under a microscope; we aren't even sure whether to look inside human brains or somewhere else. Still, although we aren't sure what linguistic information *is*, we can still theorize about it by trying to say what it is like. To be more precise, we can try to construct formal *models* that reflect certain interesting aspects of the things we are studying. This is similar in principle to what a scientist does who theorizes about some natural phenomenon. Consider, for example, a NASA physicist who is interested in the motions of the planets around the sun. He or she constructs a mathematical model. In the model, the positions and velocities of the planets and the sun are represented by vectors in a Euclidean space, their masses by positive real numbers, and their motions by the solutions to certain differential equations. The model is not the solar system, but certain features of it represent aspects of the solar system of interest to the physicist. Other aspects of the solar system, such as the size of the planets, the presence of interstellar dust, and relativistic effects that become significant only at velocities approaching the speed of light, are not taken into account in the model. If the model turns out to be inadequate, e.g. it fails to yield sufficiently accurate predictions of planetary positions for the application at hand, then it will have to be revised or augmented in various ways.

In the past several years, theoretical and computational linguists working within a number of distinct research traditions have found it useful to construct formal models of linguistic information. Instead of the NASA physicist's Euclidean spaces and differential equations, though, the formal objects of choice in information-based linguistics are things known as *feature structures*. Mathematically, a feature structure is a certain kind of connected, acyclic, finite state machine (whose final states have no transitions and possibly have values assigned to them from some fixed set of atoms). However, we will not make an effort here to present a detailed technical characterization of feature structures (the interested reader is invited to consult the relevant works cited at the end of this chapter). Instead, we will provide an informal account of feature structures, with an emphasis on their properties that typically come into play in linguistic applications.

Caution: the simple linguistic examples in this section are not part of our formal theoretical development; they are just intended to illustrate certain properties of feature structures.

2.1 Partial Information and Feature Structures

Intuitively, a feature structure is just an information-bearing object that describes or represents another thing by specifying *values* for various *attributes* of the described thing; we think of the feature structure as providing partial information about the thing described. Feature structures are standardly notated by *attribute-value matrices* (AVM's). For example, the feature structure (45a) might provide partial information about an employee named Jones:

(45) a.
$$\begin{bmatrix} \text{NAME} & \text{JONES} \\ \text{PHONE} & \text{951-4299} \\ \text{OFFICE} & \text{B21} \\ \text{DEPARTMENT} & \text{SALES} \end{bmatrix}$$

In this feature structure, the attributes are NAME, PHONE, OFFICE, and DEPARTMENT; the value specified for the NAME attribute is JONES. It is often convenient to employ an alternative form of notation, whereby a feature structure is represented graphically as in (45b):

(45) b.

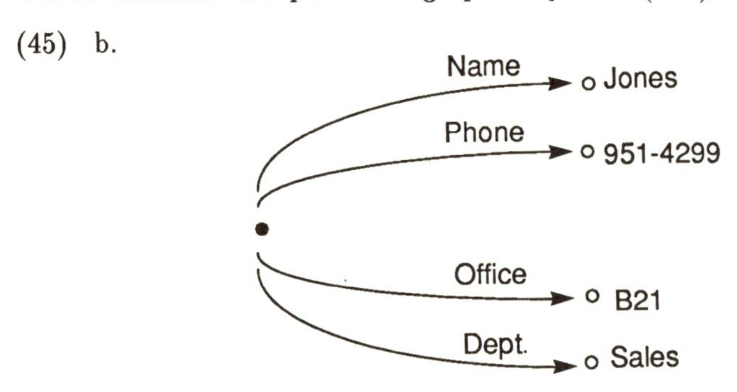

In our applications, we will think of feature structures as partial descriptions of signs (or sign tokens) and other linguistic objects which occur as parts of signs. For example, the lexical *cookie* sign is partially described by the feature structure (46):[1]

(46)
$$\begin{bmatrix} \text{PHON} & \text{cookie} \\ \text{SEM} & \text{COOKIE} \end{bmatrix}$$

[1] Names of attributes and values within attribute-value matrices are abbreviated to save space. A list of abbreviations employed appears in the Appendix.

Here the PHONOLOGY value 'cookie' represents a certain sound type, and the SEMANTICS value COOKIE represents the property of being a cookie.[2]

Another attribute of a sign, which we have not yet discussed, is its SYNTAX, which plays a principle role in determining the sign's potential for combining with other signs. The value of the SYNTAX attribute is another kind of linguistic object called a *syntactic category*. Syntactic categories in turn can be described in terms of *their* attributes. For example, the syntactic category third-singular noun might be described in terms of the attributes MAJOR (usually abbreviated MAJ) and AGREEMENT (abbreviated AGR) as shown in (47) (as we shall see in the next chapter, our analysis of syntactic categories is rather more complex than this example suggests):

(47) $$\begin{bmatrix} \text{MAJ N} \\ \text{AGR 3S} \end{bmatrix}$$

Here the attribute MAJ is the "major" attribute of syntactic categories, corresponding roughly to the traditional notion of part of speech; the MAJ value N identifies the category in question as nominal, as opposed to verbal (V) or something else. The AGR value 3S further identifies the category as third-singular.

A fundamental property of feature structures is their potential for *hierarchiality*. This means that the value of some attribute in a feature structure may itself by specified by another feature structure, rather than by an *atomic* value such as N or 3S. To put it another way, one feature structure can be embedded inside another. As an example, consider the feature structure (48):

(48) $$\begin{bmatrix} \text{PHON} & \text{cookie} \\ \text{SEM} & \text{COOKIE} \\ \text{SYN} & \begin{bmatrix} \text{MAJ N} \\ \text{AGR 3S} \end{bmatrix} \end{bmatrix}$$

Like (46), this feature structure is a partial description of the *cookie* sign, but it provides more information, viz. the information that its syntactic category is third-singular noun. Note that in (48), the value of the SYNTAX attribute is itself specified by a feature structure, the same one that appeared in (47) above.

Because of the potential for embedding of feature structures within feature structures, it is convenient to have the notion of a *path of attributes*, or simply a path. A path is just a finite sequence of attributes. We then generalize the notion of the value corresponding to an attribute to the notion of the value corresponding to a path, in the obvious way. For example,

---

[2] A more precise exposition of our theory of signs would express PHONOLOGY values in terms of phonological representations, not conventional orthographic ones. We simplify in this respect only to enhance readability.

in (48) the value corresponding to the path SEMANTICS (a path of length one) is COOKIE, while the value corresponding to the path SYNTAX|MAJ is N. By the way, it should be noted that atomic values such as N (noun) and 3S (third-singular) are themselves regarded as particularly simple feature structures in which the only path is the empty path (the sequence of attributes of length zero).

Matrices (46) and (48) also illustrate another fundamental fact about feature structures: some feature structures are *more informative* than others. In the present case, (48) is more informative than (46), since it contains all the information that (46) contains and some other information (the SYNTAX specification) besides. In general, if feature structure A is at least as informative as (i.e. equally informative as or more informative than) feature structure B, we often say A *extends* (or is an *extension* of) B, and write A $\preceq$ B. Alternatively we say that B *subsumes* A. The relation dual to $\preceq$ is usually called *subsumption*. This latter locution is connected with the obvious fact that any object that could be appropriately described by A could also be appropriately described by B: the less information you have about a thing, the wider the range of possibilities for what that thing might be. The most extreme case of subsumption is the feature structure that contains no information at all, illustrated in (49):

(49) [ ]

This feature structure subsumes all other feature structures: since it gives no information, it could be describing any object whatsoever.

Something special about subsumption must be said in the case of atomic values (recall that these are regarded as a special case of feature structures). If A and B are atoms, then evidently the only way that A can be at least as informative as B is if it actually *is* B. Thus for A and B atomic, A $\preceq$ B if and only if A and B are the same atom.

It is a standard fact about feature structures—given their mathematical characterization as finite state machines of a certain kind—that the extension relation $\preceq$ is a *reflexive partial ordering*. This means that as a binary relation on feature structures, $\preceq$ is: (1) reflexive (for every feature structure A, A $\preceq$ A); (2) transitive (if A $\preceq$ B and B $\preceq$ C, then A $\preceq$ C); and (3) antisymmetric (if A $\preceq$ B and B $\preceq$ A, then A = B).[3]

Informally: (1) every feature structure contains the same information as itself; (2) if A has no less information than B, which in turn has no less information than C, then A has no less information than C; and (3) if two feature structures each have at least as much information as the other, then in fact they are the same feature structure. Since the totally

---

[3] Equality here is to be understood in the sense of structural identity or isomorphism of finite state machines, i.e. identity of type not token.

uninformative feature structure (49) is the maximum element with respect to the $\preceq$ ordering, it is often called "Top", written $\top$.[4]

Another property of feature structures that is crucially important in linguistic applications is their ability to *share structure*. That is, two or more distinct attributes (or paths) within a feature structure may have their values specified by one and the same feature structure.[5]

By way of example, let us suppose that we analyze agreement values in terms of the attributes PER (person), NUM (number), and GEN (gender), e.g. third-singular-feminine is specified as in (50):

(50) $\begin{bmatrix} \text{PER} & \text{3RD} \\ \text{NUM} & \text{SNG} \\ \text{GEN} & \text{FEM} \end{bmatrix}$

Now suppose in addition that we have a theory of subject-verb agreement in which we analyze sentences as consisting of a subject and a predicate, and that some grammatical principle requires that subjects and predicates have the same agreement (caution: this is *not* how we will actually analyze sentences or subject-verb agreement). Then given some sentence S, we know that it is appropriately described by (51), even in the absence of any specific information about the subject and predicate themselves:

(51)

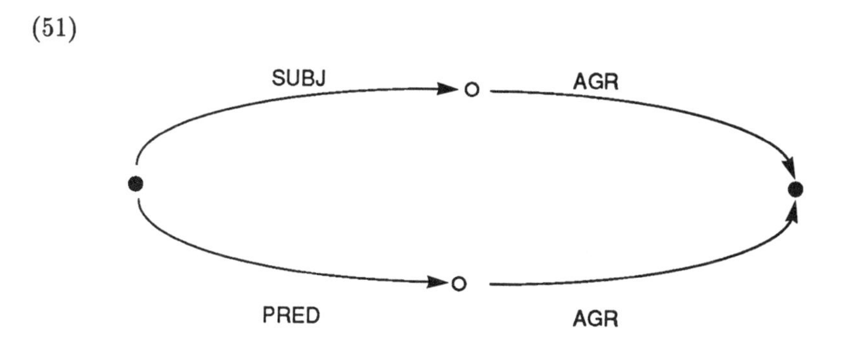

In other words, although we lack any information about the agreement values of either the subject or the predicate, we do know that, whatever they are, they are one and the same linguistic object. If we subsequently obtain the further information that the predicate is third-singular-feminine, our information about S is as shown in (52a):

---

[4] Technically, A subsumes B just in case there is a morphism from A to B in a certain mathematical subcategory of finite state machines. Such a morphism, if it exists, is necessarily unique.

[5] Here "same" is to be understood in the sense of identity of token not type.

(52) a.

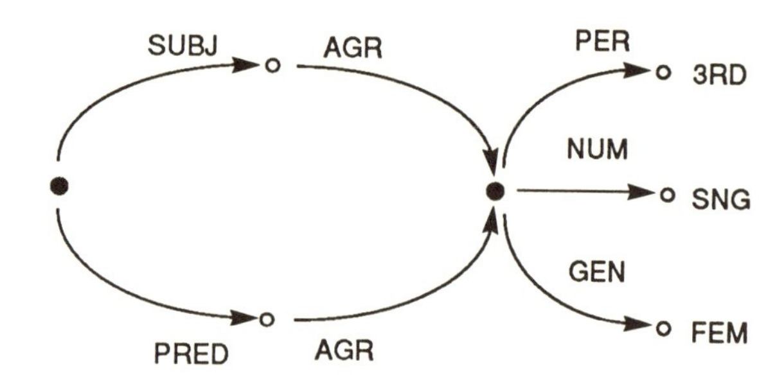

By virtue of the structure-sharing in (51), information about the predicate's agreement value also turns out to be information about the subject's agreement value.

It is evident that the graph-style notation for feature structures lends itself naturally to the representation of structure-sharing. When AVM's are used, a notational augmentation is required to indicate shared structure. The version that we adopt is illustrated in (52b):

(52) b.

$$\begin{bmatrix} \text{SUBJ} & \begin{bmatrix} \text{AGR } \boxed{1} \begin{bmatrix} \text{PER} & \text{3RD} \\ \text{NUM} & \text{SNG} \\ \text{GEN} & \text{FEM} \end{bmatrix} \end{bmatrix} \\ \text{PRED} & \begin{bmatrix} \text{AGR } \boxed{1} \end{bmatrix} \end{bmatrix}$$

Here the sharing of structure is indicated by multiple occurrences of the *tag* "$\boxed{1}$".

It is important to understand the difference between structure-sharing and merely having structurally similar values. A nonlinguistic example will help illustrate this distinction. Suppose that we use feature structures to keep track of personnel in an office, as in (53):

(53)

$$\begin{bmatrix} \text{MANAGER} & \begin{bmatrix} \text{NAME} & \text{ABRAMS} \\ \text{SS\#} & \text{309-53-2204} \\ \text{SECRETARY} & \begin{bmatrix} \text{NAME JONES} \end{bmatrix} \end{bmatrix} \\ \text{ASST-MANAGER} & \begin{bmatrix} \text{NAME} & \text{DEVITO} \\ \text{SS\#} & \text{729-85-3939} \\ \text{SECRETARY} & \begin{bmatrix} \text{NAME JONES} \end{bmatrix} \end{bmatrix} \end{bmatrix}$$

According to (53), Abrams and DeVito each have a secretary named Jones. Subsequent information might well reveal that they are two distinct people;

e.g. we might find out that Abrams' secretary and DeVito's secretary have different social security numbers. By contrast, according to (54), Abrams and DeVito *share* a secretary named Jones. Thus the information contents of (53) and (54) are quite different. In fact, (53) subsumes (54), for (54) contains all the information that (53) does, plus the information that a single secretary is shared. In this connection, it should be borne in mind that the absence of structure-sharing tags in (53) does not provide a positive indication that the two Joneses are distinct; it simply indicates the absence of information that they are the same.

(54)
$$\begin{bmatrix} \text{MANAGER} & \begin{bmatrix} \text{NAME} & \text{ABRAMS} \\ \text{SS\#} & \text{309-53-2204} \\ \text{SECRETARY} & \boxed{1}\begin{bmatrix}\text{NAME JONES}\end{bmatrix} \end{bmatrix} \\ \text{ASST-MANAGER} & \begin{bmatrix} \text{NAME} & \text{DEVITO} \\ \text{SS\#} & \text{729-85-3939} \\ \text{SECRETARY} & \boxed{1} \end{bmatrix} \end{bmatrix}$$

Equipped with the notion of structure-sharing, we can now give a formal *definition* of the subsumption relation. As mentioned above, if A and B are atomic, then $A \preceq B$ if and only if $A = B$. In the non-atomic case, subsumption can be defined recursively as follows: $A \preceq B$ just in case (i) for every path in B, the same path exists in A and its value in B subsumes its value in A; and (ii) for every pair of paths that is structure-sharing in B, the same pair of paths is structure-sharing in A.

We turn now to the centrally important notion of *unification*. The following situation often arises: we have two different feature structures A and B. Subsequently, we acquire the information that A and B actually describe the same object. In such a case, we are justified in representing the object in question by a new feature structure C which combines the information from A and B. To illustrate, let us return to the primitive agreement theory discussed above. Suppose that (55) and (56) represent what we know about a certain noun and a certain verb respectively, on the basis of their overt morphology:

(55)
$$\begin{bmatrix} \text{AGR} & \begin{bmatrix} \text{PER 3RD} \\ \text{GEN FEM} \end{bmatrix} \end{bmatrix}$$

(56)
$$\begin{bmatrix} \text{AGR} & \begin{bmatrix} \text{NUM PLU} \end{bmatrix} \end{bmatrix}$$

Suppose in addition that there is a certain sentence, about which we have the information (57) that its subject and predicate agree (note that this is just (51) in AVM format):

(57)
$$\begin{bmatrix} \text{SUBJECT} & \begin{bmatrix}\text{AGR } \boxed{1}\end{bmatrix} \\ \text{PREDICATE} & \begin{bmatrix}\text{AGR } \boxed{1}\end{bmatrix} \end{bmatrix}$$

If we subsequently learn that the noun and verb are the subject and predicate, respectively, of the sentence in question, we then have the information about the sentence shown in (58):

(58)
$$\begin{bmatrix} \text{SUBJECT} & \begin{bmatrix}\text{AGR } \boxed{1} \begin{bmatrix}\text{PER} & \text{3RD} \\ \text{GEN} & \text{FEM}\end{bmatrix}\end{bmatrix} \\ \text{PREDICATE} & \begin{bmatrix}\text{AGR } \boxed{1} \begin{bmatrix}\text{NUM PLU}\end{bmatrix}\end{bmatrix} \end{bmatrix}$$

But this could just as well have been written as (59):

(59)
$$\begin{bmatrix} \text{SUBJECT} & \begin{bmatrix}\text{AGR } \boxed{1} \begin{bmatrix}\text{PER} & \text{3RD} \\ \text{NUM} & \text{PLU} \\ \text{GEN} & \text{FEM}\end{bmatrix}\end{bmatrix} \\ \text{PREDICATE} & \begin{bmatrix}\text{AGR } \boxed{1}\end{bmatrix} \end{bmatrix}$$

In short, by virtue of having learned that the AGR values in (55) and (56) describe the same object, we combined their information to obtain (60):

(60)
$$\begin{bmatrix}\text{PER} & \text{3RD} \\ \text{NUM} & \text{PLU} \\ \text{GEN} & \text{FEM}\end{bmatrix}$$

We call (60) their *unification.*

More generally, if A, B, and C are feature structures, we call C the *unification* of A and B, written A $\wedge$ B, provided C is the least informative feature structure which is at least as informative as A and at least as informative as B. To put it another way, A $\wedge$ B has all the information of A and B, but nothing more.[6]

To take a slightly more complex example, the two noun phrase descriptions (61a) and (61b) unify to (62):

(61) a.
$$\begin{bmatrix}\text{AGR} & \begin{bmatrix}\text{PER 1ST}\end{bmatrix} \\ \text{CASE} & \text{NOM}\end{bmatrix}$$

[6] Mathematically, A $\wedge$ B is the *greatest lower bound* of A and B with respect to the subsumption ordering $\preceq$, i.e. it is the greatest feature structure which is subsumed by both A and B.

(61) b. $\begin{bmatrix} \text{AGR} & \begin{bmatrix} \text{NUM} & \text{SNG} \\ \text{GEN} & \text{MASC} \end{bmatrix} \\ \text{MAJ} & \text{N} \end{bmatrix}$

(62) $\begin{bmatrix} \text{AGR} & \begin{bmatrix} \text{PER} & \text{1ST} \\ \text{NUM} & \text{SNG} \\ \text{GEN} & \text{MASC} \end{bmatrix} \\ \text{CASE} & \text{NOM} \\ \text{MAJ} & \text{N} \end{bmatrix}$

The idea here is that unification works recursively: to unify feature structures which contain embedded feature structures, unify the corresponding substructures. In addition, if either A or B has shared structure, that too must be reflected in their unification. For example, the unification of (63a) and (63b) is (64):

(63) a. $\begin{bmatrix} \text{SUBJECT} & [\,] \\ \text{CATEGORY} & \boxed{1} \begin{bmatrix} \text{VFORM FIN} \end{bmatrix} \\ \text{PREDICATE} & \begin{bmatrix} \text{CATEGORY} & \boxed{1} \end{bmatrix} \end{bmatrix}$

b. $\begin{bmatrix} \text{PREDICATE} & \begin{bmatrix} \text{OBJECT} & [\,] \\ \text{CATEGORY} & \boxed{2} \\ \text{VERB} & \begin{bmatrix} \text{CATEGORY} & \boxed{2} \begin{bmatrix} \text{AUX} & + \end{bmatrix} \end{bmatrix} \end{bmatrix} \end{bmatrix}$

(64) $\begin{bmatrix} \text{SUBJECT} & [\,] \\ \text{CATEGORY} & \boxed{1} \begin{bmatrix} \text{VFORM} & \text{FIN} \\ \text{AUX} & + \end{bmatrix} \\ \text{PREDICATE} & \begin{bmatrix} \text{OBJECT} & [\,] \\ \text{CATEGORY} & \boxed{1} \\ \text{VERB} & \begin{bmatrix} \text{CATEGORY} & \boxed{1} \end{bmatrix} \end{bmatrix} \end{bmatrix}$

One special case is worthy of mention: in the case of atoms A and B, A and B unify if and only if they are equal.

Because of the central importance of the unification operation in information-based linguistics, grammatical formalisms which employ feature structures are often called *unification-based.* Important examples of linguistic theories based at least partially on unification are generalized phrase structure grammar (GPSG), in which feature structures are used in the analysis of syntactic categories, and lexical-functional grammar (LFG), where they are used to represent grammatical relations. Unification-based formalisms are also employed by computer scientists involved in natural language processing; the most influential ones have been the functional unification grammar (FUG) due to Martin Kay, and the PATR programming language developed at SRI International.

A note of caution is in order here: the unification of two feature structures A and B does not always exist! Usually this is because A and B contain mutually inconsistent information. It is obvious that mutually inconsistent feature structures cannot describe one and the same object. Such is the case when A and B specify different atomic values for the same attribute or path. For example, (65a) and (65b) cannot describe the same thing because they differ on the path AGR|GEN:

(65) a. $\begin{bmatrix} \text{AGR} \begin{bmatrix} \text{PER} & \text{3RD} \\ \text{GEN} & \text{FEM} \end{bmatrix} \end{bmatrix}$

b. $\begin{bmatrix} \text{AGR} \begin{bmatrix} \text{NUM} & \text{PLU} \\ \text{GEN} & \text{MASC} \end{bmatrix} \end{bmatrix}$

Similarly, (66a) and (66b) fail to unify:

(66) a. $\begin{bmatrix} \text{SUBJECT} & \text{AGR } \boxed{1} \\ \text{PREDICATE} & \text{AGR } \boxed{1} \end{bmatrix}$

b. $\begin{bmatrix} \text{SUBJECT} & \begin{bmatrix} \text{AGR} \begin{bmatrix} \text{NUM SNG} \end{bmatrix} \end{bmatrix} \\ \text{PREDICATE} & \begin{bmatrix} \text{AGR} \begin{bmatrix} \text{NUM PLU} \end{bmatrix} \end{bmatrix} \end{bmatrix}$

For according to (66a), the values SUBJECT|AGR and PREDICATE|AGR are the same, but according to (66b), they differ in number.

When the unification of two feature structures A and B does not exist, we say unification *fails*. It is common practice to use the symbol "$\perp$", read "bottom", to represent inconsistent information. Thus we write: $A \wedge B = \perp$. $\perp$ can be regarded as a sort of "improper" feature structure which contains *too much* information: it is overspecified, to the point of being inconsistent. Of course, $\perp$ cannot be an appropriate description of any object. In this sense, it is the opposite of $\top$, which is so underspecified that it can be regarded as a description of any object whatsoever. Just as $\top$ is the maximum element in the $\preceq$ ordering, $\perp$ is the minimum element. With the addition of $\perp$ to the set of feature structures, unification is always defined.

Another form of unification failure has to do with the notion of *cyclicity*. As we mentioned in passing at the beginning of this section, in mathematical terms a feature structure is a certain kind of finite state machine; in particular, it is required to be *acyclic*. This means simply that a feature structure can contain no *cycle*, i.e. a path whose value is shared with the value of a proper prefix (initial subpath) of that same path. Thus, for example, the graph (67) does not qualify as a feature structure:

(67)
$$\begin{bmatrix}\text{ATTRIBUTE1}\ \boxed{1}\begin{bmatrix}\text{ATTRIBUTE2}\ \boxed{1}\end{bmatrix}\end{bmatrix}$$

It is a perhaps surprising fact that the result of combining the information from two (acyclic) feature structures may turn out to contain a cycle. For example, the feature structures (68a) and (68b) combine to form the cyclic graph (69):

(68) a.
$$\begin{bmatrix}\text{ATTRIBUTE1} & \begin{bmatrix}\text{ATTRIBUTE1}\ \boxed{1}\end{bmatrix} \\ \text{ATTRIBUTE2} & \boxed{1}\end{bmatrix}$$

b.
$$\begin{bmatrix}\text{ATTRIBUTE1} & \boxed{2} \\ \text{ATTRIBUTE2} & \begin{bmatrix}\text{ATTRIBUTE1}\ \boxed{2}\end{bmatrix}\end{bmatrix}$$

(69)
$$\begin{bmatrix}\text{ATTRIBUTE1}\ \boxed{1} & \begin{bmatrix}\text{ATTRIBUTE1}\ \boxed{2}\end{bmatrix} \\ \text{ATTRIBUTE2}\ \boxed{2} & \begin{bmatrix}\text{ATTRIBUTE1}\ \boxed{1}\end{bmatrix}\end{bmatrix}$$

Of course, (69) does not count as the unification of (68a) and (68b) because it is not a feature structure (recall that by definition the unification of feature structures A and B is the least informative *feature structure* that is subsumed by both A and B). In fact, there is no feature structure which is subsumed by both (68a) and (68b), unless one counts $\perp$. Thus unification fails here, even though there is no path on which (68a) and (68b) differ.

In general, cyclic graphs present certain mathematical and computational complexities which are best avoided, although linguistic applications for them have been suggested from time to time. Fortunately, no need for them will arise in this book.

For reference, we assemble in (70) a few useful general facts about feature structures, subsumption, and unification:[7]

---

[7] These facts can be summarized by the statement that the feature structures under subsumption form a *meet semilattice* with top and bottom.

(70) a. (idempotency) $A \wedge A = A$

b. (commutativity) $A \wedge B = B \wedge A$

c. (associativity) $(A \wedge B) \wedge C = A \wedge (B \wedge C)$

d. (top) $\top \wedge A = A$

e. (bottom) $\bot \wedge A = \bot$

f. (interdefinability of $\preceq$ and $\wedge$) $A \preceq B$ if and only if $A \wedge B = A$

2.2 Augmentations of Feature Structures

The material presented in the preceding section constitutes something like a common core of notions related to feature structures that are present in one form or another in all unification-based formalisms. However, this rather lean system turns out to be insufficient for modelling certain aspects of linguistic information that will be of interest to us. In this section we introduce some elaborations of feature structures that will be needed in our theoretical development.

In modelling information it is often important to distinguish between cases where we *lack* information about the value of a certain attribute, and cases where that attribute is *irrelevant* for the kind of object under description. For example, suppose X is a syntactic category and Y is a sign, and our information about them is as shown in (71):

(71) a. information about category X:

$$\begin{bmatrix} \text{MAJ} & \text{V} \\ \text{VFORM} & \text{FIN} \\ \text{AUX} & + \end{bmatrix}$$

b. information about sign Y:

$$\begin{bmatrix} \text{SYN} & \begin{bmatrix} \text{MAJ} & \text{N} \end{bmatrix} \\ \text{SEM} & \text{DOG} \end{bmatrix}$$

Now neither of these feature structures bears a specification for the attribute PHONOLOGY. But the significance of that fact is very different in the two different cases. In (71b), the object Y is a sign, just the sort of thing that has phonology; we just don't know what its phonology is. To put it another way, we can regard (71b) as notational shorthand for (72):

(72) information about sign Y:

$$\begin{bmatrix} \text{SYN} & \begin{bmatrix} \text{MAJ} & \text{N} \end{bmatrix} \\ \text{SEM} & \text{DOG} \\ \text{PHON} & [\,] \end{bmatrix}$$

By virtue of not being mentioned, the PHONOLOGY attribute is *implicitly* specified as $\top$ (no information available). But in (71a), the thing X being described is a syntactic category; for such an object, the notion of phonology simply doesn't make sense. In short, different attributes make sense for different kinds of objects. A serious shortcoming of the simple feature-structure formalism presented in the preceding section is that it disregards this obvious fact. Our first augmentation of that formalism, then, is the addition of a notion of *type* for feature structures. That is, feature structures come in different *types* depending on the kind of object they describe, and a different set of attributes is appropriate for each type of feature structure.

Thus, for example, the appropriate attributes for the feature-structure type *sign* include PHONOLOGY, SYNTAX, and SEMANTICS; appropriate attributes for the type *agreement-value* include PERSON, NUMBER, and GENDER. When it is necessary to be explicit about the type of a feature structure, we subscript it at the lower left as in (73):

(73) $${}_{sign}\begin{bmatrix}\text{PHON}\\ \text{SYN}\\ \text{SEM}\end{bmatrix}$$

In most cases, though, the type of a feature structure will be evident from the context, so the subscript will be omitted. The type of a feature structure should be regarded as part of the information it provides about the described object. For example, (74a) is more informative than (74b), since the former at least tells us that the thing described is a sign, while (74b) ($\top$) tells us nothing at all:

(74) a. ${}_{sign}[\ \ ]$

b. $[\ \ ]$

It should also be clear that for different attributes, different types of values are appropriate. For example, the SYNTAX attribute for the type *sign* takes feature structures of type *syntactic-category* as values; the AGREEMENT attribute takes feature structures of type *agreement-value* as values, etc. In the case of an "atomic-valued" attribute such as the PERSON attribute for the type *agreement-value*, appropriate values are the atoms of type *person* 1ST, 2ND, and 3RD.

There is a natural connection between the subsumption ordering ($\preceq$) on feature structures and types of feature structures, which arises from the fact that one type t_1 may subsume another type t_2. In such a case we say t_2 is a *subtype* of t_1 or t_1 is a *supertype* of t_2. For example, *lexical-sign* and *phrasal-sign* are both subtypes of *sign*. Naturally, any feature structure of a given type t_1 is also considered to be of type t_2 for any t_2 that subsumes t_1, e.g. if A is a feature structure of type *phrasal-sign*, then it is also of type *sign*. Two obvious consequences of this are the following: (i) any attribute which is appropriate for a given type is also appropriate for any subtype of that type; and (ii) if a given type requires that a certain one of its attributes take values of a certain type, then the same is true for any subtype of the given type. For example PHONOLOGY, SYNTAX, and SEMANTICS are appropriate attributes for *phrasal-sign* because they are appropriate for *sign*, and the SYNTAX value in a feature structure of type *phrasal-sign* is required to be of type *syntactic-category* because that same restriction holds for feature structures of type *sign*. Thus, a feature structure type *inherits* all the attributes and corresponding type restrictions on their values from all of its supertypes.

However, in addition to the attributes and corresponding type restrictions on values that a feature structure type inherits from its supertypes, a type may also introduce attributes of its own. For example, in addition to PHONOLOGY, SYNTAX, and SEMANTICS, there is another attribute DAUGHTERS which is appropriate for the type *phrasal-sign*, but not for the type *lexical-sign*. This reflects the fact that phrasal signs have daughters (i.e. internal constituent structure) but lexical signs do not. In addition, although a type must obey any type restrictions on attributes inherited from its supertypes, it may impose further restrictions of its own. For example, as we noted before, *phrasal-sign* inherits from *sign* the type restriction *syntactic-category* on its SYNTAX attribute. But in addition, a feature structure of type *phrasal-sign* further requires that its SYNTAX value be a *phrasal* (or *nonlexical*) category, i.e. one that contains the specification [LEX –].

It should be intuitively clear that the feature structure types themselves are partially ordered by subsumption, i.e. *phrasal-sign* $\preceq$ *sign*, *lexical-sign* $\preceq$ *sign*, etc.

We turn next to some augmentations of a logical nature. Suppose that A and B are feature structures that appropriately describe a certain object X. Then we can think of A and B as expressing *true propositions* about X. Now as we saw above, since A and B describe the same thing they can be unified, and A $\wedge$ B also describes X. Conversely, if we know that C describes X and that C is A $\wedge$ B, then we also know that A and B describe X. So A $\wedge$ B expresses a true proposition about X if and only if both A and B do. Thus the unification of feature structures corresponds to the *logical conjunction* of the propositions that they express. Using the notation of propositional logic: if P is the proposition about X expressed by A and Q is the proposition about X expressed by B, then A $\wedge$ B expresses the proposition P AND Q.

But there are other operations on logical propositions besides conjunction, e.g. disjunction (P OR Q), implication (P IMPLIES Q), and negation (NOT P). Correspondingly, linguistic information can be of a disjunctive, implicative (i.e. conditional), or negative nature. Thus we need to augment our system of feature structures to include these notions.

We begin with disjunctive information. It often comes about that we know of some linguistic object X that it is appropriately described by *either* A *or* B, but we don't know which. This information is called the *disjunction* of A and B, written A ∨ B. The simplest cases of disjunction involve disjunctions of atomic values. For example, the PERSON attribute may take as values not only 1ST, 2ND, and 3RD, but also any value formed from these by disjunction: 1ST ∨ 2ND, 1ST ∨ 3RD, 2ND ∨ 3RD, and 1ST ∨ 2ND ∨ 3RD. This last value is the most general possible value for PERSON, i.e. it is equal to $_{person}[\ ]$.

In more complex cases, we have disjunctions of nonatomic feature structures. For example, case and agreement for the German article *die* might be represented as in (75):

(75)
$$\begin{bmatrix} \text{CASE} & \text{NOM} \vee \text{ACC} \\ \text{AGR} & \begin{bmatrix} \text{GEN} & \text{FEM} \\ \text{NUM} & \text{SNG} \end{bmatrix} \vee \begin{bmatrix} \text{NUM} & \text{PLU} \end{bmatrix} \end{bmatrix}$$

Thus we generalize the notion of feature structure by allowing disjunctive specifications of values. For ease of reference, we shall refer to these generalized (i.e. possibly disjunctive) feature structures simply as feature structures; to refer specifically to a feature structure which contains no disjunctions (i.e. feature structure *simpliciter* in our earlier terminology), we shall use the term *basic* feature structure.[8] There is a natural generalization of the notion of subsumption that goes along with feature structures in this new sense: if A is $A_1 \vee \ldots \vee A_n$ and B is $B_1 \vee \ldots \vee B_m$ (where the disjuncts are all basic feature structures), then we say $A \preceq B$ just in case each of the A_i is subsumed (in the original sense) by one of the B_j. (In theory, countably infinite disjunctions are also legitimate feature structures. We will not make use of them here, but some applications for them, and even some computationally tractable methods of dealing with them, have been suggested in the LFG literature under the rubric of "functional uncertainty"; for details see Kaplan, Maxwell, and Zaenen (1987) and Johnson (1987).) Notice that if A and B are basic, then this augmented notion of subsumption just reduces to the old one. The unification operation likewise generalizes: the unification A ∧ B of two (generalized) feature structures A and B is the least informative (generalized) feature structure subsumed by both A and B, and the properties summarized in (70) still hold.

By contrast, the *disjunction* of A and B, A ∨ B, is the *most* informative feature structure which *subsumes* both A and B.[9] The general properties of

---

[8] Technically, a feature structure in this generalized sense is a set of pairwise-subsumption-incomparable basic feature structures.

[9] In mathematical terms, the unification—or *conjunction*, as it is often called—of $A = A_1 \vee \ldots \vee A_n$ and $B = B_1 \vee \ldots \vee B_m$ is obtained by taking the disjunction of all the $A_i \wedge B_j$ and then discarding all nonmaximal disjuncts.

disjunction given in (76) are analogous to the properties (70) for unification. Here the variables A, B, and C range over (general) feature structures.[10]

(76)
a. (idempotency) $A \vee A = A$
b. (commutativity) $A \vee B = B \vee A$
c. (associativity) $(A \vee B) \vee C = A \vee (B \vee C)$
d. (top) $\top \vee A = \top$
e. (bottom) $\perp \vee A = A$
f. (interdefinability of $\preceq$ and $\vee$) $A \preceq B$ if and only if $A \vee B = B$

It is a useful fact that unification and disjunction of feature structures interact nicely with each other. To be more precise, they obey the laws of distributivity indicated in (77):[11]

(77) (distributivity)
$$A \wedge (B \vee C) = (A \wedge B) \vee (A \wedge C)$$
$$A \vee (B \wedge C) = (A \vee B) \wedge (A \vee C)$$

For example, (78a) and (78b) give precisely the same information:

(78) a.
$$\left(\begin{bmatrix} \text{CASE NOM} \\ \text{AGR} \begin{bmatrix} \text{PER 3RD} \end{bmatrix} \end{bmatrix} \vee \begin{bmatrix} \text{CASE ACC} \\ \text{AGR} \begin{bmatrix} \text{PER 1ST} \end{bmatrix} \end{bmatrix} \right) \wedge \begin{bmatrix} \text{AGR|NUM SNG} \end{bmatrix}$$

b.
$$\begin{bmatrix} \text{CASE NOM} \\ \text{AGR} \begin{bmatrix} \text{PER 3RD} \\ \text{NUM SNG} \end{bmatrix} \end{bmatrix} \vee \begin{bmatrix} \text{CASE ACC} \\ \text{AGR} \begin{bmatrix} \text{PER 1ST} \\ \text{NUM SNG} \end{bmatrix} \end{bmatrix}$$

In addition to the very general facts about subsumption, unification, and disjunction given in (70), (76), and (77), which are essentially facts about the logic of feature structures, there are also certain nonlogical facts which arise from our knowledge of what types of linguistic objects there

---

And, $\vee$ is the *least upper bound* operation with respect to the subsumption ordering $\preceq$. It is obtained by taking the disjunction of all the A_i and B_j, discarding all nonmaximal disjuncts.

[10] Together with (70), these facts can be summarized by the statement that feature structures under subsumption form a *lattice* with top and bottom, with unification as the lattice meet and disjunction as the lattice join. Caution: this lattice is "upside down" from the point of view of many computer scientists who are accustomed to identifying "bigger" with "more information". But it is "rightside up" from the point of view of standard logic, in the sense that $\wedge$ and $\vee$ correspond to conjunction and disjunction respectively. The best mnemonic here is that one feature structure is bigger than another if it appropriately describes a bigger set of objects.

[11] Thus the subsumption lattice of feature structures is a distributive lattice.

are and the relationships between them. For example, the only possibilities for signs are that they be either lexical or phrasal, so we have (79):

(79) $\quad {}_{sign}[\ ] = {}_{lexical\text{-}sign}[\ ] \vee {}_{phrasal\text{-}sign}[\ ]$

Moreover, since being lexical and being phrasal are mutually incompatible possibilities, we also have (80):

(80) $\quad {}_{lexical\text{-}sign}[\ ] \wedge {}_{phrasal\text{-}sign}[\ ] = \bot$

In general, such facts about relationships among types of linguistic objects will be obvious, and we will not explicitly state them.

We introduced feature structures (in the generalized sense) in order to model disjunctive information. As it turns out, they are sufficient for modelling conditional (implicative) and negative information as well. We begin with conditional information; negative information, as we shall see, is a special case of conditional information. It often comes about that we know of a linguistic object X that *if* it satisfies description A, then it must also satisfy description B. Principles of universal grammar are generally of this form. For example, to simplify very slightly, the *Head Feature Principle* says: if sign X is phrasal and Y is the head daughter of X, then X and Y share the same value for the path SYNTAX|LOCAL|HEAD. (Note: as we shall see in the next chapter, syntactic categories are analyzed as having the two attributes LOCAL and BINDING, while LOCAL values in turn have the attributes HEAD, LEX, and SUBCAT. The significance of these distinctions is irrelevant to the present discussion). This principle can be expressed as the CONDITIONAL feature structure (81):

(81) $$ {}_{phrasal\text{-}sign}[\ ] \Rightarrow \begin{bmatrix} \text{SYN}|\text{LOC}|\text{HEAD}\ \boxed{1} \\ \text{DTRS}|\text{HEAD-DTR}|\text{SYN}|\text{LOC}|\text{HEAD}\ \boxed{1} \end{bmatrix} $$

The symbol '⇒' here denotes a certain binary operation on feature structures. In terms of information content, the ⇒ operation can be described as follows: if A and B are feature structures, then A ⇒ B is the greatest (i.e. least informative) feature structure whose unification with A is subsumed by B. The most important consequence of this from our point of view is that if X is a linguistic object which is appropriately described by both C and A ⇒ B, and C is subsumed by A, then $C' = C \wedge B$ is also an appropriate description of X. Suppose, for example, that X is an English sign token and that our current information about X is given by some feature structure C. Let us also suppose C includes the information that X is phrasal, i.e. $C \preceq {}_{phrasal\text{-}sign}[\ ]$. Now since X is a sign and universal principles hold for all signs, X is also appropriately described by (81). It follows that X is appropriately described by the feature structure C′ obtained by unifying C with the right-hand side of (81), i.e. we can add to our information about X that its head features are the same as those on its head daughter.[12]

The significance of a universal principle such as (81) can best be grasped by first understanding how it fits into our overall linguistic theory. We distinguish between a theory of universal grammar and a theory of a particular natural language. A theory of universal grammar is simply what we get when we unify all universal principles such as (81): it is a theoretical model of universal linguistic knowledge, the information about language that is available to all normal adult humans by virtue of their shared genetic endowment, independent of which language communities they belong to. To say that (81) is a universal principle is to say: human beings implicitly have the information about any linguistic object—in any language whatsoever—that if it is a phrasal sign then its head features coincide with the head features on its head daughter. If $P_1, \ldots, P_n$ are the complete inventory of such principles, then our theory of universal grammar, UG, is (82), where one of the P_i, let us say P_1, is the Head Feature Principle:

(82) $\mathrm{UG} = P_1 \wedge \ldots \wedge P_n$

Then what would a theory of a particular language, such as English, amount to? Of course, it has to be subsumed by (82), for each language is subject to the constraints imposed by universal grammar. In addition, each language will impose a set of *language-specific principles* $P_{n+1}, \ldots, P_{n+m}$ which are not valid cross-linguistically but which apply to all linguistic objects of the language in question. An example of an English-specific principle is the constraint that if X is a phrasal sign whose head daughter is a lexical sign Y, then Y linearly precedes any of X's complement daughters. (This principle clearly does not apply, for example, to Japanese, where the head occurs phrase-finally.) In addition, each language makes available a different set of options for what counts as a lexical sign and what counts as a phrasal sign, i.e. each language has its own lexicon and grammar rules. Thus, if $L_1, \ldots, L_p$ correspond to the lexical signs of English and $R_1, \ldots, R_q$ to its grammar rules, then a theory of English takes the form (83):

(83) $\mathrm{English} = P_1 \wedge \ldots \wedge P_{n+m} \wedge (L_1 \vee \ldots \vee L_p \vee R_1 \vee \ldots \vee R_q)$

That is, a linguistic object is an English sign token just in case (i) either it instantiates one of the lexical signs or it instantiates one of the grammar

---

[12] Mathematically speaking, $\Rightarrow$ is the *relative pseudocomplement* operation in the subsumption lattice. Because this operation can be shown to be well-defined, the subsumption lattice of feature structures constitutes a distributive lattice of a special kind called a *Heyting algebra*. It is not hard to show that $A \Rightarrow B$ can be an infinite disjunction even if neither A nor B is; fortunately such cases do not arise in our applications.

rules, and (ii) it satisfies all the universal and English-specific grammatical principles.

The last of the logical notions we consider for feature structures is *negation*. This is just a special case of $\Rightarrow$: if A is a feature structure, then its negation, $\neg$A, is just A $\Rightarrow$ $\perp$. This is simply the most general feature structure which fails to unify with A. As with A $\Rightarrow$ B in general, we can always express $\neg$A as a (possibly infinite) disjunction of basic feature structures, although it is seldom practical to do so. On the other hand, we often employ negation to avoid writing out a long disjunction. Suppose, for example, we know of some sign that its agreement is not third-singular (e.g. because it is the SYNTAX of some sign which is known to be the subject of the finite verb *go*). We could describe our information about the agreement value disjunctively as in (84a):

(84) a. $_{agr\text{-}value}[\text{NUM PLU}] \vee {}_{agr\text{-}value}\begin{bmatrix}\text{PER 1ST}\\ \text{NUM SNG}\end{bmatrix} \vee {}_{agr\text{-}value}\begin{bmatrix}\text{PER 2ND}\\ \text{NUM SNG}\end{bmatrix}$

But the same information can be expressed more compactly in the form (84b):

(84) b. $\neg\,{}_{agr\text{-}value}\begin{bmatrix}\text{PER 3RD}\\ \text{NUM SNG}\end{bmatrix}$

So far, we have limited our attention to feature structures which are either atoms, simple feature structures, or logical combinations thereof. We conclude our overview of feature structures with a discussion of some augmentations allowing partial information structures which are specified in more complex ways: list descriptions, set descriptions, and functionally dependent values.

List descriptions, written as a list of feature structure descriptions between angle brackets, are appropriate when the thing being described is itself a list (or sequence) of objects. For example, in the next chapter we will introduce an attribute of syntactic categories called SUBCAT which gives information about the *subcategorization* of a sign, i.e. restrictions on the other signs—subject, objects, verbal complements, etc.—that the sign co-occurs with. Thus the SUBCAT value for the verb *persuade* is (roughly) the list ⟨VP[INF], NP, NP⟩ where the symbols VP[INF] and NP are themselves abbreviations for feature structures corresponding to signs with certain syntactic properties. The order of elements in a SUBCAT list is significant: it corresponds to the notion of *obliqueness* in traditional grammar, with the rightmost element being least oblique (i.e. the grammatical subject). Subsumption and unification for list values are defined componentwise (like vector addition), as indicated in (85):

(85) a. $\langle A_1, \ldots, A_n\rangle \preceq \langle B_1, \ldots, B_n\rangle$ iff $A_i \preceq B_i$, $i = 1, \ldots, n$.

b. $\langle A_1, \ldots, A_n\rangle \wedge \langle B_1, \ldots, B_n\rangle = \langle A_1 \wedge B_1, \ldots, A_n \wedge B_n\rangle$.

Intuitively, a list description of length n should be thought of as describing something which is itself a list of length *n*. Obviously, then, list descriptions of different lengths must fail to unify, since they give conflicting information about the list of objects which they purport to describe.

Another key application of lists, which also makes crucial use of feature structures' potential for recursive embedding, may require a little reorientation on the part of readers whose background is primarily in generative-transformational linguistics. This application arises in the representation of signs with internal constituent structure, traditionally presented in the form of phrase structure trees. Simplifying somewhat, the information contained in a typical phrase structure tree like (86) can be rendered in terms of feature structures as (87).

(86)

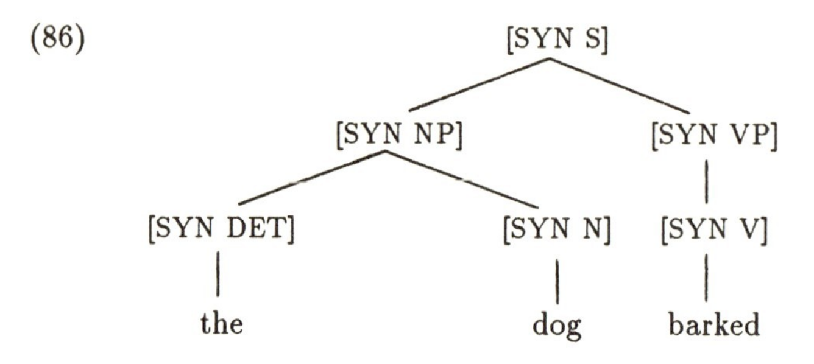

(87)

$$\begin{bmatrix} \text{PHON} & \text{the dog barked} \\ \text{SYN} & \text{S} \\ \text{DTRS} & \left\langle \begin{bmatrix} \text{PHON the dog} \\ \text{SYN NP} \\ \text{DTRS} \left\langle \begin{bmatrix} \text{PHON the} \\ \text{SYN} \quad \text{DET} \end{bmatrix}, \begin{bmatrix} \text{PHON dog} \\ \text{SYN} \quad \text{N} \end{bmatrix} \right\rangle \end{bmatrix}, \begin{bmatrix} \text{PHON barked} \\ \text{SYN VP} \\ \text{DTRS} \left\langle \begin{bmatrix} \text{PHON barked} \\ \text{SYN} \quad \text{V} \end{bmatrix} \right\rangle \end{bmatrix} \right\rangle \end{bmatrix}$$

In this simplified illustration, we use the order of elements on the DAUGHTERS list to encode the "surface order" of sister constituents (i.e. the temporal order of the corresponding phonological realizations). There is an obvious redundancy here, for evidently the PHONOLOGY value of each constituent is predictable from the DAUGHTERS values once the PHONOLOGY values of the "leaf nodes" are given; this redundancy will be absent from the structures we actually use in subsequent chapters, where the list order of elements within DAUGHTERS values does not directly reflect surface order but rather an abstract order of grammatical relations corresponding to the traditional notion of *obliqueness.*

Set descriptions, written as a list of feature structure descriptions between curly brackets, are in order when the thing being described is itself a set of objects. Unlike list descriptions, the order of elements in a set description is not significant. A cautionary note is in order here: just as with usual set-theoretic notation, there is no prohibition against set descriptions of the form $\{A_1, \ldots, A_n\}$ where two of the A_i turn out to be descriptions of the same object. Thus, (88) might describe the contents of a parking lot, even if there are only two cars in the lot:

(88)
$$\left\{ \begin{bmatrix} \text{MAKE TOYOTA} \\ \text{YEAR 1984} \end{bmatrix}, \begin{bmatrix} \text{MAKE DATSUN} \\ \text{YEAR 1985} \end{bmatrix}, \begin{bmatrix} \text{COLOR RED} \end{bmatrix} \right\}$$

Set description (88) gives the information that the lot contains a Toyota, a Datsun, and a red car. But there is no way to tell on the basis of (88) alone whether the red car is the Toyota, the Datsun, or a third car about which no further information is available. On the other hand, we will assume that (i) every object in the set under description is described by at least one of the descriptions in the set description; and (ii) each description in the set description gives information about only one member of the set being described. To put it another way, there is a (possibly many-to-one) onto function which associates to each element of the set description a member of the set being described. Thus (88) cannot be an appropriate description of a parking lot with more than three cars on it.

Unification of set values is rather difficult to describe formally, although the intuition is simple: if S_1 and S_2 are two set descriptions, then $S_1 \wedge S_2$ describes any set which could have been described by *both* S_1 and S_2. The basic idea is illustrated by (89a) and (89b), whose unification is (89c):

(89) a.
$$\left\{ \begin{bmatrix} \text{MAKE TOYOTA} \end{bmatrix}, \begin{bmatrix} \text{MAKE DATSUN} \end{bmatrix} \right\}$$

b.
$$\left\{ \begin{bmatrix} \text{COLOR WHITE} \end{bmatrix}, \begin{bmatrix} \text{COLOR RED} \end{bmatrix} \right\}$$

c.
$$\left\{ \begin{bmatrix} \text{MAKE TOYOTA} \\ \text{COLOR WHITE} \end{bmatrix}, \begin{bmatrix} \text{MAKE DATSUN} \\ \text{COLOR RED} \end{bmatrix} \right\} \vee$$
$$\left\{ \begin{bmatrix} \text{MAKE DATSUN} \\ \text{COLOR WHITE} \end{bmatrix}, \begin{bmatrix} \text{MAKE TOYOTA} \\ \text{COLOR RED} \end{bmatrix} \right\}$$

The complexity arises from the fact that in general we do not know which feature structures in the first set description correspond to which feature structures in the second, so that we have to consider disjunctions over all possible ways of matching them up. Another example of set-value unification is given in (90):

(90) $\{[\ ], [\ ]\} \wedge \{[\ ]\} = \{[\ ]\}$.

Here the left conjunct on the left-hand side could have described a set with either one or two elements, but the right conjunct can describe only a singleton set; hence the possibility of a two-element set is eliminated.

Finally, we consider the notion of *functionally dependent values.* It often happens that our information about the value of some path p in a feature structure is in this form: if the value of path p_1 is x_1 and the value of path p_2 is x_2, then whatever x_1 and x_2 may be, the value of path p is $F(x_1, x_2)$, where F is some specified function. (More generally, F may be a function of arbitrarily many arguments.) That is, one value functionally depends on other values in the same feature structure.

In our applications, the functions involved in such dependencies are usually list operations or set operations. For example, simplifying only slightly, one of the principles of universal grammar that we will introduce later says that the SUBCAT value on the head daughter of a phrasal sign is always the list obtained by joining together the list of complement daughters with the SUBCAT value on the sign itself. To put it another way: the subcategorization of a phrasal sign is the subcategorization of its head less those requirements that are actually satisfied by complement daughters of the phrasal sign. This principle can be expressed by the conditional feature structure (91):

(91) $_{\textit{phrasal-sign}}[\ ] \Rightarrow$

$$\begin{bmatrix} \text{SYN|LOC|SUBCAT } \boxed{2} \\ \text{DTRS} \begin{bmatrix} \text{HEAD-DTR|SYN|LOC|SUBCAT append(} \boxed{1}, \boxed{2} \text{)} \\ \text{COMP-DTRS } \boxed{1} \end{bmatrix} \end{bmatrix}$$

Here "append" denotes the function which joins two lists as in (92):

(92) $\text{append}(\langle A_1, \ldots, A_n \rangle, \langle B_1, \ldots, B_m \rangle) = \langle A_1, \ldots, A_n, B_1, \ldots, B_m \rangle$

Another operation which arises frequently in functional dependencies is set union, which is defined in (93):

(93) $\text{union}(\{A_1, \ldots, A_n\}, \{B_1, \ldots, B_m\}) = \{A_1, \ldots, A_n, B_1, \ldots, B_m\}$

This operation takes as arguments two set descriptions and returns as value a description which is appropriate to any set which is the union of two sets appropriately described by the two argument set descriptions. It is important to be aware that set union is different from set unification . For example, the union of (90a) and (90b) is not (90c) but rather (94):

(94) {[MAKE TOYOTA], [MAKE DATSUN], [COLOR WHITE], [COLOR RED]}

Note that this could describe lots containing anywhere from two to four cars. This is very different from the situation with set unification, where the descriptions being unified are necessarily regarded as descriptions of the same set.

Various other list and set operations involved in the specification of functionally dependent values will be introduced as the need arises.

With these formal tools in place, we now proceed with the task of building up a particular theory of natural language syntax and semantics of the general form given in (83) above, using feature structures to describe signs, rules, principles, and the other linguistic objects of which they are composed.

2.3 Suggestions for Further Reading

The use of feature structures in syntax originates under the name "functional descriptions" in Kay's (1979) functional grammar (called functional unification grammar (FUG) in Kay (1984, 1985)), where they are used to represent both lexical entries and rules (and therefore, by disjunction, the grammar itself). This formalism was an important early influence on the development of LFG (see especially Kaplan and Bresnan (1982)), where feature structures make their appearance in the form of "functional structures", the linguistic level where information about grammatical functions is represented. The use of feature structures to model syntactic categories in GPSG work is introduced in Pollard (ms. 1) and Gazdar and Pullum (1982); unification is used extensively in Gazdar et al. (1985) and even more so in the closely related HG of Pollard (1984). In the past two years, there has been a resurgence of interest in categorial grammars enriched by insights from unification-based formalisms, represented by Karttunen (1986b), Uzskoreit (1986a), and Zeevat et al. (1987).

The possibility of using feature structures in both syntax and semantics simultaneously seems also to have originated with Kay (1984). The first systematic semantic applications that we are aware of are Fenstad et al. (1985) and Pollard (ms. 2), which are remarkably similar in their situation-oriented semantic analyses and overall perspective, despite differences in syntactic orientation (LFG and HPSG respectively). Also very close to the semantic approach of this book is the unification-based approach to DRS theory represented by Johnson and Klein (1986) and Zeevat et al. (1987).

One line of work which has played a special role in the unification-based community has been the development at SRI International of PATR-II, which is not a linguistic theory but rather a computer language for constructing unification-based implementations of a wide range of linguistic theories; in addition to providing tools for theory construction, this work has also contributed importantly to the establishment of mathematical and computational foundations for such theories. PATR-II and related work are well documented in Shieber et al. (1983), Karttunen (1984), Pereira and Shieber (1984), Shieber (1984), and Karttunen (1986a); the most accessible introduction can be found in Shieber (1986), which is also provides an excellent overview of unification-based grammar formalisms in general.

As for works concerned with the mathematical technicalities which underly feature structures, we have been most influenced by the logical approach of Rounds and Kasper (1986), Kasper and Rounds (1986), and Moshier and Rounds (1987); and by Ait-Kaci's (1984) algebraic approach in terms of lattices of data types.

3 Syntactic Features and Syntactic Categories

As we saw in the preceding chapter, a sign such as the English lexical sign *cookie* can be partially described by a feature structure employing the attributes PHONOLOGY and SEMANTICS, as in (95):

(95) $$\begin{bmatrix} \text{PHON} & \text{cookie} \\ \text{SEM} & \text{COOKIE} \end{bmatrix}$$

And if English consisted of nothing but words, without the possibility of combining simple expressions to form complex ones, then we might imagine getting by on such things alone: our whole theory of English would just be a big disjunction of feature structures like (95). But of course natural languages are more complicated than that; words and phrases of different kinds characteristically combine with phrases of certain other kinds, in accordance with rules and principles of grammar, to form new phrases that can be used to convey more complex messages. And for this to be possible, a sign must include, in addition to specifications of its phonological and semantic properties, information about its combinatorial potential with respect to other signs, i.e. its *syntactic* properties. In a sense, then, syntax is the glue that holds phonology and semantics together.

Now syntax is an aspect of language that Saussure had notoriously little to say about; he regarded it as outside the realm of *langue*. Given the absence of any notion of a recursive set of rules in the linguistics of his day, it is scarcely surprising that Saussure was not disposed to perceive combinatorial potential as part of the sign system. We, however, shall have a good deal to say about the syntax of signs, and accordingly we introduce the SYNTAX attribute to serve as the repository of syntactic information in feature structures of type *sign*. Thus the information associated with a sign in general has the form (96):

(96) $$\begin{bmatrix} \text{PHON} \\ \text{SYN} \\ \text{SEM} \end{bmatrix}$$

The linguistic objects that serve as values of the SYNTAX attribute are called *syntactic categories*, or simply categories. The attributes (or paths) that are appropriate for describing categories are usually called *syntactic features*, or simply features. In this chapter, we will give an overview of the syntactic features employed in our theory, together with an indication of restrictions on their possible values and the nature of the linguistic distinctions that they reflect.

We begin by drawing a fundamental distinction between *local* features and *binding* features. Local features in general specify inherent syntactic properties of a sign, such as part of speech, inflection, case, subcategorization (including the traditional notion of government), and lexicality (whether a sign is lexical or phrasal). Binding features, on the other hand, provide information about dependent elements of various kinds contained as constituents within a sign, such as "missing" elements (often called *gaps* or *traces*), relative pronouns, and interrogative expressions. Such information is nonlocal in the sense that the kinds of syntactic dependencies involved (e.g. between a gap and its "filler" or between a relative pronoun and the antecedent noun) may extend over arbitrarily long distances. As we will see, these two types of grammatical information are governed by distinct grammatical principles, and hence are propagated through linguistic structures along different kinds of paths, in a manner to be made precise in subsequent chapters.

Among the local syntactic features, a three-way distinction is to be drawn. First there are *head* features, which specify syntactic properties that a lexical sign shares with its projections (i.e. the phrasal signs headed by that lexical sign). Second, the feature SUBCAT gives information about the valence of a sign, i.e. the number and kind of phrasal signs that the sign in question *subcategorizes for* (or characteristically combines with). And third, the binary feature LEX is used to distinguish between lexical and non-lexical signs; this distinction plays much the same role as the distinction between X^0 categories and X^n categories with $n>0$ in familiar versions of "$\overline{X}$-theory".

As for binding features, there are three that will be discussed in this book. The SLASH feature provides information about gaps within a sign which have not yet been bound to an appropriate filler (or "dislocated" constituent); the REL and QUE features give information about unbound relative and interrogative elements within the sign.

Thus the overall structure of a sign is as indicated in (97):

(97)

$$\begin{bmatrix} \text{PHON} & \\ \text{SYN} & \begin{bmatrix} \text{LOC} & \begin{bmatrix} \text{HEAD} \\ \text{SUBCAT} \\ \text{LEX} \end{bmatrix} \\ \text{BIND} & \begin{bmatrix} \text{SLASH} \\ \text{REL} \\ \text{QUE} \end{bmatrix} \end{bmatrix} \\ \text{SEM} & \end{bmatrix}$$

3.1 Head Features and Constituent Structure Types

The notion of the *head* of a phrase is one with a long history, stemming from traditional grammar and playing a central role in recent syntactic frameworks such as GB and GPSG. The underlying intuition is simply that each phrase contains a certain word which is centrally important in the sense that it determines many of the syntactic properties of the phrase as a whole; that word is called the *lexical head* of the phrase. Thus the lexical head of a verb phrase or sentence is a verb, the lexical head of a prepositional phrase is a preposition, etc.; in fact, the very terms "verb phrase" (VP) "noun phrase" (NP), "adjective phrase" (AP), and "prepositional phrase" (PP) are used to classify phrases on the basis of their lexical head's part of speech.[1] More generally, the *head* of a phrase is that daughter (immediate constituent) of the phrase which either is or contains the phrase's lexical head. For example, in the sentence *Sandy likes bagels*, the head daughter is the verb phrase *likes bagels*. The verb *likes* in turn is the head of the verb phrase, and it is also the lexical head of both the verb phrase and the sentence.

A few simple examples will suffice to illustrate the central importance of the lexical head in a phrase. First, it is clear that the part of speech of the lexical head is a major determinant of a phrase's combinatory properties. For example, as (98a) shows, the English copula (*be* and its inflected forms) can be followed by an NP, AP, VP, or PP:

(98) a. Mary was {
the tallest skateboard champion in central Idaho.
so drunk she couldn't remember her own name.
leaving on the the next train.
kicked by a deranged wildebeest.
under the station clock.
}

But *become* can be followed only by an NP or AP, as shown in (98b):

(98) b. Mary became {
the tallest skateboard champion in central Idaho.
so drunk she couldn't remember her own name.
*leaving on the the next train.
*kicked by a deranged wildebeest.
*under the station clock.
}

And (98c)–(98e) give examples of verbs which can be followed only by NP, AP, PP, and VP respectively:

(98) c. Kim devoured {
the three-day-old bagel.
*melancholy.
*on her eccentric uncle Pavel.
*leave on the next train.
}

---

[1] For the time being we use such terms only on an informal basis. In the following section, we shall actually define them in terms of feature structures.

(98) d. Kim waxed { *the three-day-old bagel. / melancholy. / *on her eccentric uncle Pavel. / *leave on the next train. }

e. Sandy depended { *the three-day-old bagel. / *melancholy. / on her eccentric uncle Pavel. / *leave on the next train. }

f. Chris must { *the three-day-old bagel. / *melancholy. / *on her eccentric uncle Pavel. / leave on the next train. }

Similarly, it is easy to see that the combinatory possibilities of a clause depend on the form of the head verb.

(99) a. I believe that { *John leave tomorrow. / John leaves tomorrow. / *John leaving tomorrow. }

b. Bagels, { *John like. / John likes. / *John liking. }

c. I demand that { John leave tomorrow. / *John leaves tomorrow. / *John leaving tomorrow. }

d. With { *John leave tomorrow / *John leaves tomorrow / John leaving tomorrow / John in New York / John dead }, things sure will be dull.

Thus, as (99a) and (99b) show, a clause headed by a finite verb (but not by a base-form or present participle) can occur as complement to the verb *believe* and also in the topicalization construction. On the other hand, the verb *demand* takes a clausal complement only if it is headed by a base-form verb (99c). And (99d) shows that a clause headed by a verb in present-participial form (but not in finite or base form) shares with predicative prepositional and adjectival clauses the ability to function as a sentential adjunct marked by *with*. From these examples we see that verb form is not a property simply of the verb itself, but also of the entire clause headed by the verb. For this reason, we speak of finite clauses, present-participial clauses, etc.

And in the same way, the combinatory potential of a prepositional phrase depends on the precise form of the preposition that heads it. For example, some verbs require a prepositional phrase complement headed by the preposition *on*, as illustrated in (100):

(100) a. Kim depends { *to Sandy. / *of Sandy. / on Sandy. / *above Sandy. / *over Sandy. }

b. Kim blames all his misfortunes { *to Sandy. / *of Sandy. / on Sandy. / *above Sandy. / *over Sandy. }

The features VFORM (verb form), PFORM (preposition form), and MAJ (the "major", or part-of-speech feature) —as well as a number of other features to be discussed below—are all classified as head features. That is, appropriate values for the attribute HEAD in a syntactic category are described by feature structures with attributes MAJ, VFORM, etc.

Before proceeding with our inventory of head features and their possible values, however, it may be instructive to sketch briefly how the sharing of head features between lexical signs and their phrasal projections will be accounted for in our theory. This will require anticipating a few notions which will be explained in full detail in chapters to come. First, there is a fundamental division of all signs into those which have internal constituent structure (*phrasal* signs or simply *phrases*), and those which do not (*lexical* signs, or simply *words*); corresponding to this distinction are the two subtypes of (the feature-structure type) *sign*, *lexical-sign* and *phrasal-sign*. (We defer the important question of just what phrases there are in English until Chapter 6, where we introduce grammar rules.) In addition to the usual sign attributes PHONOLOGY, SYNTAX, and SEMANTICS, feature structures of type *phrasal-sign* bear a fourth attribute DAUGHTERS that gives information about the (lexical or phrasal) signs which are the immediate constituents of the sign in question.

The DAUGHTERS attribute provides the kind of information about constituency (but *not* about relative order of constituents) that is contained in conventional constituent-structure tree diagrams. But in addition, it is important to distinguish the various daughters of a sign according to what kinds of information they contribute to the sign as a whole. Thus daughters are classified, *inter alia*, as *heads* (those which share their head features with the mother), *complements* (those which discharge subcategorization requirements on the head), *fillers* (those which discharge binding requirements on the head), *conjuncts* (coequal daughters in coordinate constructions), etc. Correspondingly, appropriate values of DAUGHTERS are feature structures of type *constituent-structure*, which have such attributes as HEAD-DTR (head daughter), COMP-DTRS (complement daughters), FILLER-DTR (filler daughter), CONJ-DTRS (conjunct daughters), etc.

Constituent structures are then classified on the basis of the kinds of daughters that appear in them. For example, one important subtype of *constituent-structure* is *coordinate-structure*, one of whose attributes is CONJ-DTRS. Another important subtype of *constituent-structure*, in fact the one that will principally concern us in this book, is *headed-structure*, which at minimum bears the attributes HEAD-DTR and COMP-DTRS. Headed structures in turn are subclassified according to what kinds of non-head daughters they have; thus we have such subtypes of *headed-structure* as *head-complement-structure* (which bears the attributes HEAD-DTR and COMP-DTRS), *head-filler-structure* (which requires the empty list ⟨ ⟩ as its value for COMP-DTRS and additionally bears the attribute FILLER-DTR), etc.

By way of illustration, the sign corresponding to the topicalized sentence *Bagels, John likes* is partially described by (101a):[2]

(101) a.

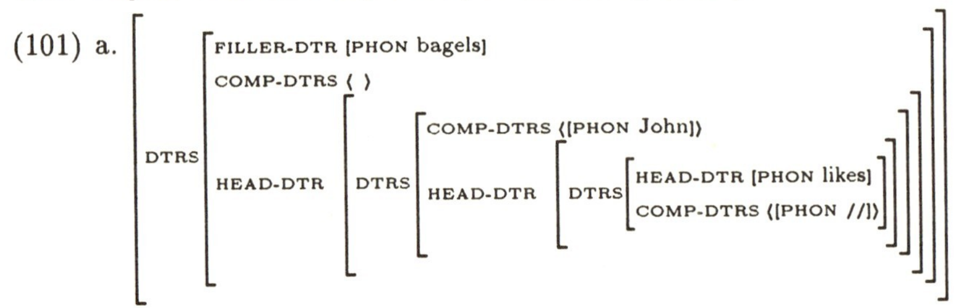

For emphasis, the SYNTAX and SEMANTICS attributes (as well as the PHONOLOGY attributes on phrasal constituents) have been omitted. The important thing to note here is that, in the description of a phrasal sign, the phrase's constituent signs (daughters) themselves are described by feature structures of type *sign* which occur as substructures within the DTRS attribute of the top-level description. Thus the values of FILLER-DTR and HEAD-DTR are just feature structures of type sign (since a sign has at most one filler daughter or head daughter), but the value of COMP-DTRS is a *list* of signs (since a sign may have several complement daughters). For familiarity, we will often use an alternative notation to describe phrasal signs, as illustrated in (101b):

[2] The symbol "//" denotes the empty phonological string.

(101) b.

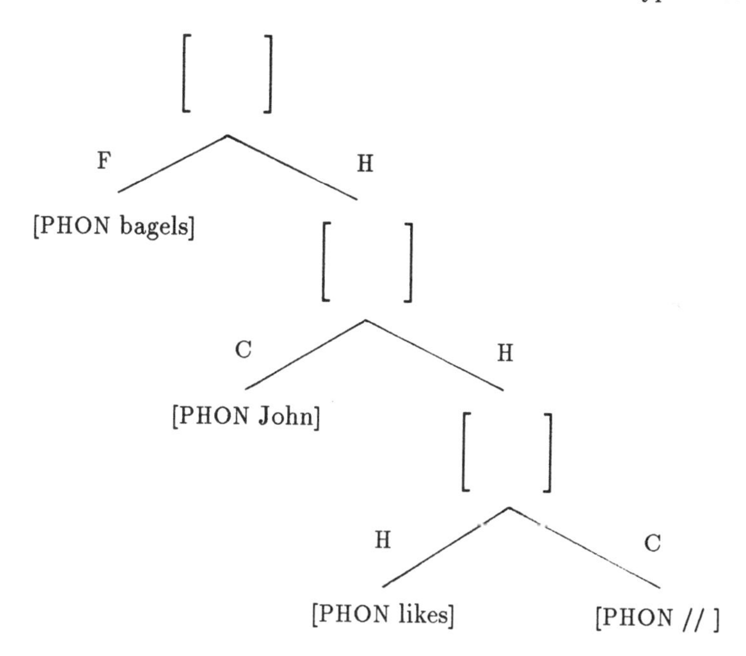

In this notation, which is intended to be suggestive of the tree diagrams conventionally favored by syntacticians, the feature structure corresponding to the phrase under description appears at the top with all of its attributes indicated as in standard AVM notation, *except* for the DTRS attribute. Instead of being notated by an AVM in the usual way, the constituent structure which is the value of the DTRS attribute is indicated by labelled "branches" descending from the top AVM; the labels "F", "H", and "C" on the branches correspond to the constituent-structure attributes FILLER-DTR, HEAD-DTR, and COMP-DTRS respectively. The same descriptive convention applies recursively, so that e.g. the AVM description (101a) with multiple levels of recursive embedding takes the form of a labelled tree (101b) with correspondingly many levels of branching. Of course, in the labelled tree notation, the "leaves", which have no constituent structure, simply appear as normal AVM's. Caution: in the case of a constituent with more than one complement daughter (e.g. the node in (133) which dominates *appealed to him to leave*) there is a branch labelled "C" for *each* complement daughter; unlike conventional linguistic tree notation, the left-to-right order of multiple complement daughters reflects increasing obliqueness, *not* the temporal order of the corresponding phonological realizations.

We call the longest path of branches labelled "H" leading upward from a lexical sign its *projection path*; in terms of feature structures, a projection path is just a path of the form DTRS|HEAD-DTR...DTRS|HEAD-DTR whose value is a lexical sign. The *projections* of a lexical sign within a phrase are just the phrases that lie on the projection path. Thus, in the present example, the phrases *likes*, *John likes*, and *Bagels, John likes* are all projections of the lexical sign *likes*.

Now what about the sharing of head features between lexical heads and their projections? This is accounted for by a principle of universal grammar called the Head Feature Principle (HFP), stated in (102):

(102) Head Feature Principle

$$\left[\text{DTRS}\ _{\textit{headed-structure}}[\ ]\right] \Rightarrow \left[\begin{array}{l}\text{SYN}|\text{LOC}|\text{HEAD}\ \boxed{1}\\ \text{DTRS}|\text{HEAD-DTR}|\text{SYN}|\text{LOC}|\text{HEAD}\ \boxed{1}\end{array}\right]$$

(An historical note: the HFP is a reformulation in feature structure terms of the Head Feature Convention of GPSG.) This says simply: if a phrase has a head daughter, then they share the same head features. In the case of the preceding example, the effect of the HFP is indicated in (103):

(103)

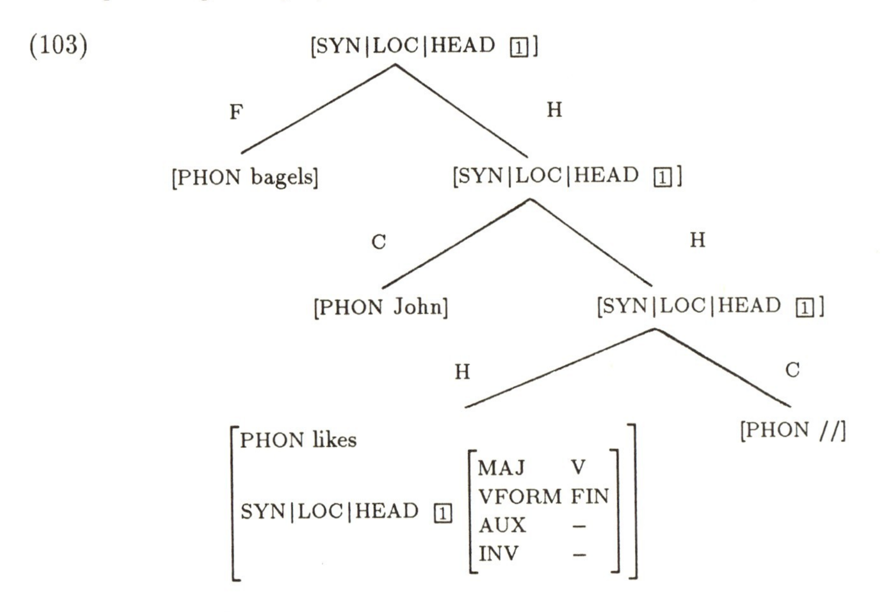

Speaking metaphorically, we sometimes describe such a situation by saying that the head features of the lexical head are "propagated", or "flow", up the tree along the projection path to all the phrasal projections. Of course, there is no actual *movement* of information; what is really involved is a *sharing* of information between the lexical head and its projections. (Similarly, as we will see below, the relationship between a filler and a gap is explained not in terms of movement, as in transformational grammar, but rather in terms of a sharing of information between the filler and the gap.)

We turn now to an inventory of the head features used in our analysis of English. With a few minor differences, these correspond to the head features of GPSG. A general remark: there is a theoretical question as to whether the inventory of syntactic features (and their possible values) varies from language to language, or whether universal grammar makes available a fixed stock of them from which each particular language selects a certain subset. We will not take a position on this question here, for it does not seem clear to us what would count as evidence one way or the other; but it should be borne in mind that some of the features used in this book may well be cross-linguistically significant.

As we have seen above, the MAJ (major) feature corresponds to the familiar notion of part of speech. English MAJ values include those listed in (104) (as well as disjunctions thereof):

(104)

MAJ	Values
N	(nominal signs, e.g. nouns and NP's, including pronouns)
V	(verbal signs, e.g. verbs, VP's, and sentences)
A	(adjectives, AP's, and adjunct clauses headed by AP's)
P	(prepositions, PP's, and adjunct clauses headed by PP's)
D	(determiners)
ADV	(adverbs and adverb phrases)

This list of MAJ values does not pretend to be exhaustive or definitive; the important thing is that part of speech be treated as a head feature. As we shall see in Chapter 6, this permits a highly schematic, cross-categorial formulation of the grammar rules that build head-complement structures, i.e. a single rule will do duty for a vast array of conventional phrase structure rules such as VP $\rightarrow$ V NP, PP $\rightarrow$ P NP, AP $\rightarrow$ A PP, etc.

Another HEAD feature is CASE. In numerous languages, the various inflected forms of nouns are specified in terms of differing values for CASE, and in virtue of the HFP the CASE specifications are inherited by the NP's that the nouns project. Thus when a given verb subcategorizes for (governs) a NP marked as [CASE GEN] or [CASE DAT] (the specifications corresponding to the traditional distinctions of genitive and dative case, respectively), this has immediate consequences for the form of the head noun of the governed NP (as well as for the form of any determiners or modifiers whose CASE specifications are required to coincide with those of the head noun). In English, of course, the case system is highly degenerate. Only pronouns are lexically specified for CASE: *I*, *he*, *she*, *we* and *they* are marked [CASE NOM] (nominative case); *me*, *him*, *her*, *us*, *them*, and *whom* are marked [CASE ACC]. All other nouns and pronouns (except for possessives, discussed below) are unspecified for CASE; technically, this means they are assigned the value $_{\textit{case-value}}[\ ]$, which is equivalent to the disjunction of all possible English CASE values (NOM, ACC, and possibly GEN).

At first blush, it seems reasonable to specify the possessive pronouns *my*, *your*, *our*, *his*, *her*, *its*, *their*, and *whose* as [CASE GEN], in order to distinguish them from nominative and accusative NP's. However, the question then arises of how to treat non-pronominal possessives, which in English are formed by attaching the clitic *-'s* after a non-pronominal NP:

(105) a. [The ambassador from Bulgaria]'s hat was stolen.

b. [The candidate I talked to]'s resume was outstanding.

If the noun phrase (which is unspecified for CASE) is the head of the possessive phrase, then evidently the latter cannot be [CASE GEN], for the head noun bears no genitive inflection. Perhaps the right thing to say here is that the clitic *-s*, not the NP, is the head; in that case, possessive phrases are not really NP's at all. (Consider, for example, the fact that possessive phrases, but no other NP's, can serve as noun determiners.) For the time being, we will leave this issue unresolved.

Verb inflections are analyzed in terms of the head feature VFORM, whose possible values are indicated in (106):

(106)

VFORM	Values
FIN	(finite, or tensed forms, e.g. *speaks*, *spoke*, *was*)
BSE	(base, or uninflected forms, e.g. *speak*, *be*)
PSP	(past participle forms, e.g. *spoken, been*)
PRP	(present participle forms, e.g. *speaking, being*)
PAS	(passive participle forms, e.g. *spoken, rumored*)
INF	(the VFORM value assigned to the infinitival marker *to*, which is considered the head of infinitival phrases such as *to leave*)
GER	(verbal gerundive forms, e.g. *speaking, having, being*)

As we shall see in Chapter 8, for most verbs in English it is sufficient to list the base form only, since the existence and precise phonology of inflected forms can be predicted by *lexical rules*. However, not all verbs display the full range of inflected forms. For example, modal auxiliary verbs (such as *may, might, shall, should, can, could, and must*) have only finite forms, and *rumored* appears only in the passive, as (107) and (108) show:

(107) Pat may take the exam. (FIN)
*Pat will may take the exam. (BSE)
*Pat has mayed take the exam. (PSP)
*Pat is maying take the exam. (PRP)
*Pat would like to may take the exam. (INF)
*Maying take the exam bothered Pat. (GER)

(108) *They rumored Sandy to be a spy. (FIN)
Sandy was rumored to be a spy. (PAS)
*They may rumor Sandy to be a spy. (BSE)
*They had rumored Sandy to be a spy. (PSP)
*They are rumoring Sandy to be a spy. (PRP)
*Rumoring Sandy to be a spy caused endless trouble. (GER)

In such cases the inflected forms must be given explicitly.

VFORM plays an important role in subcategorization, as many verbs and adjectives in English select for VP or sentential complements that are restricted to one or another VFORM specification. For example, the modal auxiliaries require VP complements in BSE form, while progressive-aspect *be* and perfective-aspect *have* take VP complements in PSP and PRP forms respectively.

Some remarks on specific verb forms follow.

FIN: all finite verb forms are considered simply [VFORM FIN] irrespective of tense and agreement distinctions (including so-called "syntactic agreement"), which we take to be semantic in nature. The analysis of agreement is taken up in detail in Volume 2.

PRP: present participles without exception end in *-ing*.

PAS: some verbs (e.g. auxiliaries and other verbs which are followed immediately by a verbal complement) lack the passive form; but if there is a passive form, it invariably coincides in phonology (and spelling) with the past participle.

INF: we analyze the infinitive marker *to* as a defective auxiliary verb with the specification [VFORM INF]; thus an infinitival phrase such as *to leave tomorrow* is analyzed as *to* (the lexical head) followed by *leave tomorrow* (a base-form VP complement).

GER: like present participles, verbal gerunds invariably end in *-ing*. It is important to distinguish verbal gerunds from certain "deverbative" nouns, sometimes called nominal gerunds, which also end in *-ing*. Like other verbs, verbal gerunds can have NP direct objects and adverbial modifiers; like other nouns, nominal gerunds cannot. For example, in (109) below, the verbal gerund (b) forms pattern like the finite (a) forms. The nominalized form of *execute*, however, is not a nominal gerund, but rather the noun *execution*.

(109) a. The government troops methodically butchered/executed the rebel leaders. (FIN)

b. The government troops' methodically butchering/executing the rebel leaders followed a long-established pattern. (GER)

c. The government troops' methodical butchering/*executing/execution of the rebel leaders followed a long-established pattern. (N)

As noted above in (100), many verbs and adjectives subcategorize for prepositional phrases whose heads are particular prepositions. Correspondingly, in order for information about the identity of the head preposition to be transmitted to a prepositional phrase, we introduce the head feature PFORM (prepositional form); appropriate values, such as TO, FOR, BY, OF, etc. correspond to particular choices of prepositional head. The preposition *on*, for example, is the only lexical sign which bears the specification [PFORM ON]; the requirement that a verb such as *depend* combine with a PP headed by *on* is then treated by including in its SUBCAT value (see the next section)) a specification containing the HEAD value [PFORM ON]. The transmission of this specification from the preposition itself to the PP complement, of course, is a consequence of the HFP.

The head feature NFORM (noun form) is used to distinguish "normal" noun phrases and pronouns, which refer to objects or quantify over objects (e.g. *Kim*, *she*, *most skateboard champions from central Idaho*), from the *expletive* pronouns (also called *dummy* pronouns) *it* and *there* which have very special syntactic properties. (These are treated in detail in Volume 2). Corresponding values are as in (110):

(110)

NFORM	Values
THERE	(the expletive pronoun *there* in existential constructions, e.g. *there is a moon out tonight.*)
IT	(the expletive pronoun *it*, e.g. in extraposition (*it bothers me that he resigned*), weather (*it's raining*), and pseudocleft (*it's bagels that I want*) constructions)
NORM	(all other NP's and nouns)

All lexical common and proper nouns are specified as [NFORM NORM]. By the HFP, this specification is transmitted to any NP headed by a common noun, thereby preventing it from occurring in a position requiring an expletive pronoun. This is illustrated in (111) and (112):

(111) a. There were two employees absent.

b. *Kim and Sandy were two employees absent.

(112) a. It is snowing.

b. *The weather is snowing.

Two closely related head features, which arise in the analysis of auxiliary verbs, are the binary features AUX (auxiliary) and INV (inverted). (Technically, a binary feature is a feature whose value must be of type *boolean*, i.e. either + or −.) AUX distinguishes auxiliary verbs from all other words (main verbs and nonverbs). To be more precise, all lexical signs are specified [AUX −] except for auxiliary verbs, which are marked [AUX +]. These include: the modals listed above; perfective-aspect *have*;

all forms of *be*, also called the *copula*; *do* (auxiliary *do*, which has only finite forms, must be distinguished from the main transitive verb *do*, which has the normal range of inflected forms); the infinitive marker *to*; certain uses of *ought*, *need*, and *dare*; and perhaps a small set of additional verbs (varying somewhat across different varieties of English). Characteristic syntactic properties of auxiliaries include the following: (a) cooccurrence with *not*; (b) the ability to undergo the lexical process of negative contraction; (c) the ability to be "stranded" by verb phrase ellipsis; (d) invertibility in interrogative (and other) constructions; and (e) occurrence in tag questions. These properties are illustrated in (113):

(113) Contrasts Involving AUX

a. Only finite [AUX +] verbs may cooccur with *not*:
Dana is not sleeping.
*Dana sleeps not.

b. Only [AUX +] verbs have negative contracted forms:
Dana isn't sleeping.
*Dana sleepsn't/sleepn'ts.

c. Only [AUX +] verbs may be stranded in verb phrase ellipsis:
Lou doesn't want to work hard, but Chris does ___.
*Lou doesn't want to work hard, but Chris wants ___.

d. Only [AUX +] verbs may occur in "subject-auxiliary inversion":
Will Pat vote for Proposition 61?
*Voted Pat for Proposition 61?

e. Only [AUX +] verbs may occur in tag questions:
Pat didn't vote for Proposition 61, did he?
*Pat didn't vote for Proposition 61, voted he?

In addition to AUX, our analysis of auxiliaries involves another head feature INV which distinguishes inverted (i.e. sentence-initial) from noninverted auxiliaries. At first blush, such a feature might seem unnecessary: why not simply say that each auxiliary verb can appear in both inverted and noninverted positions? Unfortunately, this is not quite true. At least one auxiliary verb, the negative contracted first-person-singular copula *aren't*, can only appear inverted; and at least one auxiliary verb, *better*, cannot invert. These facts are accounted for using the INV feature as follows: first, the grammar rule responsible for inverted sentences (see Chapter 6) requires that the head daughter bear the specification [INV +], but the rules responsible for noninverted phrases and sentences require [INV −] heads. Lexical specifications for INV are then assigned as follows: auxiliaries which must invert are [INV +]; nonauxiliaries and auxiliaries which must not invert are [INV −]; all other auxiliaries (the vast majority of them), which can occur in both inverted and noninverted positions, are unspecified for

INV, i.e. they are [INV + V −]. This explains the contrasts (114), noted originally by Gazdar, Pullum and Sag (1981), and (115):

(114) a. Aren't I in charge of refreshments?
b. *I aren't in charge of refreshments.

(115) a. We better leave early.
b. *Better we leave early?

The binary head feature PRD (predicative) corresponds to the predicative/nonpredicative distinction, which cuts across several different parts of speech. Roughly, predicative words (or their phrasal projections) are those which can occur as complement to the copula. For example, among verbs, present participles and passive participles are predicative, but other verb forms are not, as (116) shows:

(116) a. Kim was always hounding his debtors. ([VFORM PRP])
b. Kim was hounded to death by creditors. ([VFORM PAS])
c.*Kim was hounds/hounded his debtors. ([VFORM FIN])
d.*Kim was immediately fallen through the ice. ([VFORM PSP])
e.*Kim was immediately fall through the ice. ([VFORM BSE])

Thus present and passive participles are lexically marked as [PRD +]; other verb forms are [PRD −].

The predicative/nonpredicative distinction is also relevant for adjectives. To be a little more precise, among adjectives, we can distinguish three general types: (i) those which can occur after the copula but not as prenominal modifiers; (ii) those which can occur prenominally but not after the copula; and (iii) those which can appear in both prenominal and postcopular positions. Examples of the first type include a large class of adjectives starting with *a-*, such as *ablaze, ajar, asleep, awake*, etc., as well as certain other adjectives like *ready* and *through* (in the sense of "complete, finished"):

(117) a.*an asleep baby
*an ajar door
*an ablaze house

b. The house was ablaze.
The door was ajar.
The house was ablaze.

(118) a.*Butch put the ready cake on the table.
*All the through people left.

b. The cake was finally ready.
Everyone who is through can leave.

Such adjectives are lexically marked as [PRD +]. Examples of the second class, marked [PRD −], include *former, mere, utter*, and ***through*** (in the sense of "connecting") (119):

(119) a. a former senator
a mere child
an utter fool
a through street

b.*The senator was former.
*Chris is mere.
*That fool is utter.
*Hillview Terrace is not through.

Most adjectives, of course, fall into the third class, as illustrated in (120):

(120) a. a red ball
an optimistic salesman

b. Dana's ball is red.
Our salespeople have every reason to be optimistic.

Such adjectives are unspecified for the feature PRD (that is, are marked [PRD + ∨ −]).

In general, prepositional phrases seem to lead a double life, occurring in both predicative and nonpredicative positions, as shown in (121):

(121) a. Felix is on the oak library table.

b. Max relies on the oak library table to hide under during earthquakes.

Intuitively, the distinction corresponds to a semantic difference. In (121a) *on* seems to speak of a certain spatial relationship between Felix and the table. In (121b), by contrast, *on* evidently has no independent meaning at all; instead, it functions rather like a case marker, serving merely to formally mark the complement of *relies*. One way to deal with this kind of ambivalence is to leave prepositions unmarked for predicativeness. This approach, however, leaves the semantic difference unexplained. Alternatively, we might posit two distinct lexical signs for each preposition, a [PRD +] one to head predicative PP's as in (121a) and a [PRD −] "case-preposition" to head nonpredicative PP's subcategorized by certain verbs and adjectives. (Taking the latter course, we might choose to class the nonpredicative versions as something other than prepositions, perhaps grouping them with complementizers and other formal markers that do not seem to make a real semantic contribution. As yet, HPSG lacks any precise analysis of such markers.)

Like prepositional phrases, noun phrases too appear both predicatively (predicate nominals) and nonpredicatively (e.g. subjects and objects). The question of how to treat the distinction in terms of the PRD feature is a vexed one, for there are a number of delicate semantic issues to be teased out, e.g. the proper analysis of the distinction between the "*be* of identity" and the "*be* of predication" illustrated in (122):

(122) a. Mr. Canterbury is really Magnus Pym.

b. Magnus Pym is really a double agent.

We will not attempt to settle these questions here.

At this point the following question may have occurred to the reader: why posit a new feature PRD to distinguish those words and phrases that can appear in postcopular position? Why not simply say that the copula just happens to subcategorize for a disjunction of categories, including NP's, PP's, certain AP's, passive-partipial VP's, and present-participial VP's? The answer is that precisely this same collection of categories shares the ability to occur in a number of other syntactic environments; it is a natural class, not just a random hodge-podge of categories. For example, precisely those phrases that we have identified as [PRD +] can appear as the complement marked by *as* after the direct object of *regard*, as shown in (123):

(123) a. I don't regard that as a reasonable suggestion.

b. I don't regard that proposal as within the limits of decency.

c. I don't regard him as ready for such a demanding task.

d. I don't regard myself as running for office; I'm only testing the water.

e. I don't regard myself as tainted by the scandal; I was always very careful.

And the same kinds of phrases occur as controlled adjuncts, as in (124):

(124) Kim came back from Texas { a Republican. / in a boxcar. / ready for anything. / driving a Bentley. / pursued by lawmen from four states. }

Likewise, [PRD +] phrases occur as the heads of certain sentential modifiers called *predicative adjunct clauses* (125):

(125) { His father a lifelong Mason / His father on the screening committee / His father ready to do anything on his behalf / His father looming in the background / His father known to be a lifelong Mason }, Butch's membership was assured.

And except for NP's, [PRD +] phrases can occur in the existential *there* construction (126) and as "reduced relative" postnominal modifiers (127):

(126) There is a donkey { in the garden. / asleep in the garden. / sleeping in the garden. / stuffed with kapok. }

(127) The donkey { in the garden / asleep in the garden / sleeping in the garden / stuffed with kapok } startled Sabina.

To complete our inventory of head features, some discussion is in order concerning agreement. Perhaps contrary to expectation, we will not treat agreement phenomena (such as person, number, and gender) in terms of head features. Although a head feature account appears to explain in a natural way the transmission of agreement features from lexical heads (e.g. nouns and verbs) to their phrasal projections, a whole array of properties particular to agreement remain unexplained under such an account. In Volume 2, we will develop a theory of agreement in which distinctions such as person, number, and gender are associated not with syntactic categories but rather with a certain *semantic* attribute of noun phrases called the INDEX.

To sum up, many important syntactic properties of phrases are determined by their lexical heads; such properties are treated in HPSG in terms of head features. In virtue of the HFP, information embodied within head feature specifications is transmitted along the projection paths from lexical signs to their phrasal projections. The head features we have discussed in this section are summarized in (128):

(128)

Feature	Values
MAJ	N, V, A, P, D, ADV, ...
CASE	NOM, ACC, (GEN?)
VFORM	FIN, BSE, PSP, PRP, PAS, INF, GER
NFORM	NORM, IT, THERE
PFORM	OF, ON, TO, FROM, ...
AUX	+, −
INV	+, −
PRD	+, −

3.2 The Subcategorization Feature

The subcategorization, or valence, of a lexical or phrasal sign, is a specification of the number and kind of other signs that the sign in question characteristically combines with in order to become complete. For example, it is well known that different verbs combine with, or *subcategorize for*, different numbers of noun phrases in order to form a complete sentence. Thus an intransitive verb such as *sneeze* subcategorizes for only one NP (the subject) in order to make a complete sentence; a transitive verb such as *touch* subcategorizes for two NP's (the object and the subject); a ditransitive verb such as *hand* (as in *hand Kim a book*) subcategorizes for three NP's (the second object, the object, and the subject). The notion of subcategorization, of course, is relevant for phrases as well as words. Thus a VP such as *likes bagels* resembles a lexical intransitive verb in subcategorizing for a single NP; while a sentence such as *Kim likes bagels* is already complete, or *saturated*, i.e. it does not subcategorize for anything at all.

Verbs and their projections are not alone in bearing subcategorization specifications. For example, a predicative preposition such as *in* resembles a transitive verb in subcategorizing for two NP's (the prepositional object and the subject); a predicative PP such as *in New York* resembles a VP in subcategorizing for a single (subject) NP. Prepositional predicative clauses, such as the sentence-initial modifier in *Her father in New York, Kim took charge of the Duluth office* are saturated; thus they are analogous to sentences, except that their lexical heads are prepositions not verbs. We also treat common nouns (and common noun phrases such as *tall man with an axe*) as subcategorizing for the determiners they combine with, while NP's such as *Kim* and *the tall man with an axe* are saturated. Determiners themselves, however, we consider saturated.[3]

The repository of information about the subcategorization of signs is the local syntactic feature SUBCAT. Appropriate values of SUBCAT are lists of signs. Thus, a sign which subcategorizes for n other signs has as its SUBCAT value a list of n (usually very partially specified) signs. An important special case is that of saturated signs (e.g. clauses, NP's, and determiners), whose SUBCAT value is the empty list $\langle\ \rangle$.

Equipped with the notions of head features and subcategorization, we are now in a position to *define* conventional grammatical symbols such as NP, VP, etc. in terms of feature structures of type sign. Thus, starting with saturated signs, we can define the symbol "DET" to be an abbreviation for the feature structure (129a), which partially describes a determiner sign such as *every*. Likewise, (129b) and (129c) define NP and S as the saturated signs headed by nouns and verbs respectively. Simple examples of unsaturated signs are N (common noun) and VP, defined as in (129d) and (129e) respectively. (Note: the symbol "N" is used both as a value of the feature MAJ and as an abbreviation for a certain feature structure

---

[3] Other treatments are worth considering; e.g. we might propose that determiners are unsaturated, subcategorizing for the common nouns that combine with them, instead of the other way around. Consideration of such alternatives will be postponed until Chapter 5.

containing the specification [MAJ N]; which use is intended will always be clear from context.) Observe that the abbreviations are used recursively, e.g. "NP" is used in the SUBCAT specification in the definition of "VP".

(129) Definitions of Conventional Grammatical Symbols

<table>
<tr><th></th><th>Symbol</th><th>Definition</th><th>Examples</th></tr>
<tr><td>a.</td><td>DET</td><td>[SYN|LOC|HEAD|MAJ D
SUBCAT ⟨ ⟩]</td><td>every
the</td></tr>
<tr><td>b.</td><td>NP</td><td>[SYN|LOC|HEAD|MAJ N
SUBCAT ⟨ ⟩]</td><td>Kim
every cat</td></tr>
<tr><td>c.</td><td>S</td><td>[SYN|LOC|HEAD|MAJ V
SUBCAT ⟨ ⟩]</td><td>Kim left
did Kim go</td></tr>
<tr><td>d.</td><td>N</td><td>[SYN|LOC|HEAD|MAJ N
SUBCAT ⟨DET⟩]</td><td>cat
white cat</td></tr>
<tr><td>e.</td><td>VP</td><td>[SYN|LOC|HEAD|MAJ V
SUBCAT⟨NP⟩]</td><td>sneezed
liking cats</td></tr>
</table>

In addition to such standard symbols, it is convenient to use certain complex symbols as abbreviations for more specific types of phrases bearing certain values for one or more head features as INV, CASE, NFORM, VFORM, PFORM, PRD, etc. Some examples are given in (130); analogous abbreviations will then be used freely without comment.

(130) Definitions of Some Complex Symbols

<table>
<tr><th></th><th>Symbol</th><th>Definition</th><th>Examples</th></tr>
<tr><td>a.</td><td>S[+INV]</td><td>[SYN|LOC|HEAD [MAJ V
INV +]
SUBCAT ⟨ ⟩]</td><td>did Kim go</td></tr>
<tr><td>b.</td><td>NP[NOM]</td><td>[SYN|LOC|HEAD [MAJ N
CASE NOM]
SUBCAT ⟨ ⟩]</td><td>I
we</td></tr>
<tr><td>c.</td><td>NP[THERE]</td><td>[SYN|LOC|HEAD [MAJ N
NFORM THERE]
SUBCAT ⟨ ⟩]</td><td>there
as in
there is
a God</td></tr>
<tr><td>d.</td><td>VP[FIN]</td><td>[SYN|LOC|HEAD [MAJ V
VFORM FIN]
SUBCAT ⟨NP[NOM]⟩]</td><td>sneezed
saw Kim</td></tr>
</table>

(130)	Symbol	Definition	Examples
e.	VP[INF]	$\left[\begin{array}{ll}\text{SYN}\mid\text{LOC}\mid\text{HEAD} & \left[\begin{array}{ll}\text{MAJ} & \text{V}\\ \text{VFORM} & \text{INF}\end{array}\right]\\ \text{SUBCAT} & \langle\text{NP}\rangle\end{array}\right]$	*to sneeze*
f.	AP[+PRD]	$\left[\begin{array}{ll}\text{SYN}\mid\text{LOC}\mid\text{HEAD} & \left[\begin{array}{ll}\text{MAJ} & \text{A}\\ \text{PRD} & +\end{array}\right]\\ \text{SUBCAT} & \langle\text{NP}\rangle\end{array}\right]$	*adrift in space*
g.	PP[+PRD]	$\left[\begin{array}{ll}\text{SYN}\mid\text{LOC}\mid\text{HEAD} & \left[\begin{array}{ll}\text{MAJ} & \text{P}\\ \text{PRD} & +\end{array}\right]\\ \text{SUBCAT} & \langle\text{NP}\rangle\end{array}\right]$	*in Chicago* as in *Kim is in Chicago*
h.	PP[−PRD,ON]	$\left[\begin{array}{ll}\text{SYN}\mid\text{LOC}\mid\text{HEAD} & \left[\begin{array}{ll}\text{MAJ} & \text{P}\\ \text{PFORM} & \text{ON}\\ \text{PRD} & -\end{array}\right]\\ \text{SUBCAT} & \langle\ \rangle\end{array}\right]$	*on Sandy,* as in *Kim relies on Sandy*

Again, note that abbreviations (including complex symbols) are used recursively, e.g. for the nominative subject subcategorization of finite VP's (130d). (Thus, we are treating the case requirements that different heads place on the NP's that combine with them as a special case of subcategorization. We return to this point in Chapter 5.)

Of course, not just NP's are subcategorized for, as (131) illustrates:

(131) Values of SYNTAX|LOCAL|SUBCAT for representative lexical signs

a. *sneezed* ⟨NP[NOM,NORM]⟩
b. *rained* ⟨NP[IT]⟩
c. *ablaze* ⟨NP[NORM]⟩
d. *touched* ⟨NP[ACC,NORM], NP[NOM,NORM]⟩
e. *relied* ⟨PP[−PRD,ON], NP[NOM,NORM]⟩
f. *tried* ⟨VP[INF], NP[NOM,NORM]⟩
g. *fond* ⟨PP[−PRD,OF], NP[NORM]⟩
h. *on* ⟨NP[ACC,NORM], NP[NORM]⟩
i. *handed* ⟨NP[ACC,NORM], NP[ACC,NORM], NP[NOM,NORM]⟩
j. *forced* ⟨VP[INF], NP[ACC,NORM], NP[NOM,NORM]⟩

It should be noted that the order of occurrence of symbols on the SUBCAT list is *not* intended to directly reflect the surface constituent order of complements. Instead, order on the SUBCAT list corresponds to the traditional grammatical notion of *obliqueness of grammatical relations*, with more oblique elements occurring further to the left. Thus, in the case of NP complements, the last (least oblique) element corresponds to the grammatical *subject*; the second-last element corresponds to the *direct object*, and the third-last element corresponds to the *second* (or *indirect*) object. (The connection between subcategorization in HPSG and the notions of grammatical relations embodied in theories such as LFG and categorial grammar are considered in more detail in Chapter 5.) As we shall see in Chapters 6 and 7, the relationship between obliqueness order and surface constituent order is indirectly mediated by the language-specific grammar rules and principles of linear precedence.

It should be intuitively clear that the SUBCAT value of a phrase ought to be the SUBCAT value of the lexical head minus those specifications that have already been satisfied by some constituent in the phrase. For example, the SUBCAT value of *touched Fido* is just ⟨NP[NOM,NORM]⟩; for the SUBCAT of *touched* is lexically specified as ⟨NP[ACC,NORM], NP[NOM,NORM]⟩, but the specification NP[ACC,NORM] has already been satisfied within the phrase by the object *Fido*. Similarly, the SUBCAT value of *Kim touched Fido* is ⟨ ⟩ (the empty list), for now the remaining specification NP[NOM,NORM] has also been satisfied by the subject *Kim*. In HPSG, the transmission of subcategorization information up projection paths is governed by a principle of universal grammar called the Subcategorization Principle (132):

(132) Subcategorization Principle

$$\begin{bmatrix} \text{DTRS} & _{\textit{headed-structure}}[\;] \end{bmatrix} \Rightarrow$$

$$\begin{bmatrix} \text{SYN}|\text{LOC}|\text{SUBCAT} \; \boxed{2} \\ \text{DTRS} \begin{bmatrix} \text{HEAD-DTR}|\text{SYN}|\text{LOC}|\text{SUBCAT append}(\boxed{1}, \boxed{2}) \\ \text{COMP-DTRS} \; \boxed{1} \end{bmatrix} \end{bmatrix}$$

Recall that for two lists L_1 and L_2, append(L_1,L_2) is the list obtained by concatenating the two lists in the indicated order. Thus (132) entails that in any headed structure, the SUBCAT value is the list obtained by removing from the SUBCAT value of the head those specifications that were satisfied by one of the complement daughters. In addition, the structure sharing (indicated by the double occurrences of the tags '$\boxed{1}$' and '$\boxed{2}$') entails that the information from each complement daughter is actually *unified* with the corresponding subcategorization specification on the head. Thus a sign can satisfy a subcategorization specification on some head only if it is consistent with that specification; otherwise a unification failure will result, in violation of the Subcategorization Principle.

The resulting transmission of subcategorization information is illustrated by the partial description of the sentence *I appealed to him to leave* given in (133):

(133)

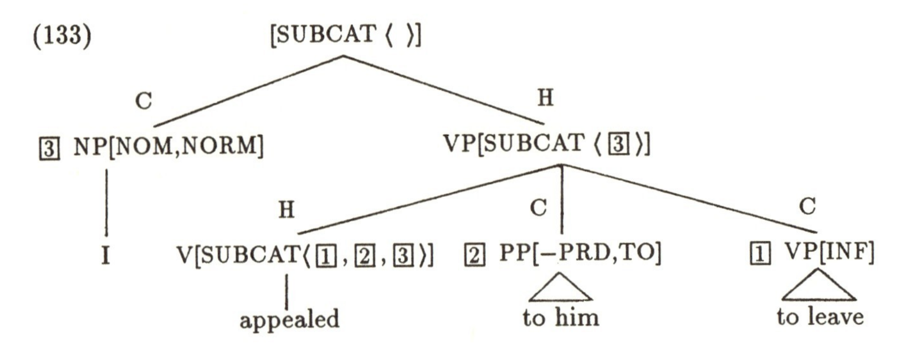

(Note: here "SUBCAT" abbreviates "SYNTAX|LOCAL|SUBCAT".) In effect, as we move up the projection path from the lexical head, subcategorization requirements are cancelled (removed from the SUBCAT list) as they are satisfied by appropriate complements. Readers familiar with categorial grammar should note that the Subcategorization Principle is analogous to the *cancellation* of categories, with heads and complements corresponding to *functor categories* and *argument categories* respectively. However, unlike standard categorial grammars, HPSG grammar rules may allow constituent structures which are not *binary-branching*; thus a phrase may have more than one complement daughter, as in the present example.

The matter of subcategorization lies at the heart of several major issues in current syntactic and semantic theory, including the nature of grammatical relations, constituent ordering principles, and the assignment of semantic roles to complements. We shall consider these and other issues as they relate to subcategorization in Chapter 5.

3.3 The Lexicality Feature

As we will see in Chapter 7, language-specific principles that determine the surface order of constituents within a phrase seem to be sensitive to whether a given constituent is lexical or phrasal. For example, it is a general principle of English constituent order that (roughly) lexical sisters precede phrasal ones. Evidently the simplest way to handle this is to key such principles to the *type* of the signs involved (i.e. *lexical-sign* or *phrasal-sign*). However, as we will see later in our discussion of coordination (Volume 2), lexicality information seems to pattern together with information about syntactic category, in the sense that conjuncts in a coordinate structure have to share it. In addition, as our discussion of long-distance dependencies (Volume 2) will show, lexicality information patterns like local syntactic information—head features and subcategorization—but unlike binding information (see next section) in the way that it is transmitted from gaps to their fillers. Thus we introduce into our descriptions of syntactic categories the local binary feature LEX, in addition to HEAD and SUBCAT.

Lexicality cannot be treated as a head feature, for phrasal signs and their head daughters typically differ with respect to lexicality.

In fact, it may well be that the distinction that we treat in terms of the LEX feature does not coincide exactly with the type distinction between lexical and phrasal signs. For example, there is evidence that noun-noun and adjective-noun structures share some syntactic properties with lexical nouns as opposed to typical common noun phrases, e.g. they can occur themselves as modifiers in noun-noun structures, as illustrated in (134):

(134) a. toxic waste
b. [toxic waste] dump
c. [[toxic waste] dump] manager
d.*[dump for toxic waste] manager

Thus, we might want to analyze such structures as [LEX +] even though they have internal constituent structure. More generally, we might divide rules of grammar into two classes: rules of word formation, including compounding rules, which introduce the specification [LEX +] on the mother, and other rules, which introduce [LEX −] on the mother. Detailed discussion of this and similar proposals is well beyond the scope of this book, and we will not pursue it here.

3.4 Binding Features

As we have seen in preceding sections, the head features and the SUBCAT feature are essentially *local* in nature, in the sense that their specifications are determined by lexical signs and transmitted only along projection paths, i.e. onto phrases from their head daughters. To put it another way, they are *lexically governed*: the information which they bear does not flow beyond the maximal projection of the lexical sign in question. In this section we introduce a class of syntactic phenomena called *binding*, or *long-distance* dependencies, which are not lexically governed; in HPSG theory, the repository of information about such dependencies is the BINDING attribute in feature structures of type *syntactic-category*. Unlike local features, binding feature specifications are transmitted more or less freely from arbitrary daughters (not just head daughters) to their mothers, in effect flowing from their points of origin upward through linguistic structures until they reach a point where they can be suitably disposed of (or *bound*).

We will be concerned with three distinct kinds of binding dependencies, associated with the three binding features SLASH, REL, and QUE. The SLASH feature mediates the flow (i.e. sharing) of information between a gap and its filler; the REL feature transmits information about relative pronouns up to the point in the structure where the relative clause is combined with the antecedent noun; and the QUE feature ensures that information about interrogative elements is propagated up to the interrogative clause or phrase that the element in question scopes over. We now illustrate these three types of binding dependency in turn. For each type, there are three principal considerations that concern us: the origin of the dependency, its transmission, and its binding.

The simplest kind of filler-gap dependency in English is the topicalization construction illustrated in (135):

(135) a. Bagels, I like ___.

b. Bagels, I know he likes ___.

c. Bagels, I thought he said he liked ___.

Topicalized sentences can be characterized simply as consisting of a "dislocated" filler constituent followed by a sentential constituent that is missing a phrase (or, "contains a gap") of the same sort as the filler. The syntactic dependency between the filler and the gap is clearly nonlocal, in the sense that it can extend across the boundaries of arbitrarily many embedded sentences.

In the case of the examples in (135), the missing phrase is an NP. But other kinds of gaps are possible; in (136), the missing elements are PP[TO]:

(136) a. To the first test tube, she added chlorine ___.

b. To the first test tube, we thought she added chlorine ___.

c. To the first test tube, we thought Kim said she added chlorine ___.

What remains constant in all these examples is that the local syntactic features of the filler must be consistent with those of the gap. Otherwise, ungrammatical sentences such as those in (137) result:

(137) a.*The first test tube, we thought she added chlorine ___.

b.*To bagels, I know he likes ___.

According to the HPSG account of long-distance dependencies presented in Volume 2, such filler-gap dependencies are mediated by the binding feature SLASH. The SLASH feature on a sign gives information about the gaps contained in the sign which have not yet been combined with a suitable filler (typically the "topic" element in a topicalization construction or a dislocated interrogative expression in a wh-question). The SLASH value itself is a set of feature structures of type *sign*, each of which describes one of the unbound missing elements. Thus a sign which contains no unbound gaps bears the specification [SLASH { }] (here { } is the empty set), while a sign containing an NP (i.e. "missing" an NP constituent) is specified [SLASH {NP}]. Such nonempty SLASH values originate from signs of a special kind called *traces*, which are phonologically empty but bear some of the same local syntactic (and semantic) information that would have been borne by a "normal" sign occupying the same position. For example, if the gap occurs in a position that would normally be occupied by a subcategorized complement, then the SLASH value on the trace coincides with (i.e. is shared with, or is unified with) the corresponding element on the SUBCAT list of the lexical head which governs (subcategorizes for) that position. This situation is exemplified by the topicalized structure in (138):

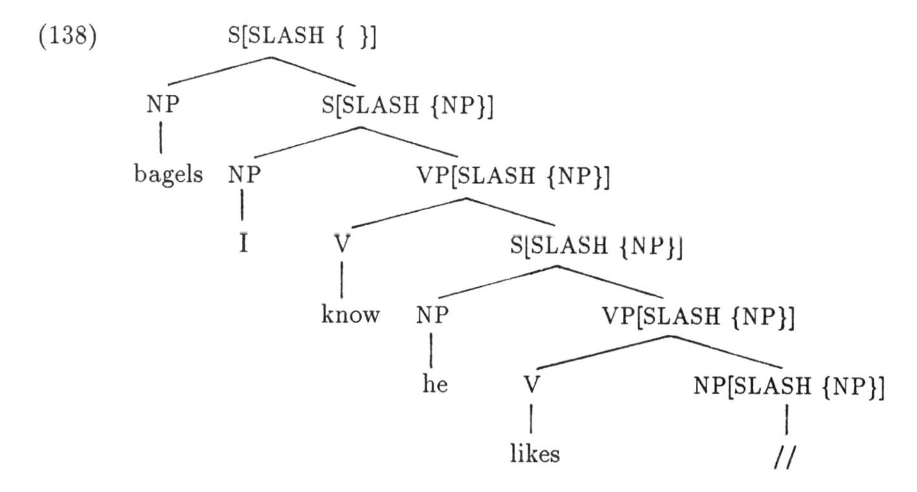

The description "NP[SLASH {NP}]" above the gap corresponds to the trace; the element NP in the SLASH value is determined by the subcategorization restriction exerted on the gap position by the lexical head *likes*. From here, the specification [SLASH {NP}] is successively transmitted from daughter to mother. As with all binding features, this transmission is governed by a further principle of universal grammar, the *Binding Inheritance Principle* (BIP), which requires that the value of SLASH (or any other binding feature) on a sign is the set union of the values on its daughters, minus those elements which have become bound. In the present example, this ensures that the information about the NP gap is passed up to the larger signs that contain it, until such a point in the structure is reached where a suitable mechanism effects the binding of the gap; at that point the newly bound element is removed from the SLASH value. In (138), the binding is effected by the grammar rule responsible for the topicalization construction, which requires, *inter alia*, that the local syntactic features of the filler be unified with those on the SLASH element being bound. The total effect is that the local features of the filler coincide with (are unified with) those on the trace, much as if the filler had actually been moved from the gap position. But on our analysis, there is no real movement from the gap to the filler, only a sharing of information between the filler and the trace.

In some cases, the SLASH set value may contain more than one element. This situation arises when a single phrase contains multiple gaps associated with distinct fillers. Such cases are rather rare in English (they are far more common in various of the Scandinavian languages), although many speakers readily accept as grammatical sentences such as those in (139):

(139) a. [Problems of this sort]$_i$, Jan$_j$ is easy to talk to $\_\_ _j$ about $\_\_ _i$.
b. [That famous old professor in Chicago]$_i$, I can't remember [which papers]$_j$ I sent copies of $\_\_ _j$ to $\_\_ _i$.
c. [Into the wastebasket]$_i$ Hilary put $\_\_ _j$ $\_\_ _i$ tearfully and Rob dropped $\_\_ _j$ $\_\_ _i$ sheet by sheet [their autographed copies of Syntactic Structures]$_j$.

Here the subscripts "i" and "j" are used to indicate informally which fillers bind which gaps; the theoretical significance of such *indices* will be discussed in the following chapter.

The binding feature REL mediates the syntactic dependency between relative expressions (e.g. the English relative pronouns *who, whom, whose*, and *which* and their antecedent nouns). Such dependencies arise in English when a noun (the antecedent) is modified by a *wh*-relative clause. A *wh*-relative clause is just a finite sentence containing a relative pronoun but not containing its antecedent; the clause may be in either canonical (S → NP VP) form, in which case the relative pronoun is within the subject NP, or in topicalized (S → XP S[SLASH {XP}]) form, in which case the relative pronoun is within the filler. Examples of the latter type are given in (140):

(140) a. They introduced the man$_i$ [[who$_i$] [Pat had been talking to __]].
b. They introduced the man$_i$ [[whose$_i$ sister] [Pat had been talking to __]].
c. They introduced the man$_i$[[to whom$_i$] [Pat had been talking __]]

Although there are a number of additional constraints on the distribution of relative pronouns, it is clear that, just as the gap may potentially be an unbounded distance away from its filler, so the relative pronoun may potentially be an unbounded distance away from its antecedent noun in the sense that it may be embedded to arbitrary depth in the relative clause. This is illustrated in (141):

(141) a. They introduced the man$_i$ [[whose$_i$ brother's friend's sister's ... uncle] [Pat had been talking to __]].
b. They looked over the government reports$_i$, [[the height of the lettering on the covers ... of which$_i$] [the government prescribes __]].

The analysis of such dependencies is analogous to the one for filler-gap dependencies. Thus the REL feature specification originates on the relative pronoun (where it is lexically specified), is propagated upward by the BIP, and is removed at the top of the relative clause where the relative pronoun becomes bound by the antecedent. (Again, we postpone discussion of the grammar rules for relativization which effect the binding.)

As with SLASH, the value of REL is a set, and the REL value is { } on any sign which contains no unbound relative pronouns. In English, the REL value set can contain at most one element, but there are indeed languages, e.g. Marathi, where multiple relative pronouns occur within a single relative clause, and are associated one-to-one (or almost so) with correlative pronouns in the main clause (see Dalrymple and Joshi (1986)).

Unlike SLASH, however, elements of REL value sets do not carry information about syntactic category. Instead, they specify a piece of semantic information, viz. the *index* of the relative pronoun. As we shall see in the next chapter, indices are similar to variables in logic; to simplify somewhat, when a relative pronoun becomes bound by its antecedent, their indices are unified. The general effect of our analysis of *wh*-relatives is sketched in (142):

(142)

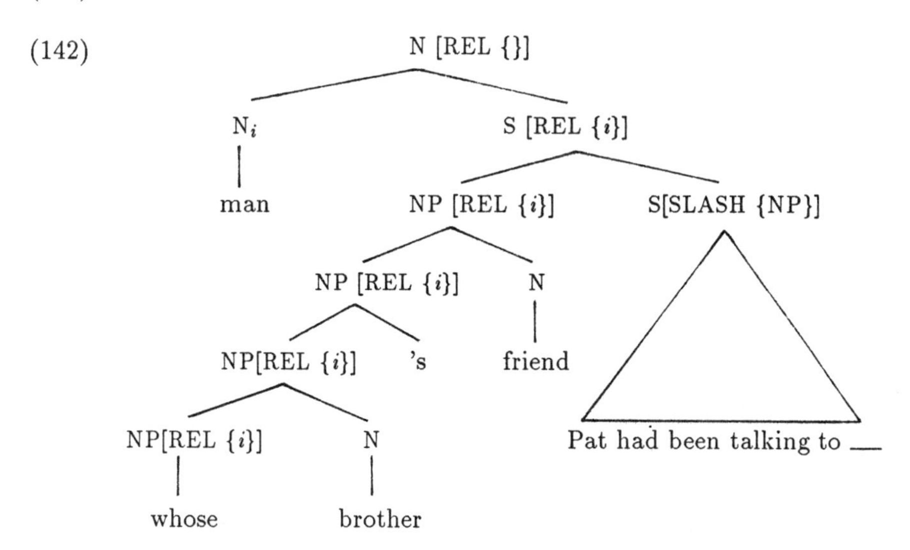

We postpone for the time being the questions of just how information about indices is encoded in feature structures, and content ourselves with the usual informal subscript notation.

The careful reader may have wondered by this point why REL specifications are considered *syntactic* information, given that their values specify only semantic indices not syntactic category information. The important point here is that whether or not a sign contains an unbound relative pronoun is syntactically significant information about that sign; for example, it determines whether or not a sentence can occur postnominally as a relative clause.

The final binding feature to be considered is QUE, whose value on a sign describes the set of unbound interrogative elements (e.g. English *who, whom, which, what, whose, when, where, how* or *why*) which it contains. In English, constituent questions are analogous in structure to *wh*-relative clauses, though there are significant differences (for example, there are multiple *wh*-questions, such as *Who ate what?*). Thus nonempty QUE values are lexically specified on interrogative words and flow up in accordance with the BIP. As with REL, the elements of QUE value sets contain semantic not syntactic information, although in the case of a QUE value element this information is more like a logical quantifier than a logical variable. They become bound (removed from the QUE value set) when an appropriate constituent (embedded question) is reached for the *wh*-quantifiers to scope over. The overall effect is illustrated in (143). Here the logic-like annotations are informal stand-ins for the *semantic contents* of signs (i.e. the value of the path SEMANTICS|CONTENT); again we postpone until Chapter 4 discussion of how semantic content is described in terms of feature structures.

(143)

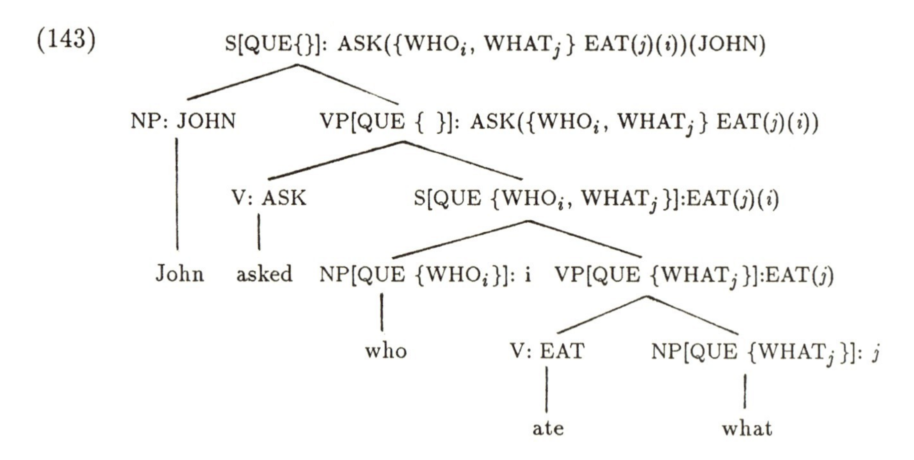

In this section, we have merely introduced some of the basic notions related to binding dependencies. We return to this important topic for a more leisurely discussion in Volume 2.

3.5 Conclusion

As we have seen in this chapter, syntactic categories in HPSG are highly complex objects, whose properties are described in terms of several distinct classes of syntactic features. Principles of universal grammar such as the Head Feature Principle, the Subcategorization Principle, and the Binding Inheritance Principle govern the flow through linguistic structures of the information encoded in syntactic features. And features themselves are classified in terms of HEAD, SUBCAT, or BINDING depending on which of these principles they obey. An additional feature, LEX, is also considered to play a role in the determination of constituent order. With these syntactic foundations in place, we turn in Chapter 4 to some fundamental semantic notions.

3.6 Suggestions for Further Reading

The theory of syntactic features and categories developed here is a synthesis and elaboration of ideas in Gazdar, Pullum and Sag (1981), Pollard (ms. 1), and Gazdar and Pullum (1982). List-valued features, and disjunction and negation for atomic values, were introduced in Pollard (1984); and the need for categories with general disjunction and negation was first recognized by Karttunen (1984). The particular inventory of head features and values used here is largely similar to that employed in GPSG work such as Gazdar et al. (1985). A clear and succinct presentation of formal foundations for the GPSG system of features and categories is contained in Gazdar et al. (1987); unlike the system of feature structures presented here (Chapter 2), negation is classical rather than intuitionistic, and some of the augmentations included here (structure sharing, list and set values) are not treated; GPSG-style "feature cooccurrence restrictions" (analogous to our feature structure types) are then enforced via a constraint language with a necessity operator.

4 Basic Semantic Notions

In the preceding chapter, we discussed the nature and structure of syntactic categories, the objects that serve as values of the SYNTAX attribute in natural language signs. In this chapter, we shift our focus to the SEMANTICS attribute. We take as our point of departure the relational theory of meaning introduced in Chapter 2, which maintains that meanings are relations of a certain kind that hold between two types of situations. Thus, to say that smoke means fire is to say that situation type A (the type of situation where there is smoke) is in some meaning relation with situation B (the type of situation where there is fire). It is characteristic of meaning relations that if situation type A means situation type B, then any situation of type A is part of a bigger situation containing as one of its parts a situation of type B. Different kinds of meanings are meaningful *to* different species or communities of organisms; or, to put it another way, different creatures are *attuned* to different meanings. A creature which is attuned to a certain meaning relation can exploit it to pick up new information about its environment from information already available.

4.1 Meaning Relations and Schemes of Individuation

We are concerned in this book with *linguistic* meaning, the relation between types of natural language utterances and the types of situations they describe. All normal adult human beings are attuned to this relation, and it is this attunement that we try to capture with principles of universal grammar. Each natural language can be regarded in turn as a subtype of linguistic meaning. What is the relation between the utterance type /kIm snizd/ and the type of situation where someone named Kim sneezes? It is the *means-in-English* relation: the first means the second in English. What kind of creature is attuned to this relation? A member of the English language community.

Of course the attunement of the English speaker includes information about the English lexicon, grammar rules, and English-specific grammatical principles, in addition to universal grammar. But such information cannot be formulated solely in terms of such things as phonemes, syntactic categories, and constituent structure types. These are necessary for classifying utterance types, but in order to exploit the English meaning relation, the English speaker must also have a way of classifying the things in the world that utterances are about. According to situation semantics, from which many of our ideas about linguistic meaning are borrowed or adapted, a way of classifying things in the world which is characteristic of a certain community is called a *scheme of individuation.* A scheme of individuation can be thought of as a system for breaking up reality into comprehensible parts, the seams along which a certain group of organisms tears the universe apart. Of course there are any number of of imaginable ways this might be done; but situation semantics assumes that human schemes of individuation consist of things called *individuals* (such as Ronald Reagan or the planet Venus), *properties* (such as being beige or being a skateboard champion from Idaho), and *relations*, such as loving or giving.

According to the realist view characteristic of situation semantics, individuals, properties, and relations are regarded as things in the world, not conceptual objects that only exist in the minds of certain organisms. To use a favorite locution of situation semantics, they are *uniformities across situations* that are individuated by humans (or, to be more precise, communities of humans). This is not to deny that one might have a concept of Ronald Reagan or a concept of giving; but the concepts should be distinguished from the things that they are concepts of. This distinction is important in accounting for the *external significance of language*, i.e. the fact that people get information about the world from linguistic utterances. If we are told by a truthful and reliable observer that Reagan ran in Reykjavik, we get information about Reagan. Of course we may also get information about the reporter's mental state (e.g. that he believes Reagan ran), but according to situation semantics, even mental states are ultimately to be characterized in terms of real individuals, properties, and relations.

So even if we think that signs are associated with concepts, we cannot give a truly *semantic* account of language unless we relate those concepts to something external. To give conceptualism its due, though, it must be conceded that the kind of realism advocated by situation semantics gives rise to a number of complex philosophical questions concerning imaginary or impossible properties (such as the property of being a unicorn or the property of being a round square) and fictitious individuals (such as Zeus or Sherlock Holmes). In the interest of practicality, though, we will simply ignore such questions, and leave it to the reader to interpret the symbolism of SEMANTICS values in a way that is consistent with his or her philosophical scruples. As a matter of expository convenience, we will usually talk about meaning in a realistic way; but the reader is urged to adopt a healthy scepticism and remain alert to the possibility of linguistic evidence which might help to resolve the conflict between realism and conceptualism one way or the other.

Roughly speaking, then, SEMANTICS values for signs will be specified by feature structures that characterize the described situation in terms of the individuals, properties, and relations that figure in it. In this chapter we will be concerned with just one attribute of such semantic values, the CONTENT attribute, which describes the main semantic contribution of the sign to the total characterization of the described situation; other attributes, to be introduced in later chapters, semantically classify the various indices (similar to logical variables) that occur in the content according to the kinds of NP's that give rise to them (e.g. referential, pronominal, reflexive, expletive, etc.). To a first approximation: the semantic content of a declarative sentence describes a type of situation, while the contributions of lexical signs to that description are individuals, properties, and relations.

But how do these contributions figure in the total characterization of the situation which the sentence containing them describes? Before we can answer this question, we first need to consider how situations are classified in terms of the individuals, properties, and relations which figure in them.

4.2 The Furniture of the World: Individuals, Relations, Circumstances, and Situations

The world is made up of objects of many different kinds, but for understanding how people approach, conceptualize, and talk about the world, we analyze them all in terms of *individuals* and *relations* (*properties* are relations of a certain kind, as we shall see below). Roughly, individuals are those persistent things that belong to the causal order of the world, the objects that we can track perceptually and affect by acting upon them: chairs, cups, donkeys, planets, protons, puddles, cabbages, and kings, for example. Some individuals are of sufficient importance to members of a linguistic community that they are given names. Kings, and people in general, fall into that category; to a lesser extent, so do donkeys and planets; protons, puddles, and cabbages almost never do. To a first approximation, the semantic content of a proper noun is just an individual, as indicated by the partial description of the lexical sign *Kim* given in (144):[1]

(144)
$$\left[\begin{array}{ll} \text{PHON Kim} & \\ \text{SYN|LOC} & \left[\begin{array}{ll}\text{HEAD} & \left[\begin{array}{ll}\text{MAJ} & \text{N}\\ \text{NFORM} & \text{NORM}\end{array}\right] \\ \text{SUBCAT} & \langle\ \rangle\end{array}\right] \\ \text{SEM|CONT KIM} & \end{array}\right]$$

That is, the semantic contribution of a token use of *Kim* is that the utterance which contains it has something to do with the individual Kim.

[1] Throughout this chapter, inessential syntactic details, e.g. specifications for head features other than MAJ, are frequently omitted from descriptions.

This is obviously an oversimplification, for *Kim* can be used to talk about *different* individuals depending on the circumstances of the utterance. We shall attempt to remedy this defect soon.

Very roughly speaking, the semantic contents of lexical signs other than proper nouns (e.g. common nouns, adjectives, verbs, and prepositions) are considered to be *relations*. To put it intuitively, relations are the kinds of goings-on of the world that objects may be involved in. Thus relations include such things as the qualities that individuals may have (such as being green or being a donkey); the states that they may get into (such as being angry, being on fire, being on top of, knowing, or loving); the activities and processes that they may participate in (such as walking, building, reading, and giving). Thus we have lexical signs such as those described in (145)–(148):

(145)
$$\begin{bmatrix} \text{PHON cookie} & \\ \text{SYN}|\text{LOC} & \begin{bmatrix} \text{HEAD} & \begin{bmatrix} \text{MAJ} & \text{N} \\ \text{NFORM} & \text{NORM} \end{bmatrix} \\ \text{SUBCAT} & \langle \text{DET} \rangle \end{bmatrix} \\ \text{SEM}|\text{CONT COOKIE} & \end{bmatrix}$$

(146)
$$\begin{bmatrix} \text{PHON fond} & \\ \text{SYN}|\text{LOC} & \begin{bmatrix} \text{HEAD} & [\text{MAJ A}] \\ \text{SUBCAT} & \langle \text{PP[OF], NP} \rangle \end{bmatrix} \\ \text{SEM}|\text{CONT FOND} & \end{bmatrix}$$

(147)
$$\begin{bmatrix} \text{PHON tickled} & \\ \text{SYN}|\text{LOC} & \begin{bmatrix} \text{HEAD} & \begin{bmatrix} \text{MAJ} & \text{V} \\ \text{VFORM} & \text{FIN} \end{bmatrix} \\ \text{SUBCAT} & \langle \text{NP[ACC], NP[NOM]} \rangle \end{bmatrix} \\ \text{SEM}|\text{CONT TICKLE} & \end{bmatrix}$$

(148)
$$\begin{bmatrix} \text{PHON on} & \\ \text{SYN}|\text{LOC} & \begin{bmatrix} \text{HEAD} & \begin{bmatrix} \text{MAJ} & \text{P} \\ \text{PFORM} & \text{ON} \end{bmatrix} \\ \text{SUBCAT} & \langle \text{NP[ACC], NP} \rangle \end{bmatrix} \\ \text{SEM}|\text{CONT ON} & \end{bmatrix}$$

Again we are simplifying away some details that will be provided in the following section. For example, (147) lacks any information as to how the things described by the object (NP[ACC]) and the subject (NP[NOM]) are involved in the tickly situation being described: we cannot tell who is tickling who.

It is a fundamental fact about relations that they vary as to the number of things that can participate in them. For each relation, that characteristic number is called the *arity* of the relation. Thus we classify relations as *unary* (arity one), *binary* (arity two), *ternary* (arity three), etc. For example, relations such as walking, dying, being brown, or being a horse evidently are unary, i.e. they involve just one participant (the thing that is walking, dying, being brown, or being a horse). Unary relations are usually called *properties*. Examples of binary relations include tickling, loving, recognizing, reading, being the mother of, and being on top of; ternary relations include giving, introducing, putting, and persuading. Warning: it is not always completely straightforward to determine the arity of a relation, as the reader may quickly discover by considering such cases as breaking, shaving, kicking, buying, and renting; there are also questions of more general applicability, e.g. whether some relations should be considered to have a location role that is played by a spatiotemporal object (region of spacetime). In fact, there is some question as to whether or not it is appropriate to speak of *the* arity of a given relation; we shall return to this point briefly in Section 5.5.

Relations also differ in the *ways* that objects participate in them. This point is easy to illustrate by considering the properties of walking, dying, and being a cat, as they apply to a given individual (let us call him Max). If Max walks, he participates in the property of walking as the doer. If he dies, the property of dying is something that befalls him. If he is a cat, he is involved in the property of felinity by virtue of being an instance of it, in the sense that there actually is a cat that is Max; properties of this kind are sometimes called *sortal* properties, or simply *sorts*. Ways of participating in relations are called *roles*. Thus an n-ary relation is a relation with n roles. Because of the rough analogy between relations in our sense and the mathematical notion of relation as a set of ordered n-tuples, roles are sometimes called *argument positions* and the objects which play the roles in relations are sometimes called *arguments*. For example there are two distinct roles that an individual might play in tickling: the one who does it or the one who is subjected to it.

Some difficult philosophical problems arise in the individuation of roles. For example, should we consider the (unique) role in walking to be the same role as the (unique) role in running, say the role of agent? Or should they be distinguished as the walker role and the runner role? Various versions of the former approach have been advocated by linguists working with such notions as *case roles*, *thematic relations*, and *theta-roles*; but no consensus has emerged as to just what case roles there are, or even as to whether the objects in question should be considered as essentially syntactic, conceptual, or real (as we take them to be). In situation semantics, by contrast, the latter approach is adopted: each relation is equipped with its own inventory of roles. One promising approach to resolving this conflict might be to view the traditional case roles posited by linguists (such as agent, patient, goal, etc.) as *properties* that roles (in the sense of situation semantics) might have; e.g. agentiveness is a property shared by the runner and walker roles.

Fortunately such philosophical problems seldom seem to confront us in our linguistic applications; for our purposes it is enough to keep the roles of any given relation distinct, without worrying about how to classify roles across different relations. (As always, the reader should view such claims with skepticism; no harm can result from remaining open to the possibility of linguistic evidence in support of such notions as agent and patient!) Thus in the case of tickling, we will refer to the tickler and ticklee roles; giving has the roles giver, given, and recipient, etc. As a matter of convenience, we will usually call the role in sortal properties the *instance* role; also, when it is too much trouble to come up with a new name for a role, we will sometimes refer to it simply as the *argument* role (abbreviated "arg").

By now, the reader should have a good intuitive grasp of individuals and relations. But what do they have to do with the situations that linguistic utterances are supposed to describe? Before we turn to that question let us tackle a prior one: what exactly are situations? They are just individuals of a certain kind, spatiotemporally limited parts of the world that can be comprehended (by the kind of organism whose scheme of individuation the situation belongs to), where various things are going on. As Barwise and Perry (1983:7) put it: "Reality consists of situations—individuals having properties and standing in relations at various spatiotemporal locations". Reagan's meeting with Gorbachev in Reykjavik was a situation. So is Carl's eating a certain apple in Office D-2 at Ventura Hall, Stanford University, at 4:45 p.m. PST, January 4, 1987, and so is Claire's having a cold on Christmas, 1986. Evidently we cognize or otherwise come to grips with situations in terms of what is going on in them, of the *circumstances* that obtain in them. In order to be more precise, though, we must say what we mean by a circumstance.

Roughly speaking, circumstances are possible ways the world might be; they are the kinds of things that obtain or do not obtain, depending on how the world is. (Caution: in situation semantics, the things we are calling circumstances are usually called *states of affairs*, or simply *soas*. We avoid this terminology because it wrongly suggests a connection with stative relations as opposed, say, to activities, events, processes. etc.) For example, Rebecca might be singing; for Rebecca to be singing is a circumstance which obtains or does not obtain depending on what the world is actually like. Likewise, Rebecca might *not* be singing; for Rebecca not to be singing is also a circumstance. A useful way to think of circumstances is as *potential facts*: a circumstance is called a fact just in case it obtains.

Circumstances are something like what philosophers call *propositions*, although great care must be taken in trying to equate the two notions. The term "proposition" is variously used to refer to assertions, statements, or something like sentence meanings construed as mental objects. But our circumstances are taken to be real, albeit somewhat abstract, objects, not syntactic or mental objects; they might well be thought of as *realistic propositions*.

The notion of circumstance is also akin to the various notions of *possible world* employed by many philosophers and semanticists (e.g. Montague semanticists). The main difference is that circumstances are only *partial* possible ways the world might be; possible worlds are usually taken to be *total* ways. For example, any possible world is supposed to settle every issue, e.g. whether or not Claire is laughing; if *w* is a possible world, then either Claire is laughing in *w* or she is not. But circumstances only settle certain issues. For Rebecca not to be singing is a circumstance that settles the issue of whether Rebecca is singing negatively, but it simply has nothing to do with whether Claire is laughing. This partiality of circumstances seems to give them an advantage over possible worlds as an analytic tool for psychologists and linguists: they are somehow small enough that we can speculate about how organisms might come to grips with them, or mentally represent them, for purposes of reasoning or language understanding; but possible worlds are so vast that it is difficult to imagine how they could have any cognitive relevance. Many fascinating philosophical and psychological questions beckon here, but in the interest of practicality we will have to make do with this rough-and-ready characterization of circumstances.

In order to do business with circumstances, it is convenient to have a notation for them. The notation introduced here is a variant of one that has become fairly standard in situation semantics. (The main difference is that we indicate roles by keywords instead of by numerical argument positions; this will ease the transition to the feature-structure notation adopted in the following section.) We start out with *basic* circumstances (basic soas in the usual terminology of situation semantics), which, to put it crudely, only have one thing going on in them. Basic circumstances are uniquely determined by specifying (i) a relation, together with (ii) an *assignment* of objects to each role of that relation, and (iii) a *polarity*, either positive or negative, written "1" and "0" respectively; basic circumstances are called *positive* or *negative* depending on their polarity. Unique determination means that if two basic circumstances have the same relation, the same assignment, and the same polarity, then they are in fact one and the same circumstance; if not, then they are different circumstances. The notation is illustrated in (149):

(149)

formal notation	*informal description*
⟨⟨laugh, laugher:Claire; 1⟩⟩	the circumstance of Claire laughing
⟨⟨cat, instance:Claire; 0⟩⟩	the circumstance of Claire not being a cat
⟨⟨tickle, tickler:Rebecca, ticklee:Claire; 1⟩⟩	the circumstance of Rebecca tickling Claire

It is crucially important to understand that notations such as those in (149) *denote* circumstances; they do *not* assert that the circumstances in question actually hold. Also, because roles are indicated by keyword rather than position, the order in which arguments appear is not significant.

Some slightly more complicated examples of basic circumstances arise in case one or more of the role players are themselves circumstances, as in (150):

(150) a. ⟨⟨want, wanter:Rebecca
wanted:⟨⟨cry, cryer:Claire; 1⟩⟩; 0⟩⟩
(the circumstance of Rebecca not wanting Claire to cry)

b. ⟨⟨try, tryer:Claire
tried:⟨⟨get, getter:Claire, gotten:Elliot; 1⟩⟩; 1⟩⟩
(the circumstance of Claire trying to get Elliot)

c. ⟨⟨believe, believer:Claire
believed:⟨⟨sleep, sleeper:Rebecca; 1⟩⟩; 1⟩⟩
(the circumstance of Claire believing that Rebecca is sleeping)

But some circumstances are nonbasic. In this category are *conjunctive* and *disjunctive* circumstances, as well as *quantificational circumstances*; these are illustrated in (151):

(151) a. (and {⟨⟨tickle, tickler:Rebecca, ticklee:Claire; 1⟩⟩,
⟨⟨laugh, laugher:Claire; 1⟩⟩})
(the circumstance of Rebecca tickling Claire and Claire laughing)

b. (or {⟨⟨tickle, tickler:Rebecca, ticklee:Claire; 1⟩⟩,
⟨⟨laugh, laugher:Claire; 1⟩⟩})
(the circumstance of Rebecca tickling Claire or Claire laughing)

c. (forall x | ⟨⟨cat, instance:x; 1⟩⟩) ⟨⟨howl, howler:x; 1⟩⟩
(the circumstance of every cat howling)

Evidently nonbasic circumstances are related to basic circumstances rather in the way that nonatomic formulas in the predicate calculus are related to atomic formulas. Indeed, notations such as those in (150) and (151) can be regarded as expressions in a formal logic of circumstances; in fact a good deal of current research in situation semantics is concerned with developing axioms, inference rules, and even a model-theoretic semantics for such a logic. Even a rough sketch of such *axiomatic situation theory* is beyond the scope of this book, but in order to avoid confusion, some basic syntactic and semantic differences between the logic of circumstances used here and standard first-order logic should be noted.

Among the syntactic differences, two arise within atomic formulas. First, as already noted, keywords instead of numerical argument position in the formula are used to distinguish the roles of a relation; and second, positive and negative atomic formulas are distinguished by their polarity instead of by the prefixing of a negation symbol. (Some writers have proposed the use of "external" negation as well as the polarities in situation semantics, but the matter is far from settled.) To enhance readability, we have chosen to write conjunctive and disjunctive formulas by prefixing the connective "AND" or "OR", and then listing the conjuncts or disjuncts between curly brackets (as in set notation). Of course, in such formulas the order of conjuncts or disjuncts is not significant. Quantification in our logic of circumstances follows natural language, but not first-order logic, in two respects. First, the variables over which we quantify are always *restricted*: instead of "for every x, x howls", we have "for every cat x, x howls". Technically, this means that a variable is always annotated by a circumstance expression in which the annotated variable itself has a free occurrence, e.g. the restricted variable "$x|\langle\langle$cat, instance:x; 1$\rangle\rangle$" in (151c). And second, in addition to the determiners "exists" and "forall" countenanced by first-order logic, we have a full range of generalized determiners such as "most", "no", "exactly three", "more-than-two-but-less-than-seven", etc.

More importantly, expressions in our logic of circumstances differ from their first-order-logic counterparts in terms of their intended interpretations. In the standard model theory of first-order logic, predicate symbols are interpreted as relations in the conventional mathematical sense, i.e. as sets of ordered n-tuples. But our relation symbols denote *realistic* relations, the goings-on of the world—qualities, states, activities, and processes that things might participate in—that we human beings can make out. Realistic relations are much richer and more finely-grained than mathematical relations in the following sense: two mathematical relations are considered to be identical just as long as precisely the same ordered n-tuples happen to be in the two relations, but this is not so for realistic relations. For example, suppose it just happened to be the case that the set of all ordered pairs $\langle a, b\rangle$ such that a has kicked, is kicking, or will kick b is precisely the same as the set of all $\langle a, b\rangle$ such that a has kissed, is kissing, or will kiss b. Then from the mathematical point of view, kicking and kissing are one and the same relation. But from the realistic point of view, this is nonsense: kicking and kissing are different because they are different kinds of goings-on, different ways that two individuals can be involved with each other, with different causal consequences; which things happen to be kicking and kissing have very little to do with what kicking and kissing are.

To give a somewhat different example: mathematically speaking, the property (unary relation) of being an equilateral triangle is the same as the property of being an equiangular triangle. In fact, not only does it happen to be the case that exactly the same triangles have these two properties, but moreover (under the assumption that mathematical truths are necessary truths), things could not have been otherwise. Yet, they are different realistic properties. To appreciate this, suppose that t is a certain triangle and Kim is a certain mathematically naive or slow-witted individual who believes t to be equiangular (perhaps because he measured the angles) but does not believe t to be equilateral (either because he doesn't know that equiangular triangles are equilateral, or because he never drew the relevant inference). Then clearly (152a) and (152b) are distinct circumstances, for (152a) is a fact but (152b) is not:

(152) a. ⟨⟨believe, believer:Kim
believed:⟨⟨equiangular-triangle, instance:t; 1⟩⟩; 1⟩⟩

b. ⟨⟨believe, believer:Kim
believed:⟨⟨equilateral-triangle, instance: t; 1⟩⟩; 1⟩⟩

Given our assumption that basic circumstances are uniquely determined by their relations, assignments, and polarities, this would be impossible if equiangular-triangle and equilateral-triangle were the same property.

Another fundamental semantic difference between our logic of circumstances and first-order logic is this: circumstance expressions such as those in (149)–(152) denote circumstances, but in first-order logic, closed formulas (i.e. formulas without free variables) only denote truth-values.

(153) a. ⟨⟨laugh, laugher:Rebecca; 1⟩⟩

b. laugh(Rebecca)

Thus (153a) denotes the circumstance of Rebecca laughing, but (153b) denotes only True (in those models or worlds where the thing denoted by "Rebecca" belongs to the set denoted by "laugh") or False (elsewhere). To put it another way, (153b) denotes True if (153a) is a fact and False otherwise. Evidently, (153a) is much more contentful than (153b), for (153b) has nothing of (153a)'s content except its facthood or nonfacthood. This crucial difference is reflected in the fact that there are no first-order formulas analogous to those in (150) or (152). For example, (154) is not well-formed:

(154) believe(Claire, sleep(Rebecca))

Expression (154) is syntactic nonsense because "sleep(Rebecca)" is a formula, not a term, and therefore cannot fill an argument position in an atomic formula. Moreover, (154) is semantic nonsense as well, in the sense that it would not have the intended interpretation even if it were syntactically well-formed. Truth values simply are not the kinds of things we believe; circumstances are.

In our linguistic applications we will often find it convenient to make use of circumstance expressions containing variables which are not bound by quantification, such as (155a):

(155) a. ⟨⟨laugh, laugher:x; 1⟩⟩

b. laugh(x)

Formally, such expressions are analogous to first-order formulas containing free variables such as (155b). The interpretation of such expressions is subtly different, however. In standard logic we consider a formula like (155b) to have a denotation only once a value has been assigned to the variable x. In situation semantics, however, the usual practice is to regard an expression such as (155a) as denoting a situation-theoretic object of a kind called a *parametrized* circumstance (in the usual terminology of situation semantics, a *parametrized state of affairs*, or simply a *psoa*). Roughly, a parametrized circumstance is like a circumstance except that certain of its argument roles—its *parameters*—have not yet been anchored to determinate objects. The reader is hereby warned that the precise philosophical status of parameters is far from settled; the basic question about them is whether they should be regarded as real, i.e. on a par with individuals, properties, and relations, or simply as analytical devices of some kind.

As usual, we will sidestep this metaphysical minefield. For our purposes, it will suffice to think of (155a) as simply denoting a *function* whose values are circumstances, just as "$5x+2$" can be taken to denote a function whose values are real numbers. Thus (155a) denotes the function which maps Claire to the circumstance ⟨⟨laugh, laugher: Claire; 1⟩⟩, etc. According to this usage, it does not matter which free variables occur in a parametrized circumstance expression as long as it is not part of another expression. For example, we consider (156a) and (156b) to denote the same parametrized circumstance:

(156) a. ⟨⟨want, wanter:x
wanted:⟨⟨tickle, tickler:y, ticklee:x; 1⟩⟩; 0⟩⟩

b. ⟨⟨want, wanter:z
wanted:⟨⟨tickle, tickler:w, ticklee:z; 1⟩⟩; 0⟩⟩

Both expressions denote one and the same function with two parameters; one of those parameters is indicated by occurrences of x in (156a) and occurrences of z in (156b), the other by the occurrence of y in (156a) and the occurrence of w in (156b). When these parameters are anchored to Claire and Rebecca respectively, this function assumes the value (157):

(157) ⟨⟨want, wanter:Claire
wanted:⟨⟨tickle, tickler:Rebecca,
ticklee:Claire; 1⟩⟩; 0⟩⟩

Just as variables bound by quantification can be restricted in their range, so parameters may be restricted as to what sorts of things they can be anchored to. Parametrized circumstances whose parameters are restricted in this way will be notated as in (158):

(158) ⟨⟨kick, kicker:x, kickee:y; 1⟩⟩
x | ⟨⟨donkey, instance:x; 1⟩⟩, y | ⟨⟨zebra, instance:y; 0⟩⟩

This denotes a circumstance-valued function of two parameters, one of which is restricted to donkeys and the other of which is restricted to non-zebras.[2]

With this rather lengthy discussion of circumstances behind us, we turn finally to the situation-theoretic objects *par excellence*, namely situations themselves. As we have said, situations are just comprehensible and spatiotemporally limited parts of the world with things going on in them (objects having or not having properties and being or not being in relations). The importance of circumstances arises from the fact that we classify, individuate, or describe situations on the basis of the circumstances that obtain in them. Conversely, circumstances are considered to obtain by virtue of obtaining in some situation or other; we say situation s *supports* circumstance c, or c *holds in* s. Supporting in this sense is regarded as a relation between situations and circumstances. Thus, if s is a situation and c a circumstance, e.g. ⟨⟨laugh; laugher:Claire; 1⟩⟩, then (159) denotes the circumstance of c holding in s:[3]

(159) ⟨⟨support, situation:s, circumstance:c; 1⟩⟩

If (159) is a fact, then so is c by virtue of there being a situation that *makes* it a fact. Conversely, c is a fact only if there is a situation s such that (159) is a fact. (Warning: there is a philosophical debate as to whether this converse should be required to hold in case c is factual by necessity e.g. c = ⟨⟨greater-than, arg1:1, arg2:2; 1⟩⟩ or c = (forall x | ⟨⟨donkey, instance:x; 1⟩⟩) ⟨⟨mammal, instance:x; 1⟩⟩.) For a given situation s, the circumstances which hold in s are called the facts *of* s.

In what sense can we use circumstances to describe or classify situations? The answer is simply that to each circumstance c there corresponds a type (or property) of situations, namely the property of being a situation in which c holds, written as (160):

(160) [{s}:⟨⟨support, situation:s, circumstance:c; 1⟩⟩]

This is a special case of a phenomenon which situation semantics calls *relation abstraction*: given any parametrized circumstance $c(x, y, \ldots)$ with parameters $x, y, \ldots$, there is assumed to be a relation $[\{x, y, \ldots\} : c(x, y, \ldots)]$ whose roles are indicated by the variables $x, y, \ldots$ For example, (161) denotes the relation that holds between two individuals x and y such that x loves y but y does not love x, i.e. the unrequited-loving relation:

---

[2] This notation is different from the one standardly used by situation semanticists, wherein restrictions are suffixed to the parameter occurrences inside the circumstance expressions themselves.

[3] In the situation semantics literature, the relation of supporting is usually denoted by "$\models$"; we eschew this notation to avoid confusion with the standard usage in model-theoretic semantics.

(161) $[\{x, y\}$: (and $\{\langle\langle$love, lover:x, beloved:y; 1$\rangle\rangle$,
$\langle\langle$love, loved:y, beloved:x; 0$\rangle\rangle\})]$

If there is just one abstracted parameter, then the relation in question is a property. For example, (162) denotes the property of being one that shaves oneself:

(162) $[\{x\}$: $\langle\langle$shave, shaver:x, shaved:x; 1$\rangle\rangle]$

Situation types such as (160) are of this kind.

As will soon be evident, we will be concerned more directly with circumstances (or parametrized circumstances) than with situations. This is because we can exploit the correspondence between circumstances and the types of situations which support them, to represent information about described situations in terms of the circumstances which hold in them. Thus, the SEMANTICS|CONTENT value in a feature structure of type *sign* corresponding to a declarative sentence will be a feature structure of type *circumstance*, which does not give information about the described situation directly, but rather characterizes it indirectly by describing the circumstances that hold in it.

Often, the situation-theoretic objects described in SEMANTICS|CONTENT values will be parametrized, with the anchoring of the parameters depending on the context of the particular sign token (language use situation). In our applications, such parameters are usually introduced by uses of NP's, with anchors corresponding to referents (for referential NP's) and antecedents (of pronouns). As we shall see in later chapters, there are many different kinds of parameters, corresponding to the different kinds of NP's which introduce them (e.g. referential NP's, quantificational NP's, ordinary pronouns, reflexive pronouns, relative pronouns, interrogative pronouns, etc.). When we turn to the study of more complex phenomena

(163)
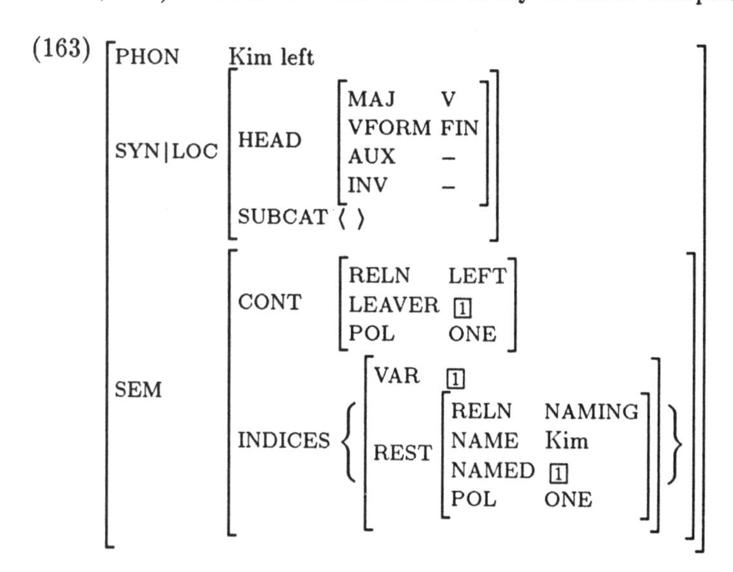

(e.g. long-distance dependencies and anaphora) which require us to keep track of the number and kind of parameters occurring in semantic contents, we will introduce additional set-valued attributes of SEMANTICS values especially for those purposes. For the time being, we can get by with just one additional attribute for managing parameters; we call this attribute INDICES. (The name is intended to suggest an affinity with the "syntactic indices" familiar from transformational grammar.) Thus, for example, the English sentential sign *Kim left* is partially described by (163) above. The SEMANTICS|CONTENT value here is a feature structure which describes the parametrized circumstance (164), with the empty feature structure indicated by "[1]" corresponding to the parameter x:

(164) $\langle\langle$leave, leaver:x; 1$\rangle\rangle$

That is, the described situation is one in which some object x leaves. Just which object x is, (163) does not tell us; that depends on who the speaker referred to with the use of *Kim*. However, the SEMANTICS|INDICES value in (163), which is simply the AVM rendering of the parameter restriction in (165), contains the information that x must be named "Kim" (i.e. x is in the naming relation with the phonological object /kIm/).

(165) $x\,|\,\langle\langle$naming, name:"Kim", named:x; 1$\rangle\rangle$

More generally, parameters are used in situation semantics to treat any aspects of linguistic meaning which depend upon the context of use, including the interpretation of tense, demonstratives, and indexical expressions such as *I*, *you*, *here*, *left*, *right*, *yesterday*, etc.; unfortunately discussion of such matters goes beyond the scope of this book.

In the next section, we turn to the basic question of how lexical signs of different kinds contribute to the semantic content of the sentences which contain them.

4.3 The Semantic Content of Signs

To get started, we will need some new types of feature structures for describing situation-theoretic objects which figure in the semantic content of signs. Notationally, all this amounts to is rewriting expressions of circumstance logic in the form of attribute-value matrices. We begin with the atomic types *individual* (e.g. KIM, SANDY, FIDO), *relation* (e.g. LEAVE, COOKIE, SEE, BELIEVE), and *polarity* (ONE and ZERO).

Circumstances are described by feature structures of type *circumstance*, with subtypes *basic-circumstance*, *compound-circumstance*,, and *quantified-circumstance*, which we consider now in turn.

Feature structures of type *basic-circumstance* minimally have the attributes RELATION and POLARITY. Various subtypes of *circumstance* require different values for the RELATION attribute and have additional attributes corresponding to the roles that are appropriate to the relation in question, as illustrated in (166) and (167):[4]

(166) a. ⟪donkey, instance:Chiquita; 1⟫

b. $$\begin{bmatrix} \text{RELN} & \text{DONKEY} \\ \text{INST} & \text{CHIQUITA} \\ \text{POL} & \text{ONE} \end{bmatrix}$$

(167) a. ⟪tickle, tickler:Rebecca, ticklee:Claire; 0⟫

b. $$\begin{bmatrix} \text{RELN} & \text{TICKLE} \\ \text{TICKLER} & \text{REBECCA} \\ \text{TICKLEE} & \text{CLAIRE} \\ \text{POL} & \text{ZERO} \end{bmatrix}$$

In practice, all the basic circumstances used in this book will have positive polarity (because we will not be dealing with negation); therefore as a matter of notational convenience we will usually omit the specification [POLARITY ONE].

Feature structures of type *compound-circumstance* have two attributes: CONNECTIVE, which takes the values AND or OR, and JUNCTS, whose value is the set of conjuncts or disjuncts as the case may be. This is illustrated for the AND case in (168):

(168) a. (and {⟪tickle, tickler:Rebecca, ticklee:Claire⟫,
⟪laugh, laugher:Claire⟫})

b. $$\begin{bmatrix} \text{CONN} & \text{AND} \\ \text{JUNCTS} & \left\{ \begin{bmatrix} \text{RELN} & \text{TICKLE} \\ \text{TICKLER} & \text{REBECCA} \\ \text{TICKLEE} & \text{CLAIRE} \end{bmatrix}, \begin{bmatrix} \text{RELN} & \text{LAUGH} \\ \text{LAUGHER} & \text{CLAIRE} \end{bmatrix} \right\} \end{bmatrix}$$

Before considering quantified and parametrized circumstances, we need to discuss the representation by feature structures of bound variables and parameters, which we refer to collectively as *variables*. For the time being, unrestricted variables will simply be be represented by empty feature structures of type *variable*; discussion of the internal structure of variables is postponed until Volume 2. Different occurrences of the same variable, of course, are indicated by structure-sharing. There is no need to distinguish notationally between bound variables and parameters: they are parameters just in case they never become bound by quantification. Restricted variables (including restricted parameters) are then represented by feature structures of type *index*, which have the two attributes VARIABLE and RESTRICTION. (The connection between our restricted variables and the

---

[4] The use of feature structures to describe circumstances is anticipated by Fenstad et al. (1985).

"syntactic indices" of transformational grammar will be discussed below.) Thus a variable which is restricted to range over (in the case of a bound variable) or to be anchored to (in the case of a parameter) cats is described as in (169):

(169)
$$\begin{bmatrix} \text{VAR} & \boxed{1} \\ \text{REST} & \begin{bmatrix} \text{RELN} & \text{CAT} \\ \text{INST} & \boxed{1} \end{bmatrix} \end{bmatrix}$$

We are now in a position to describe quantified circumstances. By way of illustration, we present in (170b) the AVM corresponding to the quantified circumstance (151c), repeated here as (170a):

(170) a. (forall $x \mid \langle\langle$cat, instance:x; 1$\rangle\rangle$) $\langle\langle$howl, howler:x; 1$\rangle\rangle$

b.
$$\begin{bmatrix} \text{QUANT} & \begin{bmatrix} \text{DET} & \text{FORALL} \\ \text{IND} & \begin{bmatrix} \text{VAR} & \boxed{1} \\ \text{REST} & \begin{bmatrix} \text{RELN} & \text{CAT} \\ \text{INST} & \boxed{1} \end{bmatrix} \end{bmatrix} \end{bmatrix} \\ \text{SCOPE} & \begin{bmatrix} \text{RELN} & \text{HOWL} \\ \text{HOWLER} & \boxed{1} \end{bmatrix} \end{bmatrix}$$

Note that a feature structure of type *quantified-circumstance* has the attributes QUANTIFIER and SCOPE. The value of QUANTIFIER is a feature structure of type *quantifier*, which in turn has the attributes DETERMINER and INDEX; here the value of INDEX is of course a feature structure of type *index* that corresponds to the restricted variable in (170a). The value of SCOPE is a feature structure of type *circumstance*; intuitively, it corresponds to the scope of the quantifier, and the variable $\boxed{1}$ bound by the quantifier occurs within it.

We turn now to the description of the SEMANTICS|CONTENT value in feature structures of type *sign*. We begin with a simplified account that ignores parameters and quantification; a more sophisticated treatment will be given in the following section.

First, let us suppose that the semantic content of a proper noun is just the individual named by the proper noun (i.e. similar to an individual constant in standard logic), as in (171):

(171)
$$\begin{bmatrix} \text{PHON} & \text{Kim} \\ \text{SYN}|\text{LOC} & \begin{bmatrix} \text{HEAD} & \begin{bmatrix} \text{MAJ} & \text{N} \\ \text{NFORM} & \text{NORM} \end{bmatrix} \\ \text{SUBCAT} & \langle\ \rangle \end{bmatrix} \\ \text{SEM}|\text{CONT} & \text{KIM} \end{bmatrix}$$

Of course this ignores the fact noted above that the individual named depends on the context of utterance; we really want a restricted parameter instead of an individual. We will remedy this defect soon, but the simplified version will provide a point of departure.

Next, let us suppose that the semantic content of a verb is just a relation, as in (172):

(172)
$$\begin{bmatrix} \text{PHON saw} & \\ \text{SYN}|\text{LOC} & \begin{bmatrix} \text{HEAD} & \begin{bmatrix} \text{MAJ} & \text{V} \\ \text{VFORM} & \text{FIN} \end{bmatrix} \\ \text{SUBCAT} & \langle \text{NP[ACC], NP[NOM]} \rangle \end{bmatrix} \\ \text{SEM}|\text{CONT SEE} & \end{bmatrix}$$

Now what about the semantic content of a sentence such as *Kim saw Sandy*? Still ignoring the context-dependence of the proper names' referents, evidently what we want is something like (173a):

(173) a.
$$\begin{bmatrix} \text{RELN} & \text{SEE} \\ \text{SEER} & \text{KIM} \\ \text{SEEN} & \text{SANDY} \end{bmatrix}$$

But where does the language user get the information that, in a sentence headed by the verb *saw*, the seer is described by the subject (the last element of the SUBCAT list) and the thing seen by the object (the second-last element of the SUBCAT list)? Why should *Kim saw Sandy* have (173a) as its content, rather than (173b) or perhaps something else altogether?

(173) b.
$$\begin{bmatrix} \text{RELN} & \text{SEE} \\ \text{SEEN} & \text{KIM} \\ \text{SEER} & \text{SANDY} \end{bmatrix}$$

Clearly, the proposed lexical sign (172) is missing some crucial information, namely the information that the subject and object of *saw* are associated with the seer and the seen respectively.

More generally, it is characteristic of non-nominal lexical heads (such as verbs, adjectives, and prepositions) that they provide a very general characterization of the described situation in terms of the kinds of things that are going on in it (properties and relations), while the complements subcategorized for by the head give information about the number and kind of things that are participating in (i.e. filling roles in) those properties and relations. To put it another way, the semantic content of the head partially describes a (possibly parametrized) basic circumstance, while the complements of the head fill in the description with information about the objects filling the roles in the circumstance. Very roughly, in order to capture this general semantic fact about heads and complements, the proposed lexical sign representation (172) needs to be replaced with something like (174a):

(174) a.
$$\begin{bmatrix} \text{PHON saw} & \\ \text{SYN}\mid\text{LOC} & \begin{bmatrix} \text{HEAD} & \begin{bmatrix}\text{MAJ} & \text{V}\\ \text{VFORM} & \text{FIN}\end{bmatrix} \\ \text{SUBCAT} & \langle \boxed{1}\ \text{NP[ACC]},\ \boxed{2}\ \text{NP[NOM]}\ \rangle \end{bmatrix} \\ \text{SEM}\mid\text{CONT} & \begin{bmatrix} \text{RELN} & \text{SEE} \\ \text{SEER} & \boxed{2} \\ \text{SEEN} & \boxed{1}\end{bmatrix}\end{bmatrix}$$

The idea here is that somehow the subcategorized complements have to be associated with roles in the circumstance; the required association has been indicated using structure-sharing tags. Yet as it stands (174a) is nonsensical, for the structures indicated by "$\boxed{1}$" and "$\boxed{2}$" are feature structures describing linguistic signs, not the sorts of things that see and be seen. To remedy this defect, we revise (174a) so that the shared structures are not the signs subcategorized for by the head but rather their semantic contents. This revision is shown in (174b) (ignoring PHONOLOGY, as well as SYNTAX | LOCAL | HEAD values, which remain unchanged):

(174) b.
$$\begin{bmatrix} \text{SYN}\mid\text{LOC}\mid\text{SUBCAT} & \langle[\text{SEM}\mid\text{CONT}\ \boxed{1}], \\ & \quad [\text{SEM}\mid\text{CONT}\ \boxed{2}]\rangle \\ \text{SEM}\mid\text{CONT} & \begin{bmatrix} \text{RELN} & \text{SEE} \\ \text{SEER} & \boxed{2} \\ \text{SEEN} & \boxed{1}\end{bmatrix}\end{bmatrix}$$

The version given in (174b) is still not the final one, since we are still making the simplifying assumption that the semantic contents of the subcategorized NP's are atomic values like KIM and SANDY, not restricted parameters or quantifiers; but it will suffice for the moment, in order to make three general points.

First, the structure-sharing between role-fillers in the semantic content of the lexical head and the semantic contents of the SUBCAT elements clearly is related to the notion of "theta-role assignment under subcategorization" in GB theory. In that theory, subcategorized-for complements are said to have theta-roles directly assigned to them by a verb; subjects are not considered to be subcategorized for, but nonetheless they are still assumed to have their theta-roles assigned by the verb (albeit perhaps in some indirect way). Although the status of theta-roles in GB theory has not been explicitly spelled out, it is generally agreed that they are essentially syntactic in nature, and that structures in which some subcategorized-for argument fails to have a theta-role assigned are syntactically ill-formed. In HPSG theory, by contrast, the burden of theta-roles is borne by the argument roles (such as SEER and SEEN), and the assignment of roles in lexical signs is given by structure-sharing between the semantic contents of the complements and the role-players in the semantic content of the head. In this way, the essentially semantic nature of role assignment is made clear. The same idea might be incorporated into GB theory by associating theta-roles with certain variables in LF (Logical Form), for the information contained in GB's LF is largely similar to the information contained in HPSG's SEMANTICS|CONTENT.

Second, role assignment in HPSG lexical signs is also related to the occasional practice in LFG of annotating grammatical function labels with role information within PRED values of f-structures, as in (175):

(175) $\begin{bmatrix} \text{PRED 'SEE } \langle(\overset{\text{seer}}{\uparrow\text{SUBJ}})(\overset{\text{seen}}{\uparrow\text{OBJ}})\rangle\text{'} \end{bmatrix}$

In fact, it is clear that the PRED attribute in f-structures is intended to provide some of the same information that is provided by HPSG SEMANTICS|CONTENT values. The chief difference between the two theories in this respect is that LFG is usually viewed by its practitioners as a theory of *syntax*, and therefore not directly concerned with explaining just how the roles come into the picture; they are just annotations which fulfill an essentially mnemonic function. HPSG, by contrast, is in principle a theory of *signs*, and is therefore concerned with providing a direct account of the *connection* between syntactic phenomena, e.g. subcategorization, and semantic phenomena, e.g. roles in the described situation.[5]

Third, it is roughly true (at least under the simplifying assumptions about the semantic content of NP's that we are temporarily adopting) that the SEMANTICS|CONTENT value of a phrasal sign is identical with (in the sense of structure-sharing) that of the head daughter; the semantic contributions of the complements are simply unified into the appropriate roles. We can express this tentative generalization as a universal principle given in (176); this will be modified into successively more sophisticated versions as we proceed:

(176) Semantics Principle (preliminary version)

$$[\text{DTRS}\ _{\textit{headed-structure}}[\ ]] \Rightarrow \begin{bmatrix} \text{SEM|CONT } \boxed{1} \\ \text{DTRS|HEAD-DTR|SEM|CONT } \boxed{1} \end{bmatrix}$$

[5] Of course there is no obstacle to augmenting an LFG-like syntactic theory by articulating semantic information in a more explicit manner, as Fenstad et al. (1985) have shown. They too employ feature structures that contain (inter alia) both syntactic and semantic information to set up the association between semantic roles and grammatical functions; in this regard their approach differs from ours only at the level of technical detail.

The effect of (176) is illustrated in (177), which partially describes the sentential sign *Kim saw Sandy*; for convenience the paths SYNTAX|LOCAL|SUBCAT and SEMANTICS|CONTENT are abbreviated to simply SUBCAT and CONTENT respectively:

(177)

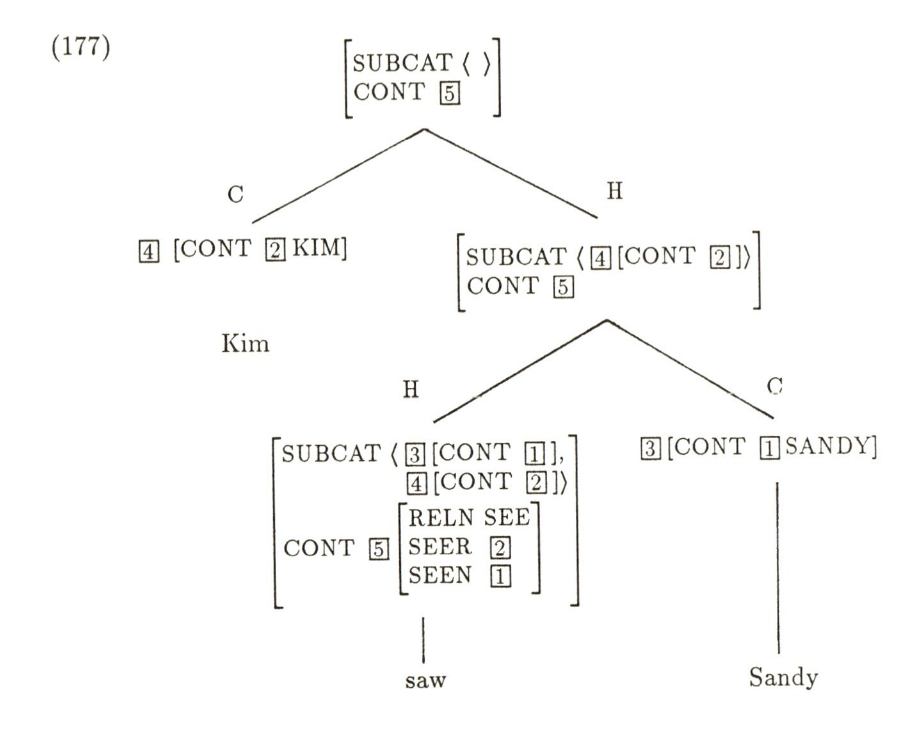

Here the lexical head is just (174b) in abbreviated form. In the VP *saw Kim*, the complement daughter *Sandy* (3) is unified with the object (second-last) element on the SUBCAT list of the head daughter *saw* and no longer appears in the SUBCAT list of the VP itself, in accordance with the Subcategorization Principle; as a consequence of this unification the SEEN value (1) in the lexical head's CONTENT is unified with the CONTENT of *Sandy*, which of course is just SANDY. In addition, the CONTENT of the VP is shared with the CONTENT (5) of the head daughter in accordance with the Semantics Principle (176). Similarly, in the whole S, the complement daughter *Kim* (4) is unified with the subject (last and only) SUBCAT element of the VP head daughter, and the SUBCAT value on the S itself is accordingly empty; this results in the unification of the subject's content KIM with the SEER value (3) in the lexical head's content. And again, the Semantics Principle ensures that the CONTENT of the whole S is just 5 again. Taking these unifications into consideration, we see that the SEMANTICS|CONTENT value of the whole sentence is precisely (173a), as desired.

4.4 Parameters, Quantifiers, and Indices

With some of the fundamental intuitions about the connection between subcategorization and semantic content in place, let us now address the fact that natural language NP's, unlike individual constants in standard logic, typically introduce restricted parameters (e.g. in the case of proper nouns) or restricted quantifiers (in the case of quantified NP's) into the overall semantic content of the sentences which contain them. To take this into account, we must revise the SEMANTICS|CONTENT values of both proper and common nouns; some of the details of role assignment and the Semantics Principle will also have to be revised accordingly. The main feature of the revision is that SEMANTICS|CONTENT values of nouns must be able to specify a restricted variable. To this end, we introduce the feature-structure type *indexed-object*, one of whose attributes is the INDEX attribute. The value of the INDEX attribute in turn will be a feature structure of type *index*; this describes the restricted variable (parameter or bound variable, as the case may be). We will also employ two subtypes of *indexed-object*, viz. *referential-object* and *quantifier* to handle proper nouns and quantified NP's respectively; as we saw above, feature structures of type *quantifier* bear the additional attribute DETERMINER.

The case of proper nouns is illustrated in (178):

(178)
$$\begin{bmatrix} \text{PHON} & \boxed{2}\,\text{Kim} \\ \text{SEM} \mid \text{CONT} & \begin{bmatrix} \text{IND} & \begin{bmatrix} \text{VAR} & \boxed{1} \\ \text{REST} & \begin{bmatrix} \text{RELN} & \text{NAMING} \\ \text{NAME} & \boxed{2} \\ \text{NAMED} & \boxed{1} \end{bmatrix} \end{bmatrix} \end{bmatrix} \end{bmatrix}$$

The SEMANTICS|CONTENT value is a feature structure of type *referential-object*. The value of the INDEX attribute is a feature structure of type *index*; the restricted parameter which it describes is of the form given in (165), repeated here as (179):

(179) $x \mid \langle\langle \text{naming, name:“Kim”, named:}x;\ 1 \rangle\rangle$

We next describe how such a semantic content contributes to the semantic content of the sentence containing the NP in question. This will require a slight revision to the way that roles are assigned to complements in the case of complements (e.g. NP's) whose SEMANTICS|CONTENT values are indexed. The basic idea is that in such cases it is just the variable of the index (in this case the parameter introduced by the use of the proper noun), not the entire semantic content of the NP, which fills a role in the semantic content of the whole sentence. An illustration is in order here. To this end, we first introduce an abbreviatory convention which facilitates reference to the value of the path SEMANTICS|CONTENT|INDEX|VARIABLE, whereby the value of that path simply appears as a subscript at the lower-right corner of a sign description. Thus, for example, "$\text{NP}_{\boxed{1}}$" abbreviates the description given in (180):

(180)
$$\begin{bmatrix} \text{SYN}|\text{LOC} & \begin{bmatrix} \text{HEAD} & [\text{MAJ N}] \\ \text{SUBCAT} & \langle\ \rangle \end{bmatrix} \\ \text{SEM}|\text{CONT}|\text{IND}|\text{VAR} & \boxed{1} \end{bmatrix}$$

(This should be compared with the standard abbreviations given in Chapter 3 (130).) We can now illustrate the required revision to the assignment of roles to complements; this is shown in (181):

(181)
$$\begin{bmatrix} \text{PHON saw} & \\ \text{SYN}|\text{LOC} & \begin{bmatrix} \text{HEAD} & \begin{bmatrix} \text{MAJ} & \text{V} \\ \text{VFORM} & \text{FIN} \end{bmatrix} \\ \text{SUBCAT} & \langle \text{NP[ACC]}_{\boxed{1}}, \text{NP[NOM]}_{\boxed{2}} \rangle \end{bmatrix} \\ \text{SEM}|\text{CONT} & \begin{bmatrix} \text{RELN} & \text{SEE} \\ \text{SEER} & \boxed{2} \\ \text{SEEN} & \boxed{1} \end{bmatrix} \end{bmatrix}$$

The effect of this revision is illustrated in (182), which improves upon the simplified version given in (177):

(182)

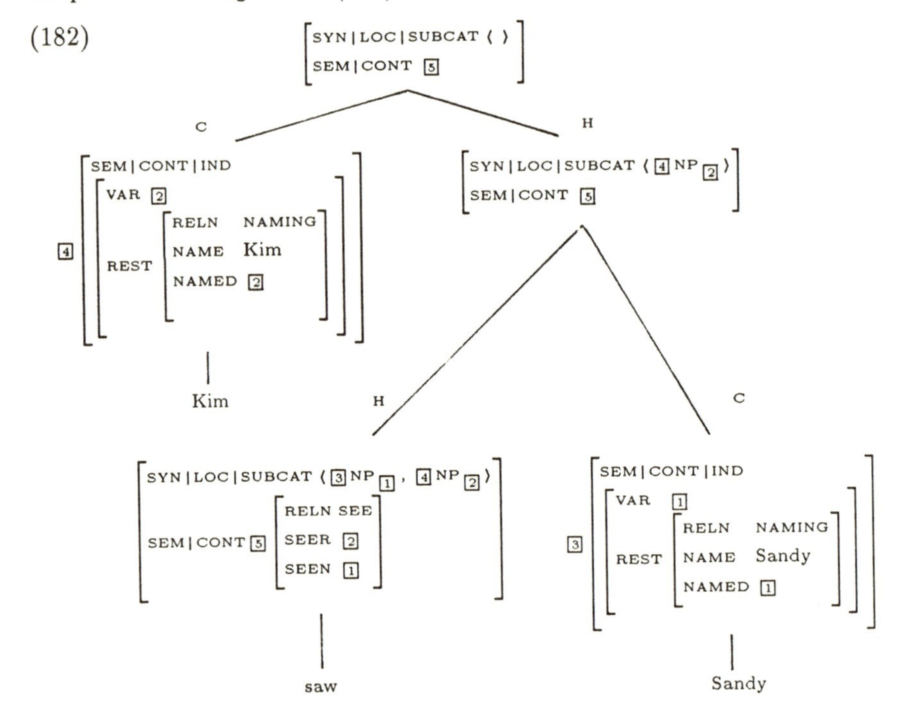

Here the SEMANTICS|CONTENT value of the whole sentence is simply (183), where [1] and [2] correspond to the parameters introduced by the uses of *Sandy* and *Kim* respectively:

(183)
$$\begin{bmatrix} \text{RELN SEE} \\ \text{SEER } \boxed{2} \\ \text{SEEN } \boxed{1} \end{bmatrix}$$

There is still some key information missing, however. The parameter [1] can only be anchored to an individual named Sandy, and [2] can only be anchored to an individual named Kim. These facts are relevant to the the semantic interpretation of the entire sentence, but somehow this information has gotten lost in the shuffle: they do not appear anywhere in the description of the semantic content of the sentence itself. What is required is some means of keeping track of information about variables (such as restrictions on what they can be anchored to or what kinds of things they can range over when bound by quantifiers) that makes it available at the sentence level. More generally, as we shall see in chapters to come, several different kinds of information about the variables introduced by uses of NP's have to be retained and made available on phrases containing those NP's; in addition to restrictions on variables, such information includes agreement features and referential type (e.g. whether the NP that introduced the variable is quantified, definite-referring, indefinite-referring, pronominal, reflexive, reciprocal, expletive, etc.). Information of this kind turns out to play an important role in determining various properties of anaphoric relations such as locality conditions on pronominal binding, so-called "disjoint reference" constraints, the potential of NP's to serve as antecedents for pronouns in subsequent sentences, etc. As the need for tracking such information arises, we will introduce appropriate attributes for storing it and corresponding mechanisms for transmitting it to the places where it is needed.

For the time being, it is sufficient to introduce a single new attribute (in addition to CONTENT) for SEMANTICS values of signs that keeps track of all the variables introduced within the sign. This is the INDICES attribute mentioned in example (163) of the preceding section. Its value will always be a set (possibly empty) of feature structures of type *index*; each index consists of a variable together with the restrictions upon that variable. As might be expected, an index originates in the INDICES value of the noun that introduces the index. For the case of proper nouns, this is illustrated below in (184), which is an elaboration of (178). Note that the INDICES value here is just a singleton set whose only member is the INDEX value in the SEMANTICS|CONTENT value of the NP itself.

In the case of phrasal signs, we assume for the time being that the INDICES value will just be the set union of the INDICES values on the daughters. This can be ensured by amending the Semantics Principle (175) to the form (185).

(184)
$$\begin{bmatrix} \text{PHON} & \boxed{2}\,\text{Kim} \\ \text{SYN|LOC} & \begin{bmatrix}\text{HEAD|MAJ} & \text{N}\\ \text{SUBCAT} & \langle\ \rangle\end{bmatrix} \\ \text{SEM} & \begin{bmatrix} \text{CONT} & \begin{bmatrix}\text{IND} & \boxed{3}\begin{bmatrix}\text{VAR} & \boxed{1}\\ \text{REST} & \begin{bmatrix}\text{RELN} & \text{NAMING}\\ \text{NAME} & \boxed{2}\\ \text{NAMED} & \boxed{1}\end{bmatrix}\end{bmatrix}\end{bmatrix} \\ \text{INDS} & \{\boxed{3}\}\end{bmatrix}\end{bmatrix}$$

(185) Semantics Principle (second version)

$$[\text{DTRS}_{\textit{headed-structure}}[\ ]] \Rightarrow$$

$$\begin{bmatrix} \text{SEMANTICS} & \begin{bmatrix}\text{CONTENT} & \boxed{1}\\ \text{INDICES} & \text{collect-indices}(\boxed{2})\end{bmatrix} \\ \text{DTRS} & \boxed{2}\ [\text{HEAD-DTR|SEM|CONT}\ \boxed{1}] \end{bmatrix}$$

What has been added is that the value of INDICES on the sign must be the set obtained by taking the union of the INDICES value sets on the daughters. Technically, this is given as a functionally dependent value (see Section 2.3); collect-indices is just the function defined on feature structures of type *constituent-structure* which takes the set union of the INDICES values on all the daughters. In the case of the simple sentence *Kim saw Sandy* (see (182) above) the resulting SEMANTICS value for the whole sentence is (186):

(186)
$$\begin{bmatrix} \text{CONT} & \begin{bmatrix}\text{REL} & \text{SEE}\\ \text{SEER} & \boxed{2}\\ \text{SEEN} & \boxed{1}\end{bmatrix} \\ \text{INDS} & \left\{ \begin{bmatrix}\text{VAR} & \boxed{1}\\ \text{REST} & \begin{bmatrix}\text{RELN} & \text{NAMING}\\ \text{NAME} & \text{Sandy}\\ \text{NAMED} & \boxed{1}\end{bmatrix}\end{bmatrix}, \begin{bmatrix}\text{VAR} & \boxed{2}\\ \text{REST} & \begin{bmatrix}\text{RELN} & \text{NAMING}\\ \text{NAME} & \text{Kim}\\ \text{NAMED} & \boxed{2}\end{bmatrix}\end{bmatrix} \right\} \end{bmatrix}$$

As we shall see later, it sometimes comes about that two NP's within a phrase share the same variable (e.g. when one NP is a gap and the other its filler, or when one NP is a pronoun and the other its antecedent). In such cases, the INDICES value set will contain distinct indices which share the same variable. For example, in the sentence *a donkey kicked herself*, *donkey* and *herself* give rise to the indices (187a) and (187b) respectively:

(187) a.
$$\begin{bmatrix} \text{VAR} & \boxed{1} \\ \text{REST} & \begin{bmatrix} \text{RELN} & \text{DONKEY} \\ \text{INST} & \boxed{1} \end{bmatrix} \end{bmatrix}$$

b.
$$\begin{bmatrix} \text{VAR} & \boxed{2} \\ \text{REST} & \begin{bmatrix} \text{RELN} & \text{FEMALE} \\ \text{INST} & \boxed{2} \end{bmatrix} \end{bmatrix}$$

A certain locality condition on the binding of reflexive pronouns (treated in Volume 2) will require that $\boxed{1}$ and $\boxed{2}$ be unified; the INDICES value of the whole sentence will then be (188):

(188)
$$\left\{ \begin{bmatrix} \text{VAR} & \boxed{1} \\ \text{REST} & \begin{bmatrix} \text{RELN} & \text{DONKEY} \\ \text{INST} & \boxed{1} \end{bmatrix} \end{bmatrix}, \begin{bmatrix} \text{VAR} & \boxed{1} \\ \text{REST} & \begin{bmatrix} \text{RELN} & \text{FEMALE} \\ \text{INST} & \boxed{1} \end{bmatrix} \end{bmatrix} \right\}$$

The net result is that the whole sentence introduces only one parameter (corresponding to the variable $\boxed{1}$), which is anchored in a given context of utterance to some female donkey or other.

It should be evident at this point that HPSG indices—or, more precisely, the variables which occur in them—are modelling essentially the same phenomena as the "syntactic indices" employed in GB theory. In both theories they are entities associated with NP tokens; in both theories two distinct NP tokens are "coindexed" under certain conditions (e.g. if they are in a filler-gap or an antecedent-pronoun relationship) and "contraindexed" (i.e. constrained to have non-identical indices) under certain other conditions. In due course (Volume 2), we shall consider a whole range of linguistic phenomena wherein coindexing or contraindexing of this kind comes into play, including the control of "understood subjects"; filler-gap dependencies and relative dependencies; intrasentential syntactic constraints on pronoun binding; and constraints on pronoun binding across sentence boundaries. By and large, this is the same territory staked out by GB theory under such rubrics as "move-alpha" and "binding theory", and in many cases the principles which we formulate will amount to recastings of principles already formulated in GB theory. The chief difference in the two approaches is that GB theory treats indices as rather mysterious abstract syntactic objects. In HPSG, by contrast, indices are essentially semantic in nature: they are components of semantic descriptions (i.e. of feature structures which model the language user's information about the situation described by an utterance) which correspond to parameters (of parametrized circumstances) and bound variables (of quantificational circumstances) which figure in the described situation. It is hoped that the approach to indices adopted here will help to demystify these objects, which have been ubiquitous in contemporary linguistic theory but little understood in their own right.

We turn next to quantified noun phrases like *every donkey*. As in the case of proper nouns, we assume that the SEMANTICS|CONTENT value of a common noun is a feature structure of type *indexed-object*. Unlike proper nouns, however, this value is of the subtype *quantifier*, which has the additional attribute DETERMINER, as illustrated by the partial description of the lexical sign *donkey* given in (189):

(189)
$$\left[\begin{array}{ll}\text{PHON} & \text{donkey} \\ \text{SEM} & \left[\begin{array}{ll}\text{CONT} & \left[\begin{array}{ll}\text{DET} & [\;] \\ \text{IND} & \boxed{2}\left[\begin{array}{ll}\text{VAR} & \boxed{1} \\ \text{REST} & \left[\begin{array}{ll}\text{RELN} & \text{DONKEY} \\ \text{INST} & \boxed{1}\end{array}\right]\end{array}\right]\end{array}\right] \\ \text{INDS} & \{\boxed{2}\}\end{array}\right]\end{array}\right]$$

Except for the precise restriction on the variable, this is similar to the lexical sign for the proper noun *Kim* given in (184). The chief difference is that the SEMANTICS|CONTENT value of the common noun has a DETERMINER attribute, whose value will depend on what determiner the common noun combines with. This semantic difference is correlated with a syntactic difference: the proper noun is saturated (i.e. its SUBCAT value is ⟨ ⟩), but the common noun subcategorizes for a determiner.

Now how does the determiner combine semantically with the common noun? The answer depends on what we think the semantic content of the determiner is. The simplest approach might be to suppose that the content of *every* is just FORALL; on this analysis (189) should be further elaborated as (190):

(190)
$$\left[\begin{array}{ll}\text{PHON} & \text{donkey} \\ \text{SYN|LOC} & \left[\begin{array}{ll}\text{HEAD|MAJ N} & \\ \text{SUBCAT} & \left\langle \left[\begin{array}{l}\text{SEM|CONT } \boxed{3} \\ \text{SYN|LOC|HEAD|MAJ D}\end{array}\right]\right\rangle\end{array}\right] \\ \text{SEM} & \left[\begin{array}{ll}\text{CONT} & \left[\begin{array}{ll}\text{DET} & \boxed{3} \\ \text{IND} & \boxed{2}\left[\begin{array}{ll}\text{VAR} & \boxed{1} \\ \text{REST} & \left[\begin{array}{ll}\text{RELN} & \text{DONKEY} \\ \text{INST} & \boxed{1}\end{array}\right]\end{array}\right]\end{array}\right] \\ \text{INDS} & \{\boxed{2}\}\end{array}\right]\end{array}\right]$$

This ensures that the semantic content of the determiner will be the value of the DETERMINER attribute in the content of the common noun (and therefore, of the whole NP, in virtue of the Semantics Principle). However, we will adopt an alternative account according to which the SEMANTICS|

CONTENT value of the determiner is itself of type *quantifier*; e.g. the lexical sign *every* is as given in (191):

(191)
$$\begin{bmatrix} \text{PHON every} \\ \text{SYN} \mid \text{LOC} \mid \text{HEAD} \mid \text{MAJ D} \\ \text{SEM} \begin{bmatrix} \text{CONT} \begin{bmatrix} \text{DET FORALL} \\ \text{IND } \boxed{2} \end{bmatrix} \\ \text{INDS } \{\boxed{2}\} \end{bmatrix} \end{bmatrix}$$

The common noun lexical sign then takes the form (192):

(192)
$$\begin{bmatrix} \text{PHON donkey} \\ \text{SYN} \mid \text{LOC} \begin{bmatrix} \text{HEAD} \mid \text{MAJ N} \\ \text{SUBCAT} \left\langle \begin{bmatrix} \text{SEM} \mid \text{CONT } \boxed{3} \\ \text{SYN} \mid \text{LOC} \mid \text{HEAD} \mid \text{MAJ D} \end{bmatrix} \right\rangle \end{bmatrix} \\ \text{SEM} \begin{bmatrix} \text{CONT } \boxed{3} \begin{bmatrix} \text{IND } \boxed{2} \begin{bmatrix} \text{VAR } \boxed{1} \\ \text{REST} \begin{bmatrix} \text{RELN DONKEY} \\ \text{INST } \boxed{1} \end{bmatrix} \end{bmatrix} \end{bmatrix} \\ \text{INDS } \{\boxed{2}\} \end{bmatrix} \end{bmatrix}$$

On this account, the semantics of the determiner and the common noun are simply unified. We are not aware of compelling arguments on behalf of either alternative, and little seems to hinge on which is adopted. The choice made here is motivated in part by the fact that many languages (including English) allow "null-headed" NP's consisting of just a determiner, as in *some like it hot*; under the analysis proposed here, it seems somewhat easier to explain how such bare determiners can carry the semantic weight normally associated with NP's. (A second possible motivation for our choice will be suggested in Volume 2.)

To close this chapter, we consider briefly the question of how the semantic content of a quantified NP figures into the content of the sentence in which it appears. Much current research in semantics is concerned with trying to answer this question, though at present there is not even much agreement as to how the question itself should be framed! We will discuss some of the issues at stake in this area at greater length in Volume 2; for the time being, we content ourselves with an attempt to articulate the question a little more clearly.

Consider a simple sentence involving a quantified NP, such as (193):

(193) Every donkey sneezed.

What is its SEMANTICS value? Given the lexical signs above for *every* and *donkey* together with the lexical sign (194) for *sneezed*, and assuming that the overall structure of the sentence is as indicated in (195), the answer provided by the Semantics Principle (185) is simply (196):

(194)

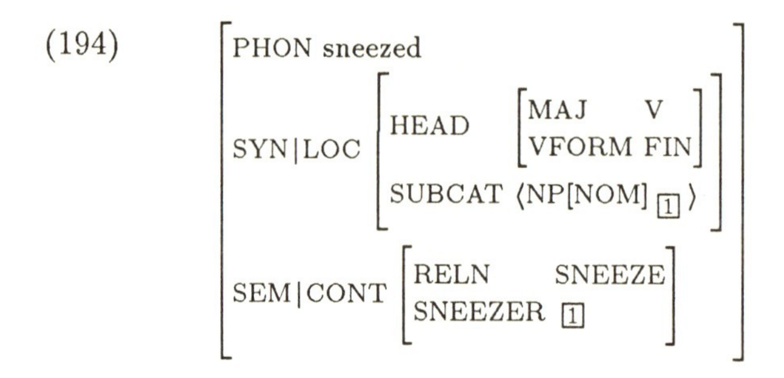

(195)

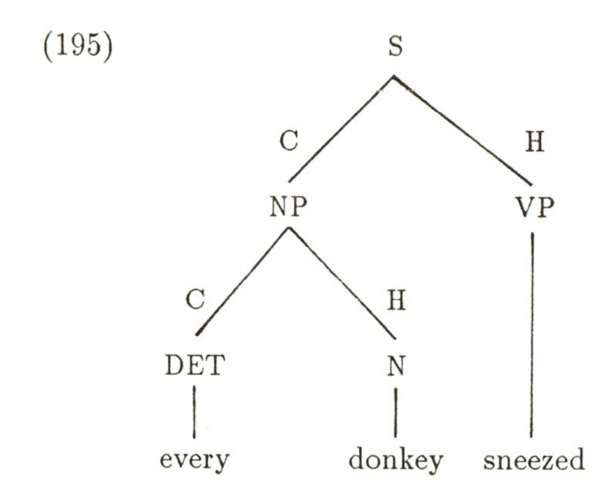

(196)

$$\begin{bmatrix} \text{CONT} & \begin{bmatrix} \text{RELN} & \text{SNEEZE} \\ \text{SNEEZER} & \boxed{1} \end{bmatrix} \\ \text{INDS} & \left\{ \begin{bmatrix} \text{VAR} & \boxed{1} \\ \text{REST} & \begin{bmatrix} \text{RELN} & \text{DONKEY} \\ \text{INST} & \boxed{1} \end{bmatrix} \end{bmatrix} \right\} \end{bmatrix}$$

This is wrong, though. The problem, of course, is that the Semantics Principle as presently formulated is now sophisticated enough to cope with the parametric account of proper names, but does not take quantification into consideration. What we should really have as the CONTENT value in (196) is the feature structure of type *quantified-circumstance* shown in (197a):

(197) a.

$$\begin{bmatrix} \text{QUANT} & \begin{bmatrix} \text{DET} & \text{FORALL} \\ \text{IND} & \begin{bmatrix} \text{VAR} & \boxed{1} \\ \text{REST} & \begin{bmatrix} \text{RELN} & \text{DONKEY} \\ \text{INST} & \boxed{1} \end{bmatrix} \end{bmatrix} \end{bmatrix} \\ \text{SCOPE} & \begin{bmatrix} \text{RELN} & \text{SNEEZE} \\ \text{SNEEZER} & \boxed{1} \end{bmatrix} \end{bmatrix}$$

This is just the AVM description of the quantified circumstance (197b):

(197) b. (forall $x \mid \langle\!\langle$donkey, instance: $x\rangle\!\rangle$) $\langle\!\langle$sneeze, sneezer:$x\rangle\!\rangle$

Roughly, then, in cases where the complement's content is a quantifier and the head's content is a circumstance, we want the mother's content to be not simply the head's content, but rather the quantified circumstance whose quantifier is the complement's content and whose scope is the head's content. We can get this effect by revising the Semantics Principle (185) again, as shown in (198):

(198) Semantics Principle (third version)

$$[\text{DTRS}_{\textit{headed-structure}}\ [\ ]] \Rightarrow$$

$$\begin{bmatrix} \text{SEM} & \begin{bmatrix} \text{CONT} & \text{combine-semantics}\ (\boxed{1}, \boxed{2}) \\ \text{IND} & \text{collect-indices}\ (\boxed{3}) \end{bmatrix} \\ \text{DTRS}\ \boxed{3} & \begin{bmatrix} \text{HEAD-DTR|SEM|CONT}\ \boxed{1} \\ \text{COMP-DTRS}\ \langle[\text{SEM|CONT}\ \boxed{2}]\rangle \end{bmatrix} \end{bmatrix}$$

The change is that the SEMANTICS|CONTENT value of the sign is now functionally dependent upon the SEMANTICS|CONTENT values of both the head daughter and the complement daughter.[6] Here the function combine-semantics is as defined in (199):

(199) combine-semantics (A,B) =

if A has type *circumstance* and
B has type *quantifier*

then $\begin{bmatrix} \text{QUANT} & \text{B} \\ \text{SCOPE} & \text{A} \end{bmatrix}$

else A

---

[6] We are adopting for the moment the simplifying assumption that there is only one complement. We will drop this assumption presently.

Here A and B are metavariables that range over feature structures; the function definition is by cases, depending on the feature-structure types of A and B. This revision has no effect on the case we have already considered, and gives the desired result for simple quantificational sentences like (193).

However, as pointed out above, (198) assumes that a headed structure has exactly one complement daughter. But some headed structures have several complement daughters, and one or more of these might be a quantified NP, as in (200):

(200)

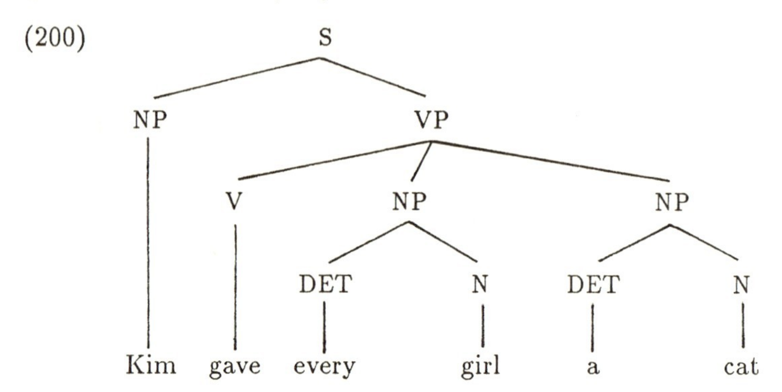

So (198) is still inadequate; it must be generalized to handle headed structures with arbitrarily many complement daughters. In (201), we present still another refinement of the Semantics Principle (198) which addresses this defect:

(201) Semantics Principle (fourth version)

$$[\text{DTRS}_{\textit{headed-structure}}\ [\ ]] \Rightarrow$$

$$\begin{bmatrix} \text{SEM} & \begin{bmatrix} \text{CONT} & \text{successively-combine-semantics}(\boxed{1}, \boxed{2}) \\ \text{INDICES} & \text{collect-indices}(\boxed{3}) \end{bmatrix} \\ \text{DTRS}\ \boxed{3} & \begin{bmatrix} \text{HEAD-DTR}|\text{SEM}|\text{CONT}\ \boxed{1} \\ \text{COMP-DTRS}\ \boxed{2} \end{bmatrix} \end{bmatrix}$$

What is new here is that now the SEMANTICS|CONTENT of the whole sign is functionally dependent on *all* the complement daughters as well as the SEMANTICS|CONTENT value of the head daughter. The new function successively-combine-semantics is defined in such a way that it has the effect of starting with the SEMANTICS|CONTENT value on the head daughter, then successively combining it with the SEMANTICS|CONTENT values of the complement daughters in the order in which they appear on the COMP-DTRS list (i.e. from more oblique to less oblique.) For readers interested in such technical details, the definition of successively-combine-semantics is given in (202):

(202) successively-combine-semantics(A,L) =

if length(L) = 0
then A
else
successively-combine-semantics
(combine-semantics (A, SEM|CONT of first(L)), rest(L)).

Here A ranges over feature structures and L ranges over lists of feature structures. Readers with some background in computer programming will note that (202) has the form of a *recursive definition*, i.e. the very function being defined is "called" in the body of the function definition. The definition also makes reference to the function combine-semantics defined in (202). Note that if L has length 1, the version of the Semantics Principle given in (201) has exactly the same effect as the version in (198).

In the case where more than one complement of the same head have quantifiers as their semantic contents, the effect of (201) is to assign "natural scope" (i.e. less oblique quantifiers scope over more oblique quantifiers). For example, (200) will have the SEMANTICS value (203a):

(203) a.

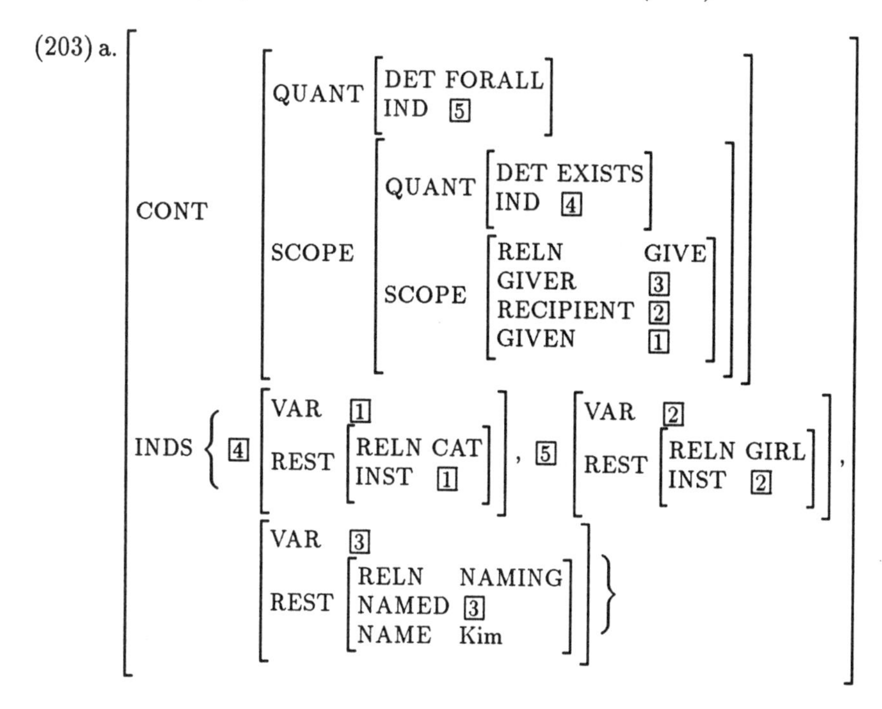

(As an exercise, the reader may wish to confirm that (203a) is indeed the SEMANTICS value determined for (200).) The CONTENT value in (203a) describes the parametrized circumstance (203b) (where x is the parameter introduced by the use of *Kim*):

(203) b. (forall y | ⟨⟨girl, instance:y; 1⟩⟩)
(exists z | ⟨⟨cat, instance:z; 1⟩⟩)
⟨⟨give, giver:x; recipient:y, given:z; 1⟩⟩

This is certainly the first reading of (200) that comes to mind, and indeed the natural scoping of quantifiers induced by (201) produces the desired result in most cases.

However, in a substantial minority of cases involving multiple quantifiers, some scoping other than the one predicted by (201) seems most appropriate. For example, in the most natural reading of (204), the universally quantified direct object *each city* has scope over the existentially quantified subject *an elected official*:

(204) An elected official represented each city at the conference.

More generally, the different scoping possibilities present in cases of multiple quantification give rise to ambiguities whose resolution may depend partly upon linguistic constraints, but often even more importantly on nonlinguistic contextual factors and general world knowledge. For example, on the most plausible reading of (205a), the quantifiers have natural scope (i.e. one and the same friend detests every James novel); but in the structurally similar (205b), only the "crossed" scoping (a different statue at each intersection) is consistent with common-sense knowledge about discrete, macroscopic physical objects and their spatial locations.

(205) a. A friend of mine detests every book by Henry James.
b. A statue of the party chief occupies every major intersection in the capital.

The proper treatment of such scopal ambiguities is the subject of much current research, and we shall discuss it more fully in Volume 2.

4.5 Suggestions for Further Reading

Our approach to semantics is indebted to situation semantics (Barwise and Perry (1983)) in its general outlook, but differs in practically every matter of technical detail. The idea of describing syntactic and situation-theoretic semantic objects within a single unification-based formalism is due to Fenstad et al. (1985). The metalinguistic notation ("logic of circumstances") is derived largely from the NFLT formalism of Creary and Pollard (1985). The realist line on semantic roles developed here is generally accepted within the situation semantics community, but scarcely anywhere else. For a sampling of recent opinion on this most controversial topic, see Carlson (ms.), Ladusaw and Dowty (ms.), Jackendoff (1987), and Rappaport and Levin (1986).

Situation semantics and situation theory are the objects of much current discussion and research, but as yet few applications to linguistic questions are to be found in print. By far the most active workers in this area have been Robin Cooper and Elisabet Engdahl, who (both singly and in joint work) have investigated a range of phenomena, including: conjunction, disjunction, and negation; quantificational and "singular" noun phrases; intensionality; tense; aspectual classes; "relational" interpretations of noun phrases; and long distance dependencies. Descriptions or reproductions of much of this work, together with further pointers to the literature, can be found in Cooper (ms.). Situation semantics is still new enough that few, if any, analyses of linguistic phenomena have achieved a canonical status comparable to (say) that accorded Montague's analyses of quantification and intensionality within the community of possible-worlds semanticists. An example of the diversity of thought still typical in this line of work is provided by the interaction between quantification and anaphora (a particularly popular topic), which is treated by (inter alia) Barwise (1986b), Rooth (1986), and Gawron and Peters (ms.).

5 Subcategorization

The term *subcategorization* is standardly used to describe differences among lexical forms of a common gross syntactic category as to the *syntactic* nature of the elements they combine with. Thus various members of the category verb are commonly assigned to distinct subcategories according to the number and syntactic nature of their dependent elements, and the dependencies that hold between these verbs and their dependent elements are referred to as *subcategorization restrictions*. The notion of subcategorization that we expound here subsumes this standard notion, but in addition treats a range of closely related phenomena commonly studied under such rubrics as *case assignment*, *government* (e.g. of particular prepositions), *role assignment*, and *verb agreement*. In this chapter we present a unified treatment of all these topics with the exception of the last, which we defer to Volume 2.

5.1 Subcategorization and Role Assignment

As we saw in Chapter 3, the feature SUBCAT is used to encode the various dependencies that hold between a lexical head and its complements (the signs that it characteristically combines with). SUBCAT takes a list of (partially specified) signs as its value; the position of an element on the list corresponds to the obliqueness of the complement sign which it describes, with the rightmost element corresponding to the least oblique dependent sign (subject). (It should be noted that we use the term "complement" to include subjects as well as NP and PP objects, VP and S complements, etc. Thus, just as in LFG (but unlike GB and GPSG), we treat subjects as subcategorized-for; the reasons for this will be discussed at some length below.) As a head combines syntactically with a complement, the grammatical information associated with the complement is unified with the partial information specified in the appropriate position on the head's SUBCAT list, as required by the Subcategorization Principle (Chapter 3, (133)). In this way, grammatical information is shared between heads and their complements, so that lexical heads in effect impose restrictions on the number and kind of complements they will combine with.

Significantly, the sign specifications that appear on the SUBCAT lists of lexical signs bear values for both SYNTAX and SEMANTICS, but *not* for DAUGHTERS; thus lexical signs can exert syntactic restrictions (e.g. subcategorization in the conventional sense, government, and case assignment) and semantic restrictions (e.g. role assignment and sortal appropriateness conditions of the kind often referred to as "semantic selection restrictions"); but such restrictions are strictly local in character (we return to this point at the end of this chapter). The semantic aspect of subcategorization is most simply illustrated by an intransitive verb such as *walk*, whose lexical sign is described in (206):

(206)

```
[PHON       walk                        ]
[           [HEAD    [MAJ V]  ]         ]
[SYN        [SUBCAT ⟨ NP[1] ⟩ ]         ]
[                                       ]
[           [RELN     WALK]             ]
[SEM|CONT   [WALKER   [1] ]             ]
```

Here the variable [1] associated with the SUBCAT element (which corresponds to the verb's subject) is identified (i.e. unified) with the variable corresponding to the walker role in the situation described by the verb itself. When the verb combines with its subject, the subject must unify with the partially specified sign on the verb's SUBCAT list in accordance with the Subcategorization Principle; in particular the variables of the subject and the SUBCAT element are unified. In consequence of these two unifications, the subject variable is unified with the variable filling the walker role in the verb's (and also the sentence's) described situation. Thus, information associated with a head is amalgamated with information associated with the complements of the head in the determination of the semantics of phrasal signs.

One essential function of the SUBCAT feature, therefore, is to set up the correspondence between grammatical relations (subject, object, etc.) and the roles in the described situation. This correspondence is reminiscent of the notion of "theta-role assignment under subcategorization," as discussed within the framework of GB theory; the fundamental difference is that HPSG treats roles not as syntactic entities but rather as constituents of semantic content. (Another difference is that HPSG does not require that every subcategorized complement be assigned a role. The significance of this fact will emerge in the treatment of raising presented in Volume 2). It is important to understand the nature of this correspondence clearly, for out of it arises the whole communicative power of lexical signs. The point of role assignment is not to make syntactic objects well-formed; it is to establish a connection between the constituents of an utterance and the constituents of the thing the utterance is about.

To give a slightly more complex example, a ditransitive verb such as *give* will assign semantic roles to all three of its subcategorized-for dependents, as shown in (207).

(207)
$$\begin{bmatrix} \text{PHON} & \text{give} \\ \text{SYN} & \begin{bmatrix} \text{HEAD} & [\text{MAJ V}] \\ \text{SUBCAT} & \langle \text{NP}_{\boxed{1}}, \text{NP}_{\boxed{2}}, \text{NP}_{\boxed{3}} \rangle \end{bmatrix} \\ \text{SEM}|\text{CONT} & \begin{bmatrix} \text{RELN} & \text{GIVE} \\ \text{GIVER} & \boxed{3} \\ \text{RECEIVER} & \boxed{2} \\ \text{GIVEN} & \boxed{1} \end{bmatrix} \end{bmatrix}$$

Syntactic combination of this form with the required complements will yield the appropriate sentence semantics as the subject, direct object and second object of the verb unify with the appropriate elements on the verb's SUBCAT list.

5.2 The Hierarchical Theory of Subcategorization

The theory of subcategorization presented here makes essential use of a *hierarchical* conception of grammatical relations. That is, notions such as *subject* and *direct object* of a verb (or, more generally, of any lexical head) are defined in terms of the order of the corresponding elements on the head's SUBCAT list. The usage adopted here is a variant of the terminology employed within the categorial grammar approach of Dowty (1982a; 1982b), which is keyed to the order of argument positions in Montague-style semantic translations. (Of course that approach is not available to us given the theory of relations sketched in Chapter 4, for the roles of a relation do not come equipped with an order.) The underlying intuition is close to the ordered conception of grammatical relations adopted in relational grammar, where subject, direct object, and indirect object are identified as *1*'s, *2*'s and *3*'s, respectively.

To be more precise, we adopt the following usages with respect to grammatical relation terms. We begin by distinguishing two basic types of complements: (i) those which do not subcategorize for anything themselves, i.e. their SUBCAT values are ⟨ ⟩ (such as nonpredicative NP's and PP's, and sentential complements); and (ii) those with a nonempty SUBCAT value (such as predicative and VP complements). These two types are distinguished as *saturated* and *unsaturated* respectively. Saturated complements are then designated as *subject*, *direct object*, and *second object* according as the corresponding SUBCAT element appears last, second-last, or third-last on the SUBCAT list, as long as an unsaturated complement does not intervene. Following LFG usage, we often refer to an unsaturated complement as *xcomp*. (The theory of *control* presented in Volume 2 is concerned in large part with the semantic interpretation of the variables associated with the "missing" subjects of xcomps.) All other complements are simply lumped together as *oblique objects*.

Before turning to a detailed justification of the notion of grammatical hierarchy, it is worth pointing out that other conceptions of grammatical relations are broadly consistent with the general framework developed here. For example, within the JPSG system of Gunji (1986), SUBCAT values are treated as (unordered) sets rather than lists; subjects and objects are then distinguished by a feature whose values include SUBJ and OBJ. Evidently any notion of obliqueness is absent here. (Indeed, one imaginable theory of grammatical relations would hold that whether or not grammatical relations participate in an obliqueness ordering is a parameter of cross-linguistic variation.) In another variant of HPSG defended by Borsley (1987), the SUBCAT feature involves non-subjects only, as in GPSG; subject selection is then handled by a new SUBJECT feature. Elsewhere, Borsley (1986) has suggested that determiners as well be split off from other dependent elements, to be treated by still another feature called SPEC. Of course, carrying this idea to its logical limit leads to a "keyword" theory of grammatical relations similar to that of LFG, wherein each grammatical relation is handled by a distinct feature. Within such a theory, SUBCAT values would resemble LFG f-structures, with the important difference that the value of each "grammatical relation feature" would be not an f-structure but rather a sign, as sketched in (208):

(208)
$$\begin{bmatrix} \text{PHON} & \\ \text{SYN}\mid\text{LOC}\mid\text{SUBCAT} & \begin{bmatrix} \text{SUBJ} & \begin{bmatrix} \text{SYN} \\ \text{SEM} \end{bmatrix} \\ \text{OBJ} & \begin{bmatrix} \text{SYN} \\ \text{SEM} \end{bmatrix} \\ \text{OBJ2} & \begin{bmatrix} \text{SYN} \\ \text{SEM} \end{bmatrix} \end{bmatrix} \\ \text{SEM} & \end{bmatrix}$$

Any such variant theories of course require modification of our principles of universal grammar, in particular the Subcategorization Principle, which can no longer be formulated in terms of list cancellation.

But why assume that grammatical relations participate in an obliqueness ordering? There are at least four different classes of linguistic generalizations which, we claim, provide motivation for the hierarchical theory of grammatical relations. These are *constituent order generalizations*, *generalizations involving the theory of control*, *generalizations about the binding of pronouns and reflexives*, and *generalizations about the functioning of lexical rules*.

In many—but by no means all—of the world's languages, the surface order of constituents (i.e. the temporal order of their phonological realizations) and their grammatical relations appear to be subject to mutual constraints. English, of course, is such a language: it is well known that the traditional notion of obliqueness corresponds closely to left-to-right order. In Chapter 7, we will argue that an array of facts about English constituent order follow from just such a *hierarchical linear precedence constraint*, viz. that a complement must linearly precede any of its sister complements whose corresponding SUBCAT elements are earlier on the head's SUBCAT list.

In virtually every current syntactic theory, some notion of "command" is assumed to play a central role in the formulation of linguistic constraints that govern the relationships (e.g. "coindexing", "disjoint reference") holding between anaphoric elements (such as personal and reflexive pronouns) and other constituents of the sentence. Depending on the theory, command is variously construed in terms of syntactic configuration (the "*c*-command" of GB), semantic predicate-argument structure (the "argument-command" of categorial grammar in the variant of Bach and Partee (1980)), or functional structure (the "*f*-command" of LFG). In Volume 2, we formulate constraints on the binding of reflexive and personal pronouns in terms of what might be called "*o*-command", where one constituent *o*-commands another provided it is a less oblique dependent of the same head. Roughly: (i) if a phrase X contains a reflexive pronoun whose antecedent is not within X, then the reflexive must be coindexed with (have the same associated variable as) an *o*-commander of X provided such exists; (ii) no (nonreflexive) pronoun can be coindexed with one of its *o*-commanders; and (iii) no constituent X can *o*-command another constituent which dominates a nonanaphoric constituent coindexed with X.[1] We will argue that such a theory of anaphora is simpler and fits the facts better than alternative accounts.

Various generalizations about the application of lexical rules also provide motivation for a hierarchical conception of grammatical relations. Passivization, for example, applies in English so as to promote a second-last NP on a SUBCAT list to a SUBCAT-final element (see Chapter 8). But, as suggested by Dowty (1982b), passive in certain other languages should be formulated so as to generalize this "promotion" to other, more oblique dependents. Indirect objects, for example, may also passivize in a number of languages, including perhaps varieties of English where examples like (209b), as well as (209a) are grammatical.

(209) a. Sandy was given a book (by Lou).

b. %A book was given Sandy (by Lou).[2]

Similarly, the analysis of languages that have impersonal passives, e.g. German *Es wird heute getanzt* 'there will be dancing today', may well

[1] These constraints are analogous to GB's binding theory principles A, B, and C respectively.

[2] We use the symbol % to indicate that a given example is acceptable in some but not all varieties of English.

motivate a schematic passivization rule that applies not just when a SUBCAT list ends in two NP's (as in standard varieties of English), but also when it ends in just one. Generalizations of this sort are naturally expressed under the assumption that subcategorization information is hierarchically represented, as with the SUBCAT feature, and that languages may set certain parameters on their lexical rules that let them apply to sublists of SUBCAT values.

We note in passing that there are a number of cross-linguistic generalizations proposed in the literature that are also naturally expressed in terms of a hierarchical view of syntactic dependents. Keenan and Comrie (1977) claim that there are generalizations about possible relative clause systems in the world's languages that have a hierarchical character; e.g. that any language permitting object relativization of the sort illustrated in (210a) also allows subject relativization as in (210b):

(210) a. The man [who Kim likes __].
b. The man [who __ likes Kim].

They argue in fact that the hierarchy in (211) expresses the relative accessibility to relativization of NP positions (in simplex main clauses).

(211) Accessibility Hierarchy [Keenan and Comrie (1977)]

SUBJECT ⇒ DIRECT OBJECT ⇒ INDIRECT OBJECT ⇒ OBLIQUES ⇒ GENITIVES ⇒ OBJECTS OF COMPARISON

That is, they claim that any language allowing relativization of any of the positions in (211) will also allow relativization of all positions to the left of that position. (So for example no language could allow relative clauses like (210a) unless it also allowed those like (210b)). Within a hierarchical theory of subcategorization like the one we are proposing, the claim would be that languages set a parameter as to how far down a SUBCAT list relativization may apply.[3] A similar approach could be taken to explain Keenan and Comrie's observation that verb agreement, cross-linguistically, obeys the Accessibility Hierarchy (languages with object agreement also exhibit subject agreement, and so forth).

In sum, there appears to be considerable evidence that syntactic phenomena of diverse sorts obey generalizations that are hierarchical in nature. The theory of subcategorization we adopt here provides a direct encoding of hierarchical relations suitable for expressing these generalizations. This is not to say that alternative theories of subcategorizations such as those mentioned above are inconsistent with the available evidence, but only that a theory with no notion of obliqueness is inadequate.

---

[3] This of course would provide no account of the behavior of genitives and objects of comparison, for which, incidentally, the evidence offered by Keenan and Comrie is the most meager.

It may be possible to develop a hybrid theory that uses the keyword approach to subjects, objects and other complements, but which uses other means to impose a hierarchical structure on syntactic elements, including optional modifiers not subcategorized for in the same sense. In Volume 2, we discuss briefly one such approach.

5.3 Category Selection

It has sometimes been proposed that lexical dependencies can be accounted for without recourse to any notion of formal category selection. The analysis of English absolutive constructions proposed by Stump (1981), for example, would seem to suggest that subcategorization can be reduced to a matter of semantic selection, as does one non-transformational analysis of unbounded dependency (filler-gap) constructions due to Cooper (1983); within the LFG framework, it is assumed that subcategorization is entirely a matter of selection for grammatical functions (such as subject, object, xcomp, etc.). But it is evident that there are subcategorization restrictions that crucially involve differences of syntactic category which cannot be reduced to semantic or functional distinctions.

First, subcategorization cannot be reduced to semantic selection. Natural languages abound with groups of verbs closely related in meaning which make different demands upon their complements with respect to either gross syntactic category or finer distinctions, such as inflectional form of the head verb in an xcomp, case of an object, or identity of the preposition which heads a prepositional phrase complement. (An important class of special cases, which involves different valences of the "same" verb, is treated in Section 5.5 below). Some examples involving gross category differences follow:

(212) a. Sandy trusts Kim.
      b.*Sandy trusts on Kim.

(213) a. Sandy depends/relies on Kim.
      b.*Sandy trusts/relies Kim of a second helping.

(214) a. Sandy spared Kim a second helping.
      b.*Sandy deprived Kim a second helping.

(215) a. Sandy deprived Kim of a second helping.
      b.*Sandy spared Kim of a second helping.

In our view, examples like these show that any adequate theory of lexical dependencies must recognize the syntactic distinction between NP's and PP's. Given the theory of syntactic features outlined in Chapter 3, the dependencies in question here are effected by positing lexical signs like the following:

(216)
$$\begin{bmatrix} \text{PHON} & \text{made} \\ \text{SYN|LOC} & \begin{bmatrix} \text{HEAD} & \begin{bmatrix} \text{MAJ} & \text{V} \\ \text{VFORM} & \text{FIN} \end{bmatrix} \\ \text{SUBCAT} & \langle \text{VP[BSE], NP, NP} \rangle \end{bmatrix} \end{bmatrix}$$

(217)
$$\begin{bmatrix} \text{PHON} & \text{forced} \\ \text{SYN|LOC} & \begin{bmatrix} \text{HEAD} & \begin{bmatrix} \text{MAJ} & \text{V} \\ \text{VFORM} & \text{FIN} \end{bmatrix} \\ \text{SUBCAT} & \langle \text{VP[INF], NP, NP} \rangle \end{bmatrix} \end{bmatrix}$$

(218)
$$\begin{bmatrix} \text{PHON} & \text{spared} \\ \text{SYN|LOC} & \begin{bmatrix} \text{HEAD} & \begin{bmatrix} \text{MAJ} & \text{V} \\ \text{VFORM} & \text{FIN} \end{bmatrix} \\ \text{SUBCAT} & \langle \text{NP, NP, NP} \rangle \end{bmatrix} \end{bmatrix}$$

(219)
$$\begin{bmatrix} \text{PHON} & \text{deprived} \\ \text{SYN|LOC} & \begin{bmatrix} \text{HEAD} & \begin{bmatrix} \text{MAJ} & \text{V} \\ \text{VFORM} & \text{FIN} \end{bmatrix} \\ \text{SUBCAT} & \langle \text{PP[OF], NP, NP} \rangle \end{bmatrix} \end{bmatrix}$$

In each case the indicated feature specifications on the appropriate signs on the verb's SUBCAT list impose the relevant restrictions on the verb's complements.

In the foregoing examples, a verb that requires an NP object is contrasted with a semantically related verb that selects a particular PP. Similarly, verbs close in meaning vary with respect to the gross category selected for the xcomp. As we noted in Chapter 3 (99a–b), forms of the English copula *be* can take NP, AP, VP, or PP complements, but *become* can be followed only by an NP or AP. The purely syntactic nature of this selectional difference is underscored by the fact that a PP xcomp for *become* is ungrammatical even if it can be paraphrased by an NP or AP:

(220) a. Terry is a complete madman.
b. Terry is quite mad.
c. Terry is out of his mind.

(221) a. Terry became a complete madman.
b. Terry became quite mad.
c.*Terry became out of his mind.

On the basis of such evidence, we further conclude that an adequate mechanism for lexical dependencies must be sensitive to the grammatical distinction between AP's and PP's. Again, the relevant selections are enforced by a specification on the appropriate (here, the first) SUBCAT element: the xcomp of *become* must be specified as [SYNTAX|LOCAL|HEAD|MAJ A∨N].

A particularly vivid illustration of idiosyncratic variation in xcomp category selection is exhibited by a family of English verbs closely related in meaning to *become*:

(222) a. Kim grew poetical.
b.*Kim grew a success.
c.*Kim grew sent more and more leaflets.
d.*Kim grew doing all the work
e. Kim grew to like anchovies.

(223) a. Kim got poetical.
b.*Kim got a success.
c. Kim got sent more and more leaflets.
d.*Kim got doing all the work
e. Kim got to like anchovies.

(224) a. Kim turned out poetical.
b. Kim turned out a success.
c.*Kim turned out sent more and more leaflets.
d.*Kim turned out doing all the work.
e. Kim turned out to like anchovies.

(225) a. Kim ended up poetical.
b. Kim ended up a success.
c.*Kim ended up sent more and more leaflets.
d. Kim ended up doing all the work.
e.*Kim ended up to like anchovies.

(226) a. Kim waxed poetical.
b.*Kim waxed a success.
c.*Kim waxed sent more and more leaflets.
d.*Kim waxed doing all the work.
e.*Kim waxed to like anchovies.

Evidently no semantic distinction will suffice to explain such lexical differences in category selection.

Similar variation is exhibited for finer syntactic selections. For instance, English verbs (including auxiliaries) differ with respect to the inflectional form required on the head verb of the xcomp, as the following examples show:

(227) a. Sandy made Kim throw up.
b.*Sandy made Kim to throw up.

(228) a. Sandy forced Kim to throw up.
b.*Sandy forced Kim throw up.

On our account, the corresponding lexical signs simply specify different values for the feature VFORM on the xcomp:

(229)
$$\begin{bmatrix} \text{PHON} & \text{made} \\ \text{SYN}|\text{LOC} & \begin{bmatrix} \text{HEAD} & \begin{bmatrix} \text{MAJ} & \text{V} \\ \text{VFORM} & \text{FIN} \end{bmatrix} \\ \text{SUBCAT} & \langle \text{VP[BSE], NP, NP} \rangle \end{bmatrix} \end{bmatrix}$$

(230)
$$\begin{bmatrix} \text{PHON} & \text{forced} \\ \text{SYN}|\text{LOC} & \begin{bmatrix} \text{HEAD} & \begin{bmatrix} \text{MAJ} & \text{V} \\ \text{VFORM} & \text{FIN} \end{bmatrix} \\ \text{SUBCAT} & \langle \text{VP[INF], NP, NP} \rangle \end{bmatrix} \end{bmatrix}$$

Precisely the same explanation accounts for variation in complement selection exhibited by English auxiliary verbs. Modal auxiliaries select VP complements whose lexical head is uninflected ([VFORM BSE]); (perfective) *have* takes complements headed by past participial phrases ([VFORM PSP]); and the verbal complements of *be* have heads that are present participial phrases ([VFORM PRP]) or passive phrases ([VFORM PAS]):[4]

(231)

modals (*may, shall,* etc.)
$$\left\langle \begin{bmatrix} \text{SYN}|\text{LOC} & \begin{bmatrix} \text{HEAD} & \begin{bmatrix} \text{MAJ} & \text{V} \\ \text{VFORM} & \text{BSE} \end{bmatrix} \\ \text{SUBCAT} & \langle \text{NP} \rangle \end{bmatrix} \end{bmatrix}, \text{NP} \right\rangle$$

(perfective) *have*
$$\left\langle \begin{bmatrix} \text{SYN}|\text{LOC} & \begin{bmatrix} \text{HEAD} & \begin{bmatrix} \text{MAJ} & \text{V} \\ \text{VFORM} & \text{PSP} \end{bmatrix} \\ \text{SUBCAT} & \langle \text{NP} \rangle \end{bmatrix} \end{bmatrix}, \text{NP} \right\rangle$$

(progressive) *be*
$$\left\langle \begin{bmatrix} \text{SYN}|\text{LOC} & \begin{bmatrix} \text{HEAD} & \begin{bmatrix} \text{MAJ} & \text{V} \\ \text{VFORM} & \text{PRP} \vee \text{PAS} \end{bmatrix} \\ \text{SUBCAT} & \langle \text{NP} \rangle \end{bmatrix} \end{bmatrix}, \text{NP} \right\rangle$$

---

[4] The correlation between certain values of VFORM and overt inflectional morphology is ensured by lexical rules which give rise to inflected forms bearing particular feature specifications. See Chapter 8.

And these specifications, taken together with the absence of nonfinite forms for modals (see Chapter 3), provide an account of such contrasts as the following:[5]

(232) a. Kim should have been eating.

b.*Kim should had eaten.

c.*Kim has shoulded eat

d.*Kim has eat.

e.*Kim is ate.

f.*Kim is eat.

g. Kim is eating.

h. Kim has eaten.

The syntactic structure of examples of this form is sketched in (233).

(233)

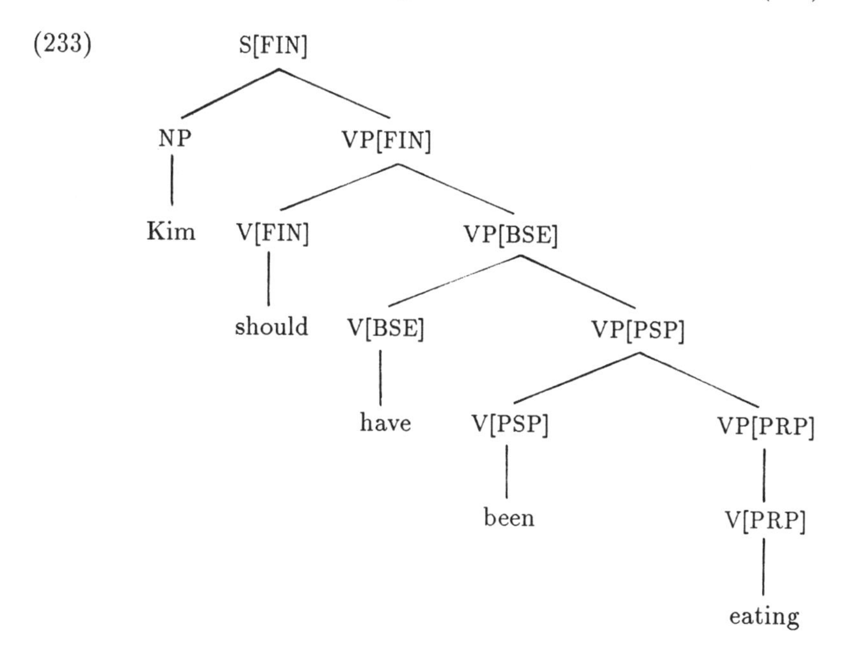

And the official representation of this structure is partially indicated in (234).

[5] As yet we lack any account of the badness of (i):
i. *Kim is having eaten.

(234)

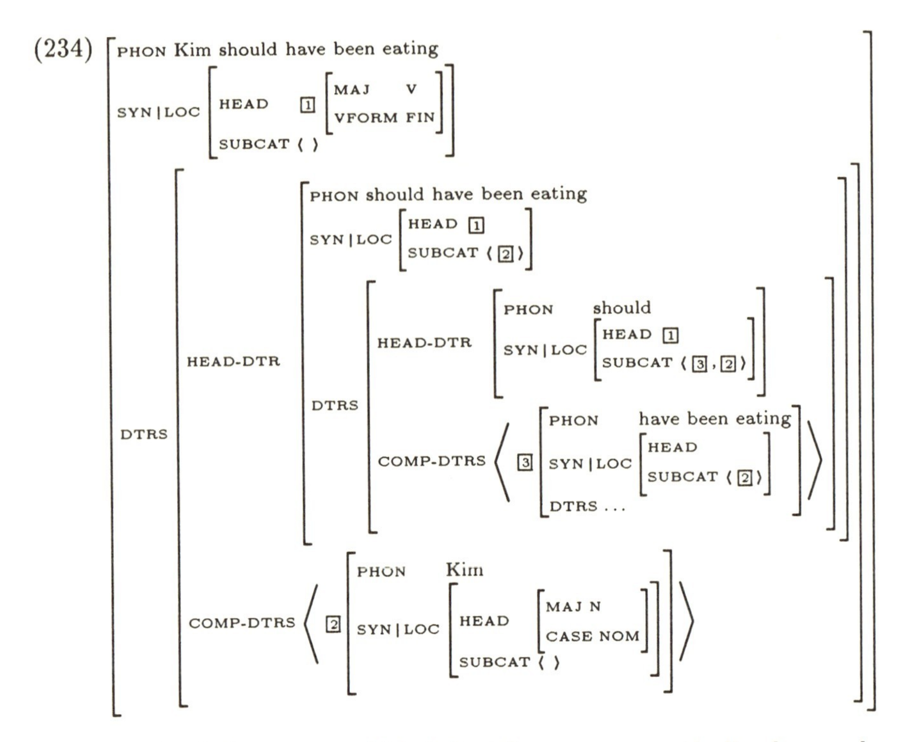

Likewise, in languages which inflect for case, semantically close verbs may require (or, in traditional terminology, govern) objects in different cases. An example of this kind is provided by the two German verbs for 'meet':

(235) a. Wem (DAT) begegneten Sie? 'Who did you meet?'

b. Wen (ACC) trafen Sie? 'Who did you meet?'

More generally, idiosyncratic selection for case forms abound in inflected languages such as Latin, Greek, Russian, or Sanskrit, where the particular case governed by individual verbs or prepositions is not semantically predictable. Such facts are too familiar to warrant further documentation here. Under our approach, case assignment too is effected via the feature SUBCAT. Since CASE is a head feature, it follows (in virtue of the Head Feature Principle) that whenever a lexical form selects a phrasal complement specified as [SYNTAX|LOCAL|HEAD|CASE ACC] or [SYNTAX|LOCAL|HEAD |CASE NOM], the lexical head of that complement is also so specified.[6]

English, of course, lacks case inflection (except rudimentarily on pronouns), but an analogous situation obtains with respect to government of

[6] Again, as with verb inflection, the correlation between overt case inflections and values of the feature CASE is determined by lexical rules (Chapter 8).

the particular preposition that heads a PP complement. It is well known that one and the same preposition can correspond to many distinct semantic roles, depending on the governing verb:

(236) a. Kim relies/depends on Sandy.
b. The authorities blamed/pinned the arson on Sandy.
c. The search committee decided/settled on Chris.

Conversely, as illustrated in (237), semantically related verbs may assign closely corresponding roles to different PP complements:

(237) a. The authorities blamed Greenpeace for/*with/*of the bombing.
b. The authorities accused Greenpeace *for/*with/of the bombing.
c. The authorities charged Greenpeace *for/with/*of the bombing.

On the basis of such examples, we conclude that government of particular prepositions is not semantically predictable; instead, different verbs which take PP complements require different values for the head feature PFORM on that complement.

If subcategorization restrictions cannot be reduced to semantics, might they be stated solely in terms of functional notions like subject, direct object, and second object? Precisely such an account is proposed within the LFG framework (Bresnan, ed. (1982)), where subcategorization restrictions are stated in terms of "functional structure", a level of syntactic representation distinct from constituent structure (*c*-structure), where certain information about "grammatical functions" (e.g. subject, direct object), "discourse functions" (e.g. topic, focus), and possibly thematic role assignment, is represented. However, there are several reasons why subcategorization restrictions cannot be stated in purely functional terms.

First, we have gross category selections of the sort considered above. For example, certain verbs like *become* select for a NP or AP xcomp, but not for PP or VP xcomps of the sort that may cooccur with the verb *be*. Such category distinctions are plainly non-functional (they are exclusively *c*-structure distinctions in LFG, for example).

Second, as Grimshaw, among others, has remarked, "a verb may govern case-marking on the head of its direct object." (Grimshaw 1982, 35). One cannot reduce such dependencies to functional dependencies. For example, in Icelandic there are verbs that select for direct object NP's specified in the dative and genitive cases.

(238) a. Ég hjalpaði honum (DAT) 'I helped him'
b. Ég mun sakna hans(GEN) 'I will miss him'

As demonstrated in detail by Zaenen, Maling and Thráinsson (1985), the dative and genitive NP's that follow *hjalpaði* ('helped') and *sakna* ('miss') respectively in these examples must both be treated as direct objects. That conclusion is based upon standard kinds of syntactic arguments, e.g. passivizability of the post-verbal NP. The verbs in question here must thus select the same grammatical function, yet they must assign distinct cases to the NP's that perform that function. (Analogous examples of case government in Icelandic for subjects are discussed in the following section.) Hence no purely functional account of subcategorization will suffice for Icelandic, unless case distinctions are also treated as "functional" in nature (as they are in Bresnan, ed. (1982), where case is regarded as an f-structure attribute).

In our opinion, any attempt to render categories of inflectional morphology such as case and verb form as functional in nature is highly questionable, for it blurs the distinction between form and function traditionally associated with such categories.[7] The formal category of dative NP, for instance, is standardly juxtaposed to various functions that the dative NP may serve, giving rise to such traditional "form-in-function" locutions as the *dative of interest*, the *dative of purpose*, and so forth. Such distinctions of form and function in this domain reflect long-standing insights into the nature of language that we are reluctant to abandon.

Analogous remarks apply to government of particular prepositions, which is treated by LFG in terms of the "semantically restricted" "oblique functions" OBL_θ (where θ ranges over some set of semantic roles). This treatment strikes us as highly problematic, for—as our discussion of examples (236–237) above indicates—one and the same preposition can correspond to numerous distinct semantic roles (and, conversely, semantically similar roles may correspond to PP's headed by different prepositions, depending on the governing verb).[8]

Indeed, if the difference in phonological form between distinct prepositions is not to be counted as a formal (as opposed to functional) difference, it is difficult to imagine what should be. Once distinctions of morphological

---

[7] Distinctions of verb inflection are treated in Bresnan, ed. (1982) in terms of the f-structure attributes TENSE (corresponding to our FINITE forms), PARTICIPIAL (our PRP, PSP, and PAS forms), INF (our BSE) and TO (our INF).

[8] The LFG treatment of PP[BY] phrases in passives in terms of the "oblique agent function" OBL_{ag} seems particularly infelicitous. As the following examples show, such phrases are by no means restricted to agentive semantic roles:

i. Kim was pleased/shocked/appalled by the report.
ii. No even integer is exceeded/equalled by any of its factors.
iii. Chris's cover was blown/goose was cooked by the ensuing chain of events.
iv. Every proposition is entailed by a contradiction.

Rather, the semantic role borne by the PP[BY] in a passive coincides with the role borne by the subject of the corresponding active form, be it agentive or not.

and phonological form, as well as such traditional functional notions as subject and object, have all been subsumed under function, why not simply abandon the notion of syntactic category altogether, and distinguish NP, VP, AP, etc. as nothing more than values of another "functional" attribute?

Of course, such a *reductio ad absurdum* is not what we propose. Rather, we believe it is more illuminating to posit a limited notion of function (in terms of the obliqueness hierarchy), in contradistinction to both selection for purely formal category distinctions (such as part of speech, verb inflection, and government of case or prepositional form) and selection for purely semantic distinctions (such as role assignment and sortal restrictions). The HPSG treatment of subcategorization dependencies allows a uniform treatment of functional, formal, and semantic selections, for the values of the feature SUBCAT contain all three kinds of information: functional information (e.g. the order of the elements on the SUBCAT list); formal information (specifications for values of the attribute SYNTAX); and semantic information (specifications for values of the attribute SEMANTICS).

5.4 Subject Selection

There can be little doubt that lexical dependencies of the type we have been discussing hold between verbs and their subjects. Subject-verb agreement, for example, is the agreement phenomenon *par excellence.* Our treatment of subject-verb agreement involves particular person and number specifications on the last member of a finite verb's SUBCAT list. Thus a finite verb like *walks* requires that the variable of its subject's semantic index be 3rd person singular in addition to imposing the syntactic requirement that the subject's case be nominative. This is illustrated in (239).

(239)
$$\begin{bmatrix} \text{PHON walks} & \\ \text{SYN}|\text{LOC} & \begin{bmatrix} \text{HEAD} & \begin{bmatrix}\text{MAJ} & \text{V}\\ \text{VFORM} & \text{FIN}\end{bmatrix} \\ \text{SUBCAT} & \left\langle \begin{bmatrix} \text{SYN}|\text{LOC}|\text{HEAD}|\text{CASE NOM} & \\ \text{SEM}|\text{CONT}|\text{IND}|\text{VAR} & \begin{bmatrix}\text{PER} & 3\\ \text{NUM} & \text{SING}\end{bmatrix}\end{bmatrix}\right\rangle \end{bmatrix}\end{bmatrix}$$

Assignment of semantic role is another respect in which verb-subject dependencies resemble the other subcategorizational dependencies we have been discussing. Despite recent attempts to distinguish the mechanism for assigning roles to subjects from the one that applies to nonsubjects (e.g. the GB notion that the "external theta-role" is assigned to the subject "indirectly" by something other than the lexical head itself), we are unaware of any evidence to support such a distinction; it seems clear that once the verb is identified, the subject role is determined to the same extent that the roles of the nonsubject complements are. It is equally clear that the possibilities for subject role assignment are comparable in range to those for objects. For all that subject roles often involve some notion of agentivity, this is by no means necessary, no more than object roles necessarily involve a notion of "patiency" or "themehood"; well-worn examples such as *like* vs. *please*, suffice to make this point.

Dependencies involving the selection of specific lexical forms, as we have seen, may involve prepositional heads and various inflected forms of non-subject arguments. But there are certainly cases of form selection that involve subjects. Here we would include expletive (or "dummy") pronouns such as English *it* and *there* and their analogues (sometimes phonetically unexpressed) in many other languages. These must be viewed as lexical dependencies, as the class of lexical items that allows expletive subjects in any language is (sometimes highly) restricted. This is a matter we return to in greater depth in Volume 2.

Case assignment too can be shown to hold between subjects and verbs, rather than between subjects and abstract disembodied clusters of morphological information (e.g. INFL), as assumed in much recent work in GB theory (e.g. Chomsky (1982, 50)). In languages like English, where subjects of finite clauses uniformly appear in nominative case, this point is not evident, but in closely related languages like Icelandic, which have been carefully studied by Thráinsson (1979), Andrews (1982), Zaenen, Maling, and Thráinsson (1985) and others, subject case assignment is not uniform. As Thráinsson and Andrews show, there are various classes of verbs in Icelandic that differ as to the case they assign to their subject NP, as illustrated in (240). (The indicated cases are the only ones possible in these examples.)

(240) a. Drengurinn kyssti stúlkuna i bílnum
the-boy (NOM) kissed the-girl(ACC) in the-car(DAT)

'The boy kissed the girl in the car.'

b. Mig langar að fara til Íslands.
me (ACC) longs to to go to Iceland

'I long to go to Iceland.'

c. Honum mæltist vel í kirkjunni.
He (DAT) spoke well in the church

'He spoke well in the church.'

d. Verkjanna gætir ekki.
the-pains (GEN) is noticeable not

'The pains are not noticeable.'

The final kind of subject selection that we will discuss here involves sentential subjects. We should point out that the conclusions we draw, as well as some of the evidence adduced, are somewhat controversial. As noted by Kajita (1967) and independently by Janet Fodor (personal communication), there are verbs in English that subcategorize for NP rather than sentential subjects, despite the fact that they would appear to be semantically compatible with sentential subject arguments:

(241) a.*That we invested when we did made us rich.
b. The fact that we invested when we did made us rich.

(242) a.*That he was late resulted in his being dismissed.
b. The fact that he was late resulted in his being dismissed.

(243) a.*That he was going bald drove him to drink.
b. The fact/idea that he was going bald drove him to drink.

(244) a.*That images are waterproof is incoherent.
b. The idea/claim/proposition that images are waterproof is incoherent.

It might be thought that some subtle semantic distinction is at stake here; to the best of our knowledge, however, no precise semantic account of the facts has ever been provided, leaving the matter squarely within the province of syntactic form. If the relevant distinction to be subcategorized for is indeed the distinction between NP's and S's, then verbs that allow only the former are specified as [SUBCAT ⟨ ..., NP⟩] , while those that allow both are specified as in (245).

(245) $$[\text{SUBCAT}\ \langle \ldots, \left[\text{SYN}|\text{LOC} \begin{bmatrix} \text{HEAD}|\text{MAJ N} \vee \text{V} \\ \text{SUBCAT} \langle\ \rangle \end{bmatrix}\right] \rangle]$$

Alternatively, sentential subjects may well be NP's of a special type, in which case they may be distinguished from non-sentential NP's by some other syntactic feature, perhaps NFORM. In this case, it is NFORM that serves to distinguish the various kinds of subject NP's that verbs select. We leave this matter unresolved here, but under whatever analysis turns out to be correct, it is clear that the feature SUBCAT can be used effectively to provide an account of the selection in question.

To summarize, as far as the full range of subcategorizational dependencies in concerned (verb-complement agreement, role assignment, case assignment, selection for particular lexical forms or particular syntactic features), the behavior of subjects is no different in kind from that of non-subject complements.

5.5 Optional Complements

As is well-known, subcategorized-for arguments are sometimes unrealized, as illustrated in (246).

(246) a. Pat will talk (to Sandy).
b. Lee has eaten (lunch).
c. The French were defeated (by the Germans).
d. We bet (Lou) five dollars (that the 49ers would win).

What is less well-known, however, is that there are at least two different kinds of unexpressed complements.

Certain complements are associated with semantic roles that are *ontologically necessary*, so that even when the complement in question is not overtly expressed, the situation described must be one where some object plays the role in question. Eating situations, for example, are of this type. When one says *Kim is eating*, the situation described must include something that is eaten. The eater and eaten roles are both ontologically necessary in the eat relation. In the kick relation, on the other hand, the kicker is necessary while the kickee is nonnecessary. That is, one can just kick without kicking anything in particular. Such observations, by the way, cast suspicion upon our claim in Chapter 4 that each relation has a characteristic arity. If there are really ontologically nonnecessary roles, it seems more appropriate to say that each relation has a characteristic *maximum* arity; other arities of the relation arise when one or more nonnecessary roles are left unfilled. That is, some relations may have *variable arity*.

The optionality of complements is a grammatical issue clearly orthogonal to the question of ontological necessity. Some of the linguistic complexities which can arise in this area are illustrated by various classes of "object deletion" verbs. In the cases of *eats* and *kicks*, the subject is obligatory and the direct object optional, while in the case of *likes*, both subject and direct object are obligatory. Using parentheses for optionality, we can represent the distinction between the *likes* and *eats* cases as follows:

(247)
$$\begin{bmatrix} \text{PHON likes} & \\ \text{SYN|LOC|SUBCAT} & \langle \text{NP}_{\boxed{1}}, \text{NP}_{\boxed{2}} \rangle \\ \text{SEM|CONT} & \begin{bmatrix} \text{RELN} & \text{LIKE} \\ \text{LIKER} & \boxed{2} \\ \text{LIKED} & \boxed{1} \end{bmatrix} \end{bmatrix}$$

(248)
$$\begin{bmatrix} \text{PHON eats} & \\ \text{SYN|LOC|SUBCAT} & \langle (\text{NP}_{\boxed{1}}), \text{NP}_{\boxed{2}} \rangle \\ \text{SEM|CONT} & \begin{bmatrix} \text{RELN} & \text{EAT} \\ \text{EATER} & \boxed{2} \\ \text{EATEN} & \boxed{1} \end{bmatrix} \end{bmatrix}$$

Here ⟨(X), Y⟩ abbreviates ⟨X,Y⟩ ∨ ⟨Y⟩. The idea is that a parameter for the role of the EATEN in the semantic content of *eats* will be present even if the optional object is not realized.

Succinctly representing the *kicks*-type optionality is a little trickier, since the KICKED role *must* be filled if the object is realized, but needn't be otherwise. Of course distinct lexical entries for transitive and intransitive *kicks* is one possibility; another way which factors out the redundancies between the two entries is this:

(249)

$$\begin{bmatrix} \text{PHON kicks} & \\ \text{SYN|LOC|HEAD} & \begin{bmatrix} \text{MAJ} & \text{V} \\ \text{VFORM} & \text{FIN} \\ \text{AUX} & - \\ \text{INV} & - \end{bmatrix} \\ \text{SEM|CONT} & \begin{bmatrix} \text{RELN} & \text{KICK} \\ \text{KICKER} & \boxed{1} \\ \text{KICKED} & \boxed{2} \end{bmatrix} \end{bmatrix} \wedge$$

$$\left([\text{SYN|LOC|SUBCAT} \ \langle \text{NP}_{\boxed{1}} \rangle] \vee \begin{bmatrix} \text{SYN|LOC|SUBCAT} \ \langle \text{NP}_{\boxed{2}}, \text{NP}_{\boxed{1}} \rangle \\ \text{SEM|CONT} \ [\text{KICKED} \ \boxed{2}] \end{bmatrix} \right)$$

Other classes, such as "inherent reflexives" (e.g. *shaved*) and "null-anaphora" object deletion (e.g. *won*) introduce additional semantic complexities which we will not attempt to sort through here.

It is well known that often two or more homophonous lexical forms which are used to refer to one and the same kind of situation may differ with respect to which (optional and obligatory) complements they subcategorize for and what semantic roles they assign to them. In such cases we speak of *polyvalency*. (N.B. Polyvalency is a *grammatical* notion, to be clearly distinguished from the ontological notion of variable arity.) Often, a pattern of polyvalency may apply across a whole class of lexical forms, e.g. the so-called "dative shift" alternation (*Kim gave the book to Sandy* vs. *Kim gave Sandy the book*), and the causative alternation (*The vase broke* vs. *Kim broke the vase*); here *lexical rules* (Chapter 8) appear to be the analytic tool of choice. For some lexical forms like *rent*, however, the pattern of alternations is idiosyncratic, as illustrated in (250):

(250) a.*Kim rented. (Kim the landlord)
  b. Kim rented. (Kim the tenant)
  c. Kim rented Apt. 3B. (Kim the landlord)
  d. Kim rented Apt. 3B. (Kim the tenant)
  e. Kim rented to Sandy.
  f. Kim rented from Sandy.
  g.*Kim rented from Chris to Sandy.

(250) h. Kim rented Sandy Apt. 3B.

i.*Kim rented Sandy. (Sandy the tenant)

j. Kim rented Apt. 3B to Sandy.

k. Kim rented Apt. 3B from Sandy.

In such cases there appears to be no recourse other than to posit distinct lexical signs. (For *rent*, three lexical signs suffice to account for the foregoing facts; the verification is left as an exercise for the reader.)

5.6 Complements vs. Adjuncts

It is important to be aware that not all optional elements are subcategorized for: optional complements must be distinguished from other optional constituents, known as *adjuncts* or *modifiers*, whose relationship to the head is of a different syntactic and semantic nature. The list given in (251), which is by no means exhaustive, illustrates a number of commonly occurring optional elements which are generally regarded as adjuncts:

(251) a. subordinate clauses:
Kim left *because/although/whenever Sandy came.*

b. predicative (small) clauses:
With Kim directing the project/off the scene/dead drunk, it was impossible to make any headway.

c. controlled adjuncts ("xadj's"):
Dead drunk, Kim ate the fish *raw.*

d. adjuncts of purpose:
She bought it *to play with.*

e. adjuncts of rationale:
Kim runs *to/in order to keep fit.*

f. manner adverbials:
Kim sang *blandly/with a lisp/with aplomb/without spilling his martini.*

g. frequentatives:
Sandy hang glides *three times a week.*

h. duratives:
Butch held forth *for two hours.*

i. full relatives:
the professor *who Kim wanted to impress*

j. complementizerless relatives:
the professor *Kim wanted to impress*

(251) k. "reduced relatives" (postnominal predicative adjuncts):
the unicorn *in the garden/asleep in the garden/insulted by the centaur*

l. infinitival relatives:
a friend *to talk to*

m. prenominal adjectives
ardent/former/alleged communist

Although there is not general agreement as to how the difference between adjuncts and complements should be characterized in theoretical terms, there are a number of rough-and-ready syntactic and semantic diagnostics which usually serve to make the distinction.

Order-dependence of content. The contribution of adjuncts to semantic content can depend upon their relative order in a way which does not apply to optional complements. This is illustrated in (252), which involves a frequentative and a durative:

(252) a. Kim jogged for 20 minutes twice a day.
b. Kim jogged twice a day for twenty years.

Note that in (252a), 20-minute duration is a property of the situation type whose frequency is described, while in (252b) twice-dailiness is a property of the situation type whose duration is described. It might be supposed that scope of quantification (over events or space-time locations, say) is at stake here. But in general such an account will not work, for an analogous meaning difference arises in (253) where the durative is replaced by an adverbial which clearly lacks any quantificational force:

(253) a. Kim jogs reluctantly twice a day.
b. Kim jogs twice a day reluctantly.

For (253b), but not (253a), a reading is available wherein twice-dailiness is part of what Kim is reluctant about. Similarly, no quantificational account will explain the meaning difference in (254):

(254) a. a self-proclaimed alleged communist
b. an alleged self-proclaimed communist

By contrast, the pair (255), which involves two optional complements, exhibits no such effect: (255a) and (255b) have the same semantic content.

(255) a. Kim complained about the neighbors to the landlord.
b. Kim complained to the landlord about the neighbors.

Constancy of semantic contribution. In general, a given adjunct can co-occur with a relatively broad range of heads while seeming to make a more-or-less uniform contribution to semantic content across that range. A given optional complement, by contrast, is typically limited in its distribution to co-occurrence with a small (and often semantically restricted) class of heads (possibly even a single item); in addition, the semantic contribution of the complement is idiosyncratically dependent upon the head. In (256a), for example, the PP[ON] is a locative adjunct. It is appropriate with any head that describes a kind of situation for which the notion of location is relevant, and its locative semantic contribution seems independent of the head.

(256) a. Kim camps/jogs/meditates on the hill.
 b. Kim depends/relies on Sandy.
 c. The authorities blamed/pinned the arson on Sandy.
 d. The search committee decided/settled on Chris.

In (256b–d), by contrast, where the PP[ON] is (obligatorily or optionally) subcategorized for, the only semantically constant feature of the PP[ON] is that it always describes the participant in one of the roles appropriate to the relation described by the head verb; but precisely which role is involved varies from one verb (or verb class) to the next.

Iterability. In general, two or more instances of the same adjunct type can combine with the same head (257a–e), but this is impossible for complements (257f–i).

(257) a. Kim and Sandy met in Baltimore in the lobby of the Hyatt in July.
 b. Dana went to Chicago without going to the conference without feeling guilty.
 c. Mary climbed Beacon Hill without oxygen to impress Bill, to show how impressionable he was.
 d. Kim sold life insurance for Mutual of the Ozarks, for her poor old mother.
 e. Heather opened the rusty lock with a key, with a pair of pliers.
 f.*The authorities blamed the arson on the vegetarians on the Luddites.
 g.*Yes, we have no bananas, pineapples.
 h.*Chris rented the gazebo to yuppies, to libertarians.
 i.*Josh longed for a gas-guzzler, for a Buick.

Relative Order. In English, at least some adjuncts tend to be ordered after complements, as indicated by the contrast between the examples in (258) and those in (259):

(258) a. The authorities blamed the arson on the skydivers without checking the facts.

b. Myra promised to intimidate the Trilateral Commission, in order to impress Orton.

c. Butch announced that coelocanths were decidable to his computational ichthyology seminar.

(259) a.*The authorities blamed the arson without checking the facts on the skydivers.

b.*Myra promised in order to impress Orton to intimidate the Trilateral Commission.

c.*Butch apologized because coelocanths were undecidable to his computational ichthyology seminar.

Possibility of internal gaps. At least some adjuncts appear to generally disallow unbound internal traces (unless they are "licensed" by another coindexed trace as described in Volume 2), such as those in (260):

(260) a.*Which hypothesis did Sandy leave for Maui [before Sandy had proved __ logically independent]?

b.*Which famous professor did Kim climb K-2 without oxygen [in order to impress __]?

c.*Which endangered species did Sandy meet someone [fond of __]?

Complements, by contrast, generally allow internal gaps, as in (261):

(261) a. Which hypothesis did Kim deny [that Sandy had proved __ logically independent]?

b. Which famous professor did Kim attempt [to impress __] by climbing K-2 without oxygen?

c. Which endangered species did Kim impress you as being most [fond of __]?

Much work in semantics, particularly within the framework of categorial grammar, has assumed that the adjunct/complement distinction reduces to a matter of whether the element in question is semantically a functor or an argument, i.e. whether it takes the head to which it attaches as an argument or vice versa. The complement half of this characterization can be imported directly into our framework, wherein complements in general are semantic arguments of their heads in the sense that their semantic contents fill roles in the relation described by the head (raising controllers constitute an important class of exceptions as described in Volume 2). This provides a point of departure for an explanation of why complements behave as they do with respect to the first three diagnostics mentioned above. Thus, the contributions of complements to semantic content is independent of surface order (at least up to scope of quantifiers) because they are determined by the roles assigned to those complements; e.g. the assignment of roles by *talks* to its optional PP[TO] and PP[ABOUT] complements is fixed, regardless of the relative surface order of their phonological realizations. The contribution of a complement with a given syntactic category (such as PP[ON]) is inconstant across the set of heads which subcategorize for it because different heads (such as *depend*, *blame*, and *decide*) assign different roles with different properties to it. No semantic account of the noniterability of complements is needed, for that is already a consequence of the Subcategorization Principle.

However, in a framework such as ours where (unlike standard categorial grammar) possible modes for combining semantic contents are not limited to functional application (or some analog of functional application), there is no clear analog of the functor notion. A finer-grained classification of semantic combinatorial modes is required in order to account for different semantic properties of different adjunct types. For example, as (252–254) above show, the semantic contributions of multiple adjuncts are often order-sensitive. But there are exceptions: (spatio-temporal) locative adjuncts, for example, seem to be freely permutable without semantic effect, as illustrated by (262):

(262) a. The conference was held on June 19, at Conundrum Pass, 13,000 feet above sea level.

b. The conference was held on June 19, 13,000 feet above sea level, at Conundrum Pass.

c. The conference was held at Conundrum Pass, on June 19, 13,000 feet above sea level.

Provided we adopt the assumption, by now conventional in situation semantics, that location is a role appropriate to a wide range of relations, then this permutability can be accounted for if we suppose further that the semantic effect of a locative adjunct is to extend information about the filler of the location role. A number of technical solutions are consistent with such an approach. For example, following Fenstad et al. (1985), we might treat locative adjuncts semantically as constraints upon a location parameter; alternatively, we might assume that locative adjuncts describe locations (spatio-temporal regions), with multiple locative adjuncts corresponding to the intersection of a set of locations (which would presumably be a location itself).

There are also finer syntactic distinctions to be made among adjuncts. The most obvious one, of course, is that different kinds of adjuncts attach to different kinds of heads, e.g. relative clauses and (nonpredicative) adjectives to nouns; subordinate clauses, adverbs, and rationale adjuncts to verbs (or their projections), etc. But how are such facts to be captured in the theory? A moment's reflection shows that there cannot be an analog to the Subcategorization Principle for adjuncts: even if we believe that heads syntactically select certain adjunct types (e.g. that common nouns select relative clauses), this must be accomplished in a way that permits iteration.

Adjuncts also differ as to how they fare with the last two of the rough diagnostics mentioned above, viz. relative ordering with respect to complements and the possibility of internal gaps. Thus, although certain adjunct types, such as those illustrated in (258–259) above, must follow complements in surface order, others are not subject to this constraint, as the examples in (263) show:

(263) a. Orton depended for most of his life on his aunt Myra.
b. Sandy speculated boldly that the Axiom of Infinity was inconsistent.
c. Kim decided after much consideration to withdraw from the Cognitive Herpetology seminar.

Likewise, although some adjunct types appear not to sanction internal gaps as illustrated in (263) above, others are more permissive:

(264) a. This is the blanket that Rebecca refuses to sleep [without __].
b. This is the bridge that Sedgewick committed *Syntactic Structures* to memory [under __].
c. Which symphony did Schubert die [without finishing __]?

Such problems with adjuncts are by and large uncharted territory, and we will not attempt to come to grips with them here. Some possible avenues for further exploration will be suggested in Chapters 6 through 8, where we consider how the rules and lexicon of a language are organized.

5.7 SUBCAT in the Noun Phrase

As noted in Chapter 3, we make the assumption that nouns, as well as other lexical signs, are specified for SUBCAT. In general, the final argument subcategorized for by a common noun is either a determiner or a possessive phrase (NP + 's), reflecting the fact that these are the two kinds of syntactic elements that common nouns combine with to form saturated nominal signs (NP's).

There is an issue as to whether each common noun should have two lexical signs, one specified as [SYNTAX|LOCAL|SUBCAT ⟨DET⟩], the other as [SYNTAX|LOCAL|SUBCAT ⟨POSP⟩] (where "POSP" abbreviates whatever formal analysis is adopted for possessive phrases), or whether a single lexical sign can be given for each noun which specifies the disjunction of the two possibilities. For languages like English where the phonological form of the noun remains invariant whether a determiner or a possessive occurs, this does not seem to be an empirical question; as far as the logic of feature structures is concerned, the two analyses are equivalent (to be more precise, the first is the disjunctive normal form of the second).

At first blush, the first alternative may seem massively redundant, but as we shall see in Chapter 8, the two lexical signs can be related by a lexical rule. Indeed, such an analysis seems to be required in the case of languages such as Hungarian where the form of the common noun systematically varies according to the syntactic nature of the element it combines with. This is illustrated in (265):

(265) a. a könyv 'the book'
b. a könyvek 'the books'
c. az író 'the writer'
d. az írók 'the writers'

(266) a. az író könyve 'the writer's book'
b. az író könyvei 'the writer's books'
c. az írók könyve 'the writers' book'
d. az írók könyvei 'the writers' books'

The nouns in (265) are all specified as [SYNTAX|LOCAL|SUBCAT ⟨DET⟩], those in (266) as [SYNTAX|LOCAL|SUBCAT ⟨NP[NOM]⟩]. Assuming that possessive phrases are in fact NP's, the relevant nominal signs for the forms of 'book' are sketched in (267)–(269).

(267)
$$\begin{bmatrix} \text{PHON} & \text{könyve} \\ \text{SYN}|\text{LOC}|\text{SUBCAT} & \langle \text{NP[NOM]} \rangle \\ \text{SEM}|\text{CONT}|\text{IND}|\text{VAR}|\text{NUM} & \text{SING} \end{bmatrix}$$

(268)
$$\begin{bmatrix} \text{PHON} & \text{könyvei} \\ \text{SYN}|\text{LOC}|\text{SUBCAT} & \langle \text{NP[NOM]} \rangle \\ \text{SEM}|\text{CONT}|\text{IND}|\text{VAR}|\text{NUM} & \text{PLU} \end{bmatrix}$$

(269)
$$\begin{bmatrix} \text{PHON} & \text{könyv} \\ \text{SYN}|\text{LOC}|\text{SUBCAT} & \langle \text{DET} \rangle \\ \text{SEM}|\text{CONT}|\text{IND}|\text{VAR}|\text{NUM} & \text{SING} \end{bmatrix}$$

(270)
$$\begin{bmatrix} \text{PHON} & \text{könyvek} \\ \text{SYN}|\text{LOC}|\text{SUBCAT} & \langle \text{DET} \rangle \\ \text{SEM}|\text{CONT}|\text{IND}|\text{VAR}|\text{NUM} & \text{PLU} \end{bmatrix}$$

On this analysis, it is essentially a morphological accident of English, that there is no phonological distinction between the forms of common nouns that combine with determiners and those that combine with possessors.

Plural common nouns and mass nouns in English of course occur with no overt determiner. Several distinct analyses suggest themselves rather naturally. One possibility would be to introduce a special grammar rule whose sole purpose is to allow these nouns to form noun phrases without combining with any determiner or possessor. However, the positing of special-purpose rules runs counter to the general approach set forth in the next chapter, and indeed to the spirit of most contemporary syntactic theorization. Within HPSG, a further technical obstacle presents itself: given the Subcategorization Principle, we are left with no account of how the noun's SUBCAT requirement is satisfied. A second possibility which avoids these difficulties would be to introduce phonologically unexpressed determiners that only these forms will combine with; but the lack of any independent syntactic motivation for such a proposal argues strongly against it. A third possibility, which strikes us as the most promising, would be that the determiner/possessive complement is *optionally* subcategorized-for by these nouns. However, the technical details of such a proposal remain to be worked out, and we leave the matter unresolved here.

Finally, we point out that in general common nouns do not subcategorize for elements other than determiners or possessors, but instead combine with various kinds of modifiers as adjuncts, which are not treated by the feature SUBCAT and are governed by a principle distinct from the Subcategorization Principle. This *Adjuncts Principle* will be discussed in greater detail in Chapter 6. However, some classes of common nouns in English appear to subcategorize—albeit optionally—for additional complements. So-called "picture nouns" appear to be of this type.[9] On such an account, the lexical sign *picture* takes the form sketched in (271):

(271)
$$\begin{bmatrix} \text{PHON picture} \\ \text{SYN|LOC} \begin{bmatrix} \text{HEAD|MAJ N} \\ \text{SUBCAT} \langle \text{(PP[OF]), DET} \rangle \end{bmatrix} \end{bmatrix}$$

This form combines with its PP complement in accordance with the same rule whereby verbs combine with their direct objects, and the resulting phrasal sign functions just as any common-noun phrase with respect to its combination with a determiner to form an NP.

Another class of English nouns which subcategorize for additional complements are so-called "deverbative" nouns or "nominalizations", nominal forms etymologically related to verbs and distinct from verbal gerunds (see Chapter 3). To a large extent, the optional complements of such nouns, as

[9] Alternatively, we might analyze the PP[OF] in *picture of Kim* as a postnominal predicative adjunct, like the one in *picture hanging on the wall.* But then it is difficult to explain the contrast between (i) and (ii):

i. *There was a picture of Kim, of Sandy.

ii. There was a picture hanging in the lobby, hanging upside down.

well as their semantic role assignments, can be predicted on the basis of the corresponding verb "sources". For example, in general, the role assigned to the subject by the verb source can be assigned by the nominalization to either a POSP (possessive phrase), an optional PP[OF], or an optional PP[BY]:

(272) a. John abdicated.
b. John's abdication
c. the abdication of/by John

If the verb subcategorizes for a direct object NP, the direct object role is typically also assignable to the POSP of the nominalization, and often (but not always!) to the PP[OF] of the nominalization as well; if both the POSP and the PP[OF] appear, then their roles must correspond to the subject and object of the verb respectively (and not vice versa). But there is idiosyncratic lexical variation here, as the following examples show:

(273) a. The barbarians destroyed the city.
b. the city's destruction (by/*of the barbarians)
c. the barbarians' destruction (of the city)
d. the destruction of the city (by the barbarians)
e. the destruction by/of the barbarians (barbarians = destroyers)

(274) a. Mineola State University rejected Orton.
b. Orton's rejection (by/*of Mineola State University) (Orton = rejectee)
c. Mineola State University's rejection (of Orton)
d. the rejection of Orton (by Mineola State University)
e. the rejection by/*of Mineola State University (MSU = rejector)

On the other hand, a role assigned by a verb to a PP complement cannot usually be assigned by the corresponding nominalization to the POSP or PP[OF];[10] instead, the assignment of the role to the PP in question is "inherited" by the nominalization:

---

[10] An obvious subclass of exceptions is composed of verbs which themselves subcategorize for a PP[OF]:
i.*Ira disapproved the project.
ii. Ira disapproved of the project.
iii. Ira's disapproval of the project
iv. the disapproval of the project by Ira
v. the project's disapproval *of/by Ira (Ira = disapprover)

(275) a. Myra depended on heroin.
b.*Heroin's dependence (by/of Myra) (Myra = addict)
c. Myra's dependence (*of/on heroin)
d. the dependence (of/by Myra) *of/on heroin
e. the dependence by/of Myra (Myra = addict)

(276) a. Orton donated the manuscript to Mineola State University.
b. Orton's donation (of the manuscript)(to/*of Mineola State University)
c. the manuscript's donation (to/*of Mineola State University) (*of/by Orton)
d.*the donation of Orton (to Mineola State University) (Orton = donor)
e. the donation of the manuscript (to Mineola State University)(by Orton)
f.*the donation of Mineola State University (by Orton) (MSU = recipient)

There are, however, a number of subtle semantic distinctions to be drawn among various subclasses of deverbative nouns, as well as subregularities and idiosyncratic variation in the assignment by such nouns of semantic roles to their arguments; this is an area which requires much further study. One or more "nominalization" lexical (Chapter 8) rules may well be appropriate in the analysis of these phenomena.

5.8 Conclusion

The feature SUBCAT provides the basis for the treatment of lexical dependencies in HPSG: subcategorized-for complements and their associated grammatical relations, category selection, case, agreement, semantic role assignment, and perhaps certain semantic selectional restrictions as well. Why should we seek to provide a single mechanism for analyzing all these seemingly diverse phenomena? There is a simple answer to this question: all the phenomena just listed share a certain *locality* property. Just as there are no verbs in any language we know of that select a sentential complement whose verb phrase is headed by a transitive rather than an intransitive verb, there are no verbs in any language that assign roles to a complement within a complement that they select. Likewise there are no verbs that assign case to some NP properly contained within one of their complements, or agree with an NP properly contained within one of their complements. Why should this be so? Our answer is that all of these locality restrictions follow from the assumption that *the* SUBCAT *elements of lexical signs specifies values for* SYNTAX *and* SEMANTICS *but crucially not the attribute* DAUGHTERS. This *Locality Principle*, we suggest, is a universal constraint on lexical signs.[11]

On the basis of the paradigm given in (277), Kajita (1967, 103) has claimed that the verb *serve* must be subcategorized for a VP complement that contains a direct object NP (which would render it a counterexample to the Locality Principle):

(277) a. The ice melted.
b.*The ice served to melt.
c. The ice chilled the beer.
d. The ice served to chill the beer.

But this claim is suspect, as noted by Higgins (1973, 173 n.5) who remarks as follows:

> One merely needs to strictly subcategorize the verb *serve* for an infinitival complement sentence. One has to say, in addition, that the subject of the complement verb must be interpretable as an instrument. (This is only a rough characterization and needs further precision.) Since any verb in English whose subject can be understood as an instrument of necessity has an object, the verb in the complement sentence must have an object. Clearly, the semantic nature of the subject of the complement sentence is not a matter to be regulated by strict subcategorization restrictions, and Chomsky's conjecture ... that selection restrictions might be a more appropriate mechanism in this case, is confirmed.

Within our framework, it is possible for a verb to exert restrictions (including restrictions on role assignment) upon the "understood subject" of an unsaturated complement (xcomp), since those restrictions are internal to the SUBCAT value of the verb. Locality is not violated since there is no phonologically unrealized subconstituent ("empty category") corresponding to the complement subject; the restriction can be exerted without illicit access to the complement's DAUGHTERS value.[12]

---

[11] The point here is that no lexical sign inherently *selects* a particular value for the DAUGHTERS attribute of its complements; of course, in any token of a lexical sign, any SUBCAT element that is unified with a phrasal constituent *bears* a value for DAUGHTERS.

[12] Similar considerations come into play in the *control* of subjects of xcomps, where under standard assumptions, a verb selects for a complement whose unexpressed subject is "coindexed" with either the subject or direct object of the matrix verb. Under our analysis of control (sketched in Volume 2) the controlled complement is specified as [SYNTAX|LOCAL|SUBCAT ⟨NP$_{\boxed{i}}$⟩],

Stuart Shieber (personal communication), who independently arrived at essentially the same conclusion as Higgins regarding the nature of the restriction on *serve*, points out that the semantic analysis is confirmed by the ungrammaticality of examples like (278), which should be grammatical if transitivity of the infinitival complement is the relevant constraining factor.

(278) *Kim served to break the window with the hammer.

The deviance of this example is in complete accord with the semantic approach suggested by Higgins and Shieber. On the other hand, examples such as (279) suggest that (pace Higgins) verbs with instrument subjects need not be transitive:

(279) a. A pair of nines can open in this game.
b. You can open with a pair of nines in this game.

Here (279a) is roughly paraphrasable by (279b). As our analysis predicts, (280) seems quite acceptable even though the complement verb is intransitive:

(280) A pair of nines will serve to open in this game.

The Locality Principle severely constrains the kind of elements that lexical signs may select. Non-local selection would require signs on SUBCAT lists to specify values for attributes such as HEAD-DTR or COMPLEMENT-DTR, as sketched in (281).

(281) $$\text{SUBCAT}\ \langle \ldots \left[\ldots\ \text{DTRS} \begin{bmatrix} \text{HEAD-DTR} & \text{X} \\ \text{COMP-DTRS} & \langle \ldots,\text{Y},\ldots \rangle \end{bmatrix} \right] \ldots \rangle$$

It is precisely specifications like these that the Locality Principle rules out. In this way, the theory of subcategorization we have outlined makes strong empirical claims about the full range of lexical dependency phenomena.

5.9 Suggestions for Further Reading

Purely syntactic aspects of the theory of subcategorization presented here, and particularly the list-valued SUBCAT feature, are derived from Pollard (1984). The treatment of semantic role assignment as an integral part of

---

where the variable i is unified with the variable corresponding to the controlling complement. Hence even if control were a lexical selection (a position which we argue against in Volume 2), the relevant variable would be locally available.

subcategorization is present, in an early formulation, in Pollard (ms. 2), where the index of a noun phrase is handled in terms of a distinct INDEX attribute; the approach adopted here, wherein the index is treated as part of the semantic content, was suggested to us by Stuart Shieber. The use of unification to ensure compatibility between complements and subcategorization requirements, also due to Pollard (1984), is essentially similar to the treatment of subcategorization in LFG (Kaplan and Bresnan (1982)), except that (1) in LFG each subcategorized element is handled by a distinct attribute, and (2) in LFG, syntactic information regarded as belonging to *c*-structure rather than *f*-structure (such as part of speech) cannot be subcategorized for. Our approach bears an even closer resemblance to the unification categorial grammar of Zeevat et al. (1987), which also employs a list encoding of "sought" dependent elements bearing both syntactic and semantic information. One variation on the subcategorization theory given here, proposed by Gunji (1986), treats the SUBCAT feature as set-valued rather than list-valued; in another, due to Borsley (in press), subject selection is handled by a distinct SUBJECT attribute.

6 Grammar Rules

In the preceding chapters, we proposed a few principles of universal grammar, including the Head Feature Principle, the Subcategorization Principle, and the Semantics Principle; others will be proposed in chapters to come. Our theory of universal grammar (UG) is the unification of all such principles, as stated in (282):

(282) $\text{UG} = \text{P}_1 \wedge \ldots \wedge \text{P}_n$

where $\text{P}_1, \ldots, \text{P}_n$ is an exhaustive list of the universal principles.

Moreover, we assume that each natural language imposes additional language-specific constraints of its own. Thus there are principles $\text{P}_{n+1}, \ldots, \text{P}_{n+m}$ which must be satisfied by all signs of English. One such principle, the *Constituent Ordering Principle*, will be discussed in Chapter 7.

In addition, each language presents a finite set of lexical signs and a finite set of *grammar rules.* A grammar rule is just a very partially specified phrasal sign which constitutes one of the options offered by the language in question for making big signs from little ones. But how do lexical signs and grammar rules fit into our theory of a particular language? To answer this question, let us suppose that $\text{L}_1, \ldots, \text{L}_p$ is an exhaustive list of the English lexical signs and $\text{R}_1, \ldots, \text{R}_q$ is an exhaustive list of the English grammar rules. Then our theory of English is (283):

(283) $\text{English} = \text{P}_1 \wedge \ldots \wedge \text{P}_{n+m} \wedge (\text{L}_1 \vee \ldots \vee \text{L}_p \vee \text{R}_1 \vee \ldots \vee \text{R}_q)$

In other words, an object is an English sign token just in case (i) it satisfies all the universal and English-specific principles, and (ii) either it instantiates one of the English lexical signs or it instantiates one of the English grammar rules.

As we saw in Chapter 3, phrasal signs differ from lexical signs in having daughters (internal constituent structure). Constituent structure is specified in feature structures of type *phrasal-sign* by means of the attribute DAUGHTERS, whose value is in turn a feature structure of type *constituent-structure.* We assume in addition that cross-linguistically, there is a small number of subtypes of *constituent-structure*, including *headed-structure*, *coordinate-structure*, and perhaps a few others; in this book, we are concerned almost exclusively with the subtype *headed-structure*, which subsumes all phrases possessing a head daughter. For reference, the three universal principles proposed so far, all of which take the form $[\text{DTRS}\ {}_{\textit{headed-structure}}[\ ]] \Rightarrow X$, are stated in (284):

(284) Three Principles of Universal Grammar

Head Feature Principle

$$[\text{DTRS}\ {}_{\textit{headed-structure}}[\ ]] \quad \Rightarrow$$

$$\begin{bmatrix} \text{SYN|LOC|HEAD}\ \boxed{1} \\ \text{DTRS|HEAD-DTR|SYN|LOC|HEAD}\ \boxed{1} \end{bmatrix}$$

Subcategorization Principle

$$[\text{DTRS}\ {}_{\textit{headed-structure}}[\ ]] \quad \Rightarrow$$

$$\begin{bmatrix} \text{SYN|LOC|SUBCAT}\ \boxed{2} & \\ \text{DTRS} & \begin{bmatrix} \text{HEAD-DTR|SYN|LOC|SUBCAT append(}\boxed{1},\boxed{2}\text{)} \\ \text{COMP-DTRS}\ \boxed{1} \end{bmatrix} \end{bmatrix}$$

Semantics Principle

$$[\text{DTRS}\ {}_{\textit{headed-structure}}[\ ]] \quad \Rightarrow$$

$$\begin{bmatrix} \text{SEM} & \begin{bmatrix} \text{CONT successively-combine-semantics(}\boxed{1},\boxed{2}\text{)} \\ \text{INDICES collect-indices(}\boxed{3}\text{)} \end{bmatrix} \\ \text{DTRS}\ \boxed{3} & \begin{bmatrix} \text{HEAD-DTR|SEM|CONT}\ \boxed{1} \\ \text{COMP-DTRS}\ \boxed{2} \end{bmatrix} \end{bmatrix}$$

Using the identity $(A \Rightarrow B) \wedge (A \Rightarrow C) = A \Rightarrow (B \wedge C)$, which is valid in any Heyting algebra, the three principles above can be unified into the more compact form (284′):

(284′) $[\text{DTRS}\ {}_{\textit{headed-structure}}[\ ]] \quad \Rightarrow$

$$\begin{bmatrix} \text{SYN|LOC} & \begin{bmatrix} \text{HEAD}\ \boxed{1} \\ \text{SUBCAT}\ \boxed{3} \end{bmatrix} \\ \text{SEM} & \begin{bmatrix} \text{CONT successively-combine-semantics(}\boxed{5},\boxed{2}\text{)} \\ \text{INDICES collect-indices(}\boxed{4}\text{)} \end{bmatrix} \\ \text{DTRS}\ \boxed{4} & \begin{bmatrix} \text{HEAD-DTR} & \begin{bmatrix} \text{SYN|LOC} & \begin{bmatrix} \text{HEAD}\ \boxed{1} \\ \text{SUBCAT append(}\boxed{2},\boxed{3}\text{)} \end{bmatrix} \\ \text{SEM|CONT}\ \boxed{5} & \end{bmatrix} \\ \text{COMP-DTRS}\ \boxed{2} & \end{bmatrix} \end{bmatrix}$$

Headed structures are further classified according to the kinds of non-head daughters (e.g. complements, fillers, adjuncts, etc.) which they contain. Thus there is a subtype *head-complement-structure* with attributes HEAD-DTR and COMP-DTRS; another subtype, *head-filler-structure* bears the additional attribute FILLER-DTR. English head-complement structures are the principal subject of this chapter; head-filler structures will be treated in detail in Volume 2.

In a feature structure of type *head-complement-structure*, the value of HEAD-DTR is always of type *sign*, while the value of COMP-DTRS is a list of feature structures of type *sign*. This is because a phrase has at most one head, but may have several complements. It is important to keep in mind that the order of elements in the COMP-DTRS value (as in SUBCAT values) corresponds to order in the hierarchy of obliqueness (with more oblique elements further to the left), *not* to the temporal order of their phonological realizations (usually called "surface order"). The correspondence between the two kinds of order is determined by language-specific constituent-ordering principles (see Chapter 7).[1]

In the next two sections, we present three grammar rules which account for English head-complement structures.

6.1 Two Rules

Grammar Rule 1, given in (285a) below, corresponds to the rules standardly expressed in the forms "S → NP VP", "NP → DET NOM", and "NP → NP[GEN] NOM". It is also responsible for small clauses (sentence-like signs headed by predicative phrases or nonfinite verb phrases).

(285) a. Rule 1

$$\begin{bmatrix} \text{SYN|LOC|SUBCAT} \ \langle\ \rangle \\ \text{DTRS} \begin{bmatrix} \text{HEAD-DTR|SYN|LOC|LEX} \ - \\ \text{COMP-DTRS} \ \langle [\ ] \rangle \end{bmatrix} \end{bmatrix}$$

The essential content of this rule is that one of the possibilities for a phrasal sign in English is to be a saturated (i.e. [SUBCAT ⟨ ⟩]) sign which has as constituents a single complement daughter (i.e. [COMP-DTRS ⟨[ ]⟩]) and a head daughter, which in turn is constrained to be a phrasal rather than a lexical sign. Recall that we treat VP's as the heads of sentences (unlike most work within GB theory); hence this rule legitimates the combination

[1] The factoring out of ordering principles from grammar rules follows the tradition of work in GPSG originating with Gazdar and Pullum (1981). However, as argued in Sag (1987), a number of problems for the GPSG theory of *linear precedence* (LP) rules can be resolved in the context of HPSG.

of VP's with subject complements to make sentences as well as the combination of unsaturated nominal constituents with DET or possessor phrase complements to form NP's.

For the sake of familiarity, we shall sometimes express a rule such as (285a) in a somewhat more standard "rewrite" notation, as in (285b).

(285) b. [SUBCAT ⟨ ⟩] → H[LEX –], C

Whenever we may write rules in this way, however, it should be understood that this is just a shorthand for the official notation in (285a). Grammar rules are always to be conceived of as partially specified phrasal signs.

Of course, the rule in (285) does not tell all there is to know about the phrases that it subsumes; it does not contain any information that is predictable from universal principles (such as (284′)) or English-specific principles (such as the Constituent Ordering Principle of Chapter 7). For example, any phrasal sign subsumed by (285) must in fact be subsumed by the more specified version of Rule 1, given in (286), which is obtained by unifying (285a) with the HFP and the Subcategorization Principle (for expository simplicity we ignore the Semantics Principle, and the SEMANTICS attribute, in the remainder of this chapter):

(286)
$$\begin{bmatrix} \text{SYN|LOC} & \begin{bmatrix}\text{HEAD} & \boxed{1}\\ \text{SUBCAT} & \langle\ \rangle\end{bmatrix} \\ \text{DTRS} & \begin{bmatrix} \text{HEAD-DTR|SYN|LOC} & \begin{bmatrix}\text{HEAD} & \boxed{1}\\ \text{SUBCAT} & \langle \boxed{2}\rangle \\ \text{LEX} & -\end{bmatrix} \\ \text{COMP-DTRS}\ \langle\boxed{2}\rangle & \end{bmatrix}\end{bmatrix}$$

Likewise, any phrasal sign subsumed by (285) (or, equivalently, by (286)) must also be subsumed by the still more specified version of Rule (1), given in (287), which is obtained by unifying (286) with the English Constituent Ordering Principle:

(287)
$$\begin{bmatrix} \text{PHON concat}(\boxed{3},\boxed{4}) & \\ \text{SYN|LOC} & \begin{bmatrix}\text{HEAD} & \boxed{1}\\ \text{SUBCAT} & \langle\ \rangle\end{bmatrix} \\ \text{DTRS} & \begin{bmatrix} \text{HEAD-DTR} & \begin{bmatrix} \text{PHON} & \boxed{4} \\ \text{SYN|LOC} & \begin{bmatrix}\text{HEAD} & \boxed{1}\\ \text{SUBCAT} & \langle \boxed{2}\rangle \\ \text{LEX} & -\end{bmatrix}\end{bmatrix} \\ \text{COMP-DTRS}\ \langle\boxed{2}[\text{PHON}\ \boxed{3}]\rangle & \end{bmatrix}\end{bmatrix}$$

The architecture of the theory is simply such that properties of phrases that follow from universal or language-specific principles need not be specified on individual grammar rules. (287) differs from (286) in that it contains the information that the complement daughter precedes the head daughter in surface order.

Rule 2 is the rule that subsumes unsaturated phrasal signs such as VP's. It says simply that another one of the options for English is to be a phrasal sign one dependent short of being saturated (i.e. whose SUBCAT value is a list of length one) whose head daughter is an uninverted ([INV −]) lexical sign. This is shown in (288):

(288) Rule 2

$$\begin{bmatrix} \text{SYN}|\text{LOC SUBCAT } \langle [\ ] \rangle \\ \text{DTRS}|\text{HEAD-DTR}|\text{SYN}|\text{LOC} \begin{bmatrix} \text{HEAD}|\text{INV} - \\ \text{LEX} + \end{bmatrix} \end{bmatrix}$$

The specification [INV −] in this rule prevents verbs marked [INV +], e.g. 1st person singular *aren't*, from being the head of a verb phrase (and hence accounts for the ungrammaticality of examples like **I aren't going to the store*). In the familiar rewrite notation, Rule 2 takes the form (289).

(289) $[\text{SUBCAT } \langle [\ ] \rangle] \rightarrow \text{H}[\text{INV} -, \text{LEX} +], \text{C}^*$

Again, this grammar rule says very little, since much of the structure of the phrases which it subsumes is obtained from the principles of universal grammar and the English Constituent Ordering Principle. The HFP will again enforce the identity of the phrase's head feature values with those on the head daughter (in this case the lexical head); the Subcategorization Principle will guarantee that the lexical head have a SUBCAT list whose length is exactly one greater than the number of complement daughters, and that those complement daughters actually satisfy the subcategorization restrictions specified on the lexical head. In addition, the Constituent Ordering Principle will ensure that in the corresponding utterance tokens, the realization of the lexical head precedes the realization of the complements, that the direct object precedes the indirect object (if any), etc. Thus, for example, a transitive verb will combine with exactly one complement (the direct object) to form a verb phrase, i.e. a [MAJ V] phrasal sign that still requires one additional complement (the subject) in order to become saturated.

Because so many conventional phrase structure rules are schematized by Rules 1 and 2, the two together account for a very substantial subtype ("fragment") of English: the non-inverted head-complement structures. Such a structure is partially illustrated in (290):

(290)

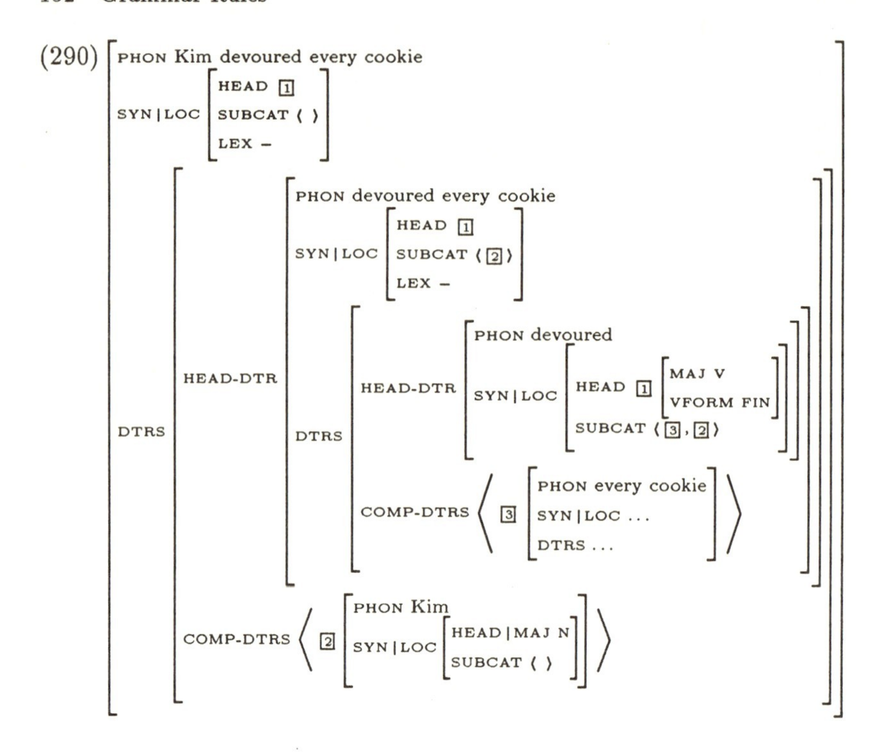

The connection between the structure of a complex sign according to HPSG theory and conventional constituent structure trees is seen at once by considering diagram (291), where the DTRS attributes have been notated by arcs labelled 'H' and 'C' (for HEAD-DTRS and COMP-DTRS respectively).

For ease of reference, each node of the tree is labelled by the number of the rule that subsumes it. To enhance readability, specifications for some head features are omitted. For the same reason, structure-sharing required by the HFP and the Subcategorization Principle (i.e. identity of HEAD between phrases and their head daughters, and identity of complement daughters with the subcategorization specifications that they satisfy) has not been explicitly indicated. Note that in the derivation of the nominal phrase *cookie*, the lexical sign *cookie* has combined according to Rule 2, but with no complements. Intransitive verbs are built into verb phrases in similar fashion.

This same tree is displayed again in (292), this time with the relevant structure-sharing explicitly indicated.

In similar fashion, Rules 1 and 2 interact to provide an account of possessor constructions (recall that common nouns also may be specified as [SUBCAT ⟨POSP⟩], where "POSP" abbreviates whatever analysis is adopted for possessive NP's) and "small clauses" (sentence-like phrases whose heads are not finite verbs). This is illustrated by the partial descriptions in (293) and (294).

(291)

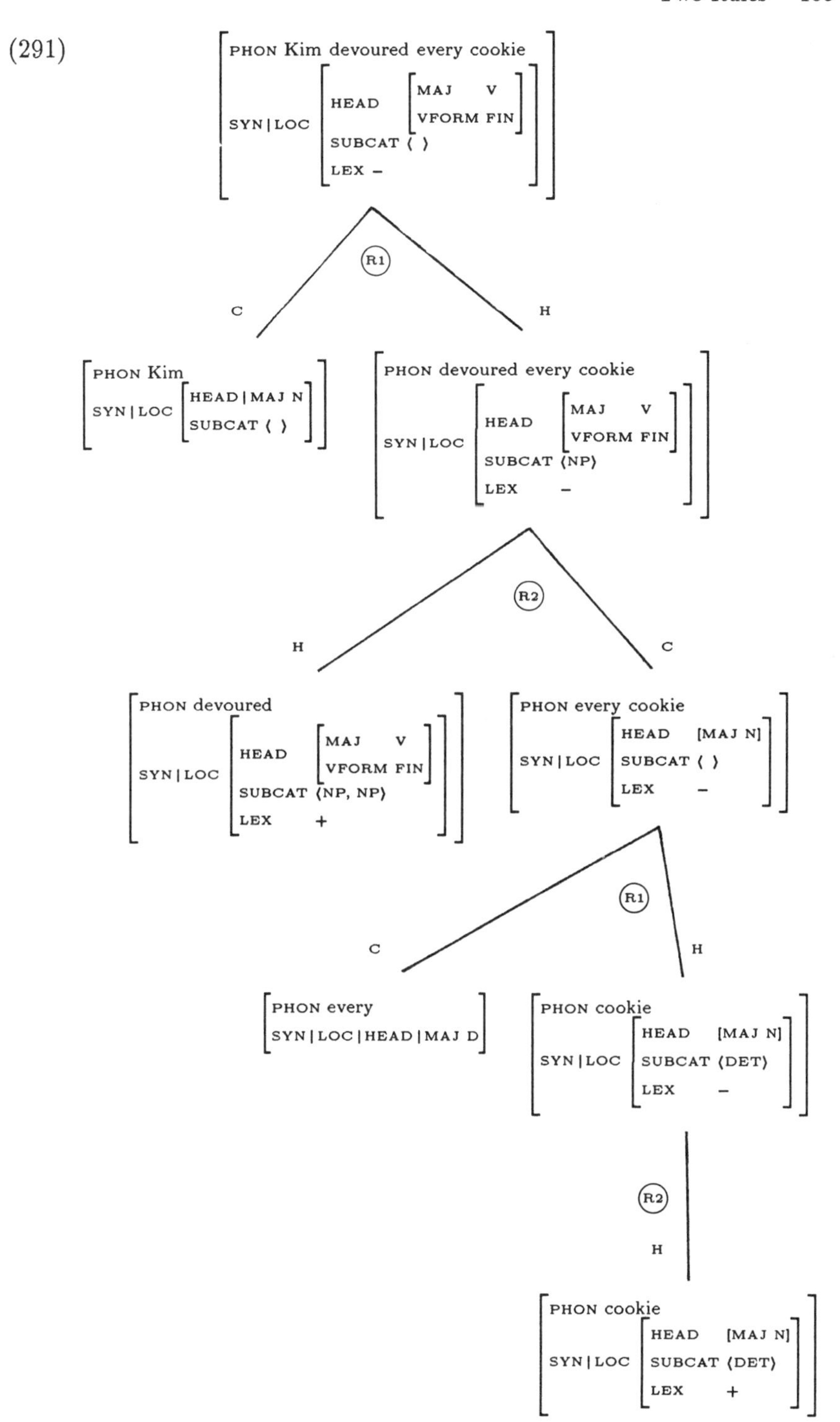
PHON Kim devoured every cookie
SYN | LOC
HEAD
MAJ V
VFORM FIN
SUBCAT ⟨ ⟩
LEX –
R1
C
H
PHON Kim
SYN | LOC
HEAD | MAJ N
SUBCAT ⟨ ⟩
PHON devoured every cookie
SYN | LOC
HEAD
MAJ V
VFORM FIN
SUBCAT ⟨NP⟩
LEX –
R2
H
C
PHON devoured
SYN | LOC
HEAD
MAJ V
VFORM FIN
SUBCAT ⟨NP, NP⟩
LEX +
PHON every cookie
SYN | LOC
HEAD [MAJ N]
SUBCAT ⟨ ⟩
LEX –
R1
C
H
PHON every
SYN | LOC | HEAD | MAJ D
PHON cookie
SYN | LOC
HEAD [MAJ N]
SUBCAT ⟨DET⟩
LEX –
R2
H
PHON cookie
SYN | LOC
HEAD [MAJ N]
SUBCAT ⟨DET⟩
LEX +

(292)

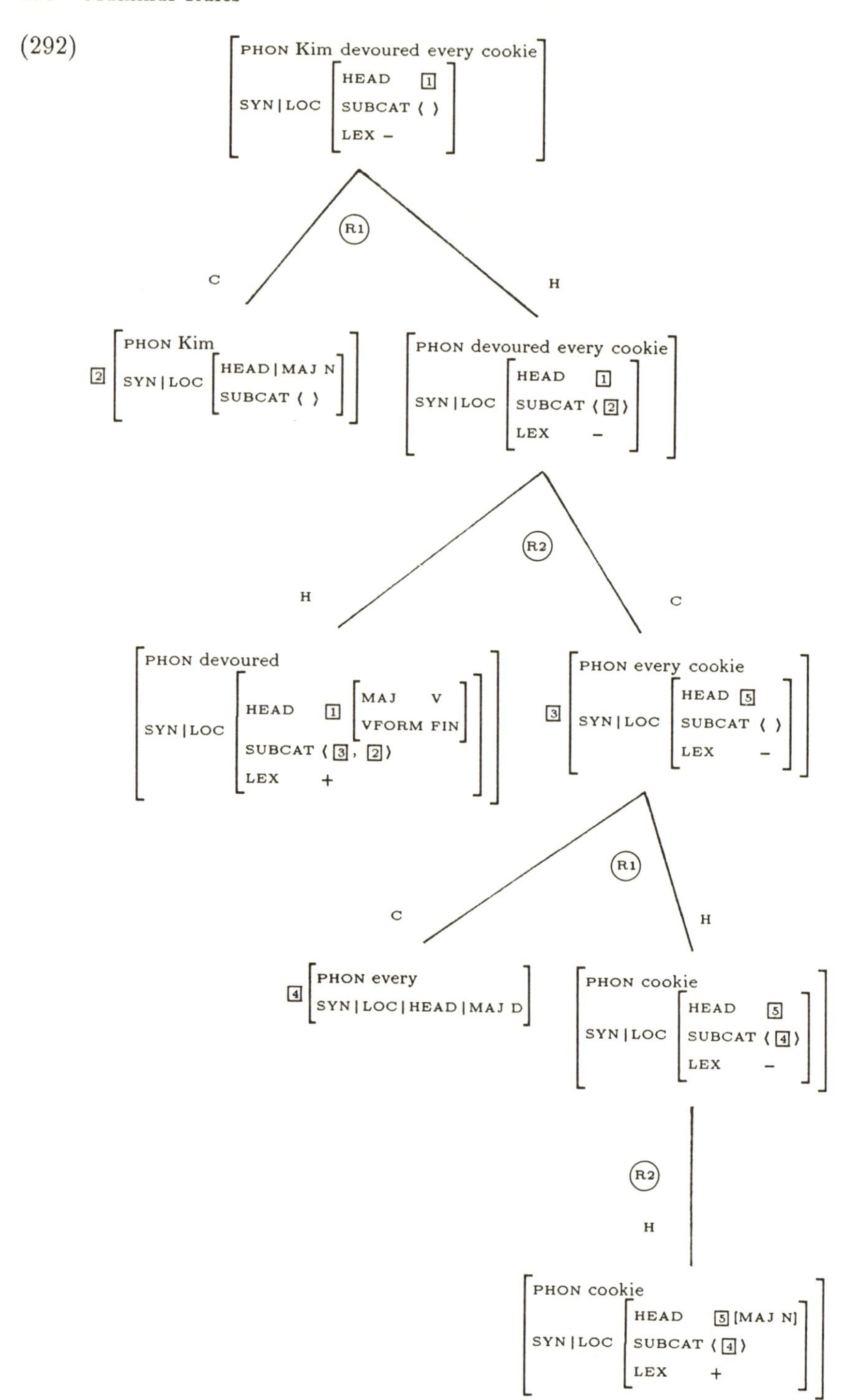
PHON Kim devoured every cookie
SYN | LOC
HEAD 1
SUBCAT ⟨ ⟩
LEX –
R1
C
H
2
PHON Kim
SYN | LOC
HEAD | MAJ N
SUBCAT ⟨ ⟩
PHON devoured every cookie
SYN | LOC
HEAD 1
SUBCAT ⟨ 2 ⟩
LEX –
R2
H
C
PHON devoured
SYN | LOC
HEAD 1
MAJ V
VFORM FIN
SUBCAT ⟨ 3, 2 ⟩
LEX +
3
PHON every cookie
SYN | LOC
HEAD 5
SUBCAT ⟨ ⟩
LEX –
R1
C
H
4
PHON every
SYN | LOC | HEAD | MAJ D
PHON cookie
SYN | LOC
HEAD 5
SUBCAT ⟨ 4 ⟩
LEX –
R2
H
PHON cookie
SYN | LOC
HEAD 5 [MAJ N]
SUBCAT ⟨ 4 ⟩
LEX +

(293)

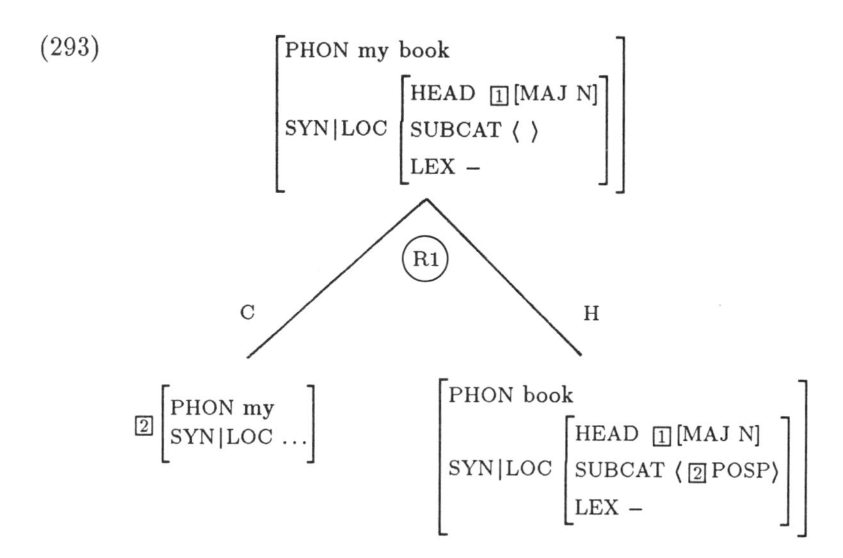

(294)

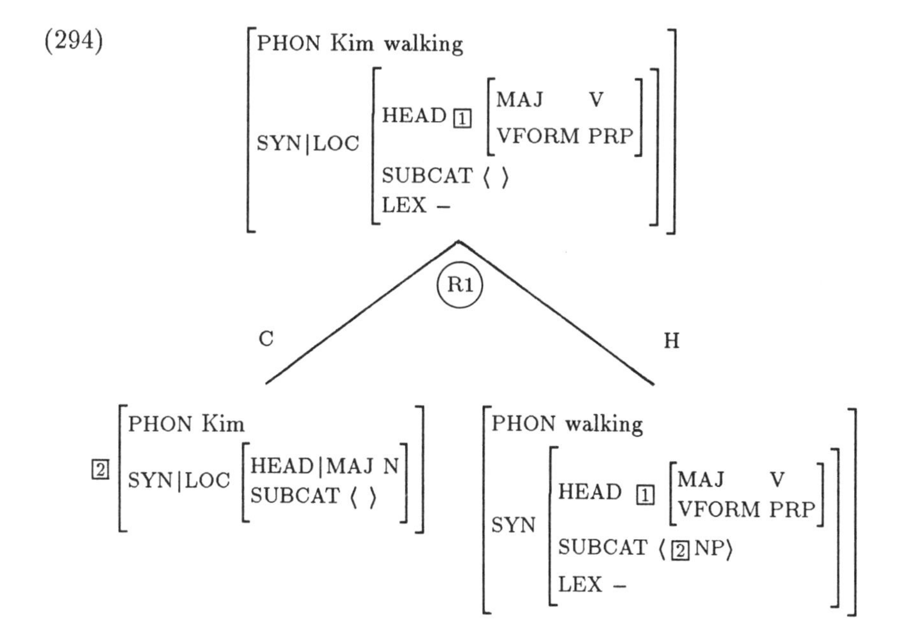

Small clauses like the one in (294) occur as predicative adjunct clauses (either marked by *with* or *not*), as in (295):

(295) With Kim walking, we can throw away the crutches.

6.2 Inverted Structures

Inverted clauses in standard varieties of English occur in a number of different main (or "root") clause construction types, some of which are illustrated in (296).[2]

(296) a. Is Dana walking to the store? (Polar ("yes-no") question)
b. Whose brother will Lou visit __?(Constituent ("Wh") question)
c. Never have I seen a taller tree. ("Negative Adverb Preposing")
d. Did she ever ace the test! (Exclamation)

The verbs that introduce such clauses, as noted in Chapter 3, are all compatible with the specification [INV +]. In fact, all invertible verbs in English (as opposed to other Germanic languages) are also specified as [AUX +].

To allow for this clause type, we posit the grammar rule given in its official form in (297) and in unofficial rewrite notation in (298).

(297) Rule 3

$$\begin{bmatrix} \text{SYN|LOC|SUBCAT}\ \langle\ \rangle \\ \text{DTRS|HEAD-DTR|SYN|LOC} \begin{bmatrix} \text{HEAD|INV}\ + \\ \text{LEX}\ + \end{bmatrix} \end{bmatrix}$$

(298) $[\text{SUBCAT}\ \langle\ \rangle] \rightarrow \text{H}[\text{INV}\ +, \text{LEX}\ +], \text{C}^*$

In virtue of the HFP, the Subcategorization Principle, the English Constituent Ordering Principle, the fact that every lexical sign specified as [INV +] is a finite auxiliary verb, and the fact that auxiliary verbs always have SUBCAT lists of length 2, it follows that inverted phrasal signs will also be subsumed by the more specified version of Rule 3 shown in (299):

(299)

$$\begin{bmatrix} \text{PHON}\ \langle \boxed{4}, \boxed{5}, \boxed{6} \rangle \\ \text{SYN|LOC} \begin{bmatrix} \text{HEAD} & \boxed{1} \\ \text{SUBCAT} & \langle\ \rangle \\ \text{LEX} & - \end{bmatrix} \\ \text{DTRS} \begin{bmatrix} \text{HEAD-DTR} \begin{bmatrix} \text{PHON}\ \boxed{4} \\ \text{SYN|LOC} \begin{bmatrix} \text{HEAD} & \boxed{1} \begin{bmatrix} \text{MAJ V} \\ \text{VFORM FIN} \\ \text{INV}\ + \\ \text{AUX}\ + \end{bmatrix} \\ \text{SUBCAT} & \langle \boxed{2}, \boxed{3} \rangle \\ \text{LEX} & + \end{bmatrix} \end{bmatrix} \\ \text{COMP-DTRS}\ \langle \boxed{2}[\text{PHON}\ \boxed{6}], \boxed{3}[\text{PHON}\ \boxed{5}] \rangle \end{bmatrix} \end{bmatrix}$$

---

[2] There are non-standard varieties of English where inverted clauses appear as embedded polar interrogatives as well, e.g. *I asked did he go* as a variant of *I asked if he went* or *I asked whether he went*.

Thus Rule 3, taken together with universal principles and independently motivated English-specific constraints on constituent ordering, allows for inverted clauses of the sort sketched in (300):

(300)

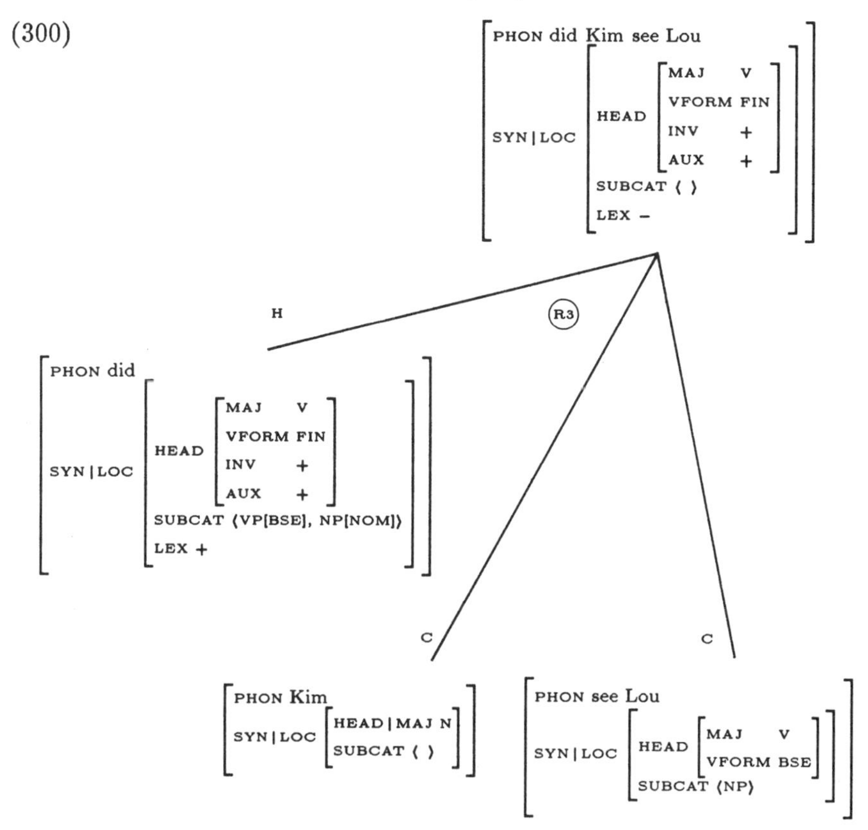

Since INV is a head feature, the specification [INV +] is inherited by clauses projected from [INV +] lexical heads. If we assume that verbs which take sentential complements subcategorize for S[INV –], we can then account for the fact that inverted clauses in standard English are always root clauses.

6.3 The Syntax of Adjuncts

The three rules presented so far account for a significant fragment of English, viz. structures in which every constituent is either a head or a complement. But not all constituents are heads or complements; two important classes of cases include filler daughters in *head-filler structures* (treated in Volume 2), such as "topicalized" phrases and "dislocated" wh-phrases in constituent questions and relative clauses; and conjunct daughters in coordinate structures (also treated in Volume 2). The residue consists for the most part of *adjuncts* (see Section 5.7 above), such as relative-clause, adjectival, and postnominal-predicative (so-called "reduced relative") modifiers of nouns; adverbial modifiers of adjectives, and various kinds of adjuncts to verbs (or verb phrases) and sentences.

In HPSG theory, as in linguistic theory at large, the analysis of adjuncts is at a very primitive stage. Indeed, it is difficult to come up with a natural characterization of the notion adjunct, other than the purely negative one which subsumes all constituents that do not fit any of the other well-defined daughter types (head, complement, filler, or conjunct). A rough approximation is that an adjunct daughter in a phrase is one which is *loosely* dependent upon the head in the senses that: (i) the syntactic categories of the adjunct and the head are mutually constraining (e.g. a relative clause cannot modify a verb phrase, nor an adverb a noun); and (ii) the contribution of the adjunct to the semantic content of the whole phrase is other than the filling of some role in the relation contributed by the head. This should be seen in contrast with the tighter kind of dependence relation that holds between a complement and the head that subcategorizes for it; for a partial and informal inventory of the differences, see Section 5.6.

Among the basic questions that arise in conjunction with the syntactic analysis of adjuncts are the following. How should we characterize adjunct selection? Do heads select for adjuncts or vice versa? What principles determine whether adjuncts precede or follow their heads? Can adjuncts be sisters of complements? How should the introduction of adjuncts be treated by rules of grammar? How are "extraposed" modifiers to be analyzed? We will not pretend to answer any of these questions here; instead, we will merely try to refine some of the questions and suggest some directions for further study.

Adjunct selection is syntactically different from complement selection in at least two respects. First, the class of signs that a given category of adjuncts (e.g. relative clauses, adjectives, manner adverbials, etc.) can modify is much broader than the class of signs that selects a given category of complements. Thus, generally speaking, a relative clause can modify any common noun and a locative adjunct can modify any verb;[3] but only certain nouns (e.g. *reliance*) subcategorize for a PP[ON] complement and only certain verbs (e.g. modal auxiliaries) subcategorize for a VP[BSE] xcomp. And second, while a complement daughter discharges, or cancels, the subcategorization requirement that it matches, an adjunct does not: for a given head there can be at most one PP[ON] complement or at most one VP[BSE] xcomp, but there can be arbitrarily many relative clauses or locative adjuncts. How should such differences be captured within our theory?

One possible approach is to assume that the dependency between a type of adjunct and a type of head is determined not by specification on

---

[3] Of course, the result may be semantically anomalous: e.g. *the eggplant that ate Chicago, two equals three in Tuscon.*

either the head or the adjunct itself, but rather by means of a grammar rule. On such an approach, a common noun does not contain the information that it is compatible with a relative clause modifier, nor does a relative clause contain the information that it can modify a common noun; but instead, we assume that the grammar contains a rule that in some way combines nouns and relative clauses. In order to formulate such a rule, let us first suppose that the constituent-structure type *headed-structure* has a subtype *head-adjunct-structure* with attributes HEAD-DAUGHTER, COMPLEMENT-DAUGHTERS, and ADJUNCT-DAUGHTER; let us also assume that this subtype requires the value ⟨ ⟩ (the empty list) for the attribute COMPLEMENT-DAUGHTERS.[4] Then our rule for relative clauses might take roughly the form (301):

(301)
$$\left[\text{DTRS}\left[\begin{array}{ll}\text{HEAD-DTR}\mid\text{SYN}\mid\text{LOC} & \left[\begin{array}{ll}\text{HEAD} & \left[\begin{array}{ll}\text{MAJ} & \text{N}\\ \text{NFORM} & \text{NORM}\end{array}\right]\\ \text{LEX} & -\end{array}\right]\\ \text{ADJ-DTR}\mid\text{SYN RELCLAUSE} & \end{array}\right]\right]$$

where RELCLAUSE abbreviates whatever official analysis we adopt for the category of relative clauses (see Volume 2).[5] As stated, this rule allows for the attachment of relative clauses to either NP's or common noun phrases ($\overline{\text{N}}$'s); the specification [NFORM NORM] prevents the head noun from being an expletive pronoun (*it* or *there*). This rule allows for structures such as (302):

---

[4] Thus, we are assuming that (i) adjuncts are never sisters to complements, and (ii) at most one adjunct can be sister to the same head. This is for specificity only; we hold no brief for these particular assumptions. In fact, we will call both of these assumptions into question below; to replace the second assumption with its denial, simply assume that the type *head-adjunct-structure* bears an attribute ADJUNCT-DAUGHTERS (not ADJUNCT-DAUGHTER), whose value is a nonempty set of signs. To achieve greater generality, we assume that head-adjunct structures actually have a COMPLEMENT-DAUGHTERS attribute with value ⟨ ⟩ (instead of assuming that they simply lack the attribute COMPLEMENT-DAUGHTERS): this way the Subcategorization Principle extends without revision to head-adjunct structures, simply passing the SUBCAT value of the head up to the mother.

[5] This rule incorporates the conventional assumption that adjuncts attach to phrasal, not lexical, heads. We will question this assumption below when we consider the possibility of adjuncts and complements which are sisters of the same (possibly lexical) head. Discussion of the semantics of relative clauses is postponed until Volume 2; roughly, the relative clause makes an additional contribution to the RESTRICTION attribute in the semantic content of the noun. Nothing is said about surface order of the daughters; as with other rules, we suppose that order is taken care of by the language-specific constituent ordering principles, e.g. LP constraints (Chapter 7).

(302)

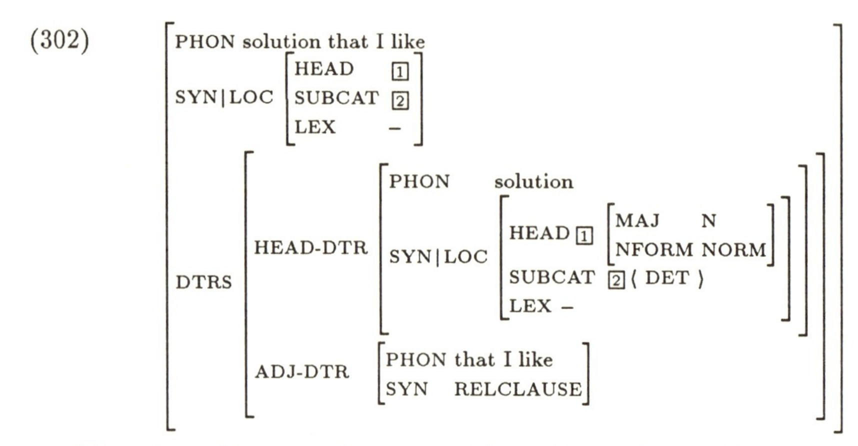

There is nothing exactly wrong with positing rules of this kind; however, if the full range of acceptable head-adjunct pairings is to be accounted for, a very large number of structurally similar additional rules will be needed. It would be more in the spirit of our enterprise to introduce a single highly schematic head-adjunct rule and leave the matter of compatibility to a certain unification stated within the rule, requiring one of the daughters to be consistent with some selectional requirement on the other. But who is selecting for whom? Do relative clauses specify that they can modify nouns, or do nouns specify that they can be modified by relative clauses?

At first blush, the former approach may seem attractive, for it is consistent with the conventional wisdom that in head-adjunct structures (unlike head-complement structures) the head is the "argument", not the "functor". Unfortunately, it is very difficult to formalize this intuition within HPSG (or any other formal syntactic-semantic theory, for that matter). Roughly, we would like there to be a syntactic feature—let us call it MODIFIED-HEAD—such that, for any sign which could function as an adjunct, the value of that attribute for that sign would be a specification of the kind of head that the the sign in question could modify; e.g. any relative clause would bear the specification (303):

(303) [SYN|LOC|MOD-HEAD|SYN|LOC [MAJ N, NFORM NORM]]

But it is far from clear how this can be arranged, short of introducing large numbers of ad hoc language-specific constraints such as (304):

(304) [SYN RELCLAUSE] ⇒

[SYN|LOC|MOD-HEAD|SYN|LOC [MAJ N, NFORM NORM]]

The alternative approach, letting modified heads select their adjuncts, appears to be more promising. The reason for this is that the class of signs that can be modified by a given adjunct can typically be characterized as a class of phrasal projections of some lexical category; e.g. relative clauses modify projections of the category [MAJ N, NFORM NORM, LEX +]; manner adverbials modify projections of the category [MAJ V, LEX +]; etc. Consequently, if we posit a set-of-categories-valued feature ADJUNCTS, whose value specifies the categories of adjuncts that can modify projections of a given lexical head, that value will be passed up to phrasal projections of that head *as long as we assume that* ADJUNCTS *is a head feature.*

Let us attempt a more specific formulation along these lines. First, we assume that each lexical sign specifies a value (some finite set of syntactic categories) for the head feature ADJUNCTS. For example, we assume that every lexical common noun bears the specification [SYNTAX|LOCAL|HEAD|ADJUNCTS {RELCLAUSE,...}].[6] Next, we posit the highly schematic head-adjunct rule (305):

(305) Rule 4

$$\left[\text{DTRS}\left[\begin{array}{ll}\text{HEAD-DTR|SYN|LOC} & \left[\begin{array}{l}\text{HEAD|ADJUNCTS } \{\ldots,\boxed{1},\ldots\}\\ \text{LEX } -\end{array}\right]\\ \text{ADJ-DTR|SYN } \boxed{1} & \end{array}\right]\right]$$

The basic idea here is that an adjunct daughter in a head-adjunct structure is sanctioned as long as its SYNTAX unifies with one of the members of the ADJUNCTS value-set on the head daughter, which in turn is inherited from the head-daughter's lexical head by virtue of the HFP. Thus the proliferation of special-purpose head-adjunct rules (such as (301) above) is avoided, while compatibility between heads and adjuncts is maintained; example (302) is then produced with the structure (306) below.

And under the assumption that verbs include a specification for adverbial phrases in their ADJUNCTS value-set, the same grammar rule gives rise to nested VP structures as shown in (306).

---

[6] It may appear that this move introduces massive redundancy into the grammar, inasmuch as, e.g. every single lexical common noun will have to be individually specified as [SYN|LOC|HEAD|ADJUNCTS {RELCLAUSE, ...}]. However, in Chapter 8 we will show that, by representing the lexicon as an inheritance hierarchy of types, such stipulations need be made only once in the grammar (at the appropriate node of the lexical hierarchy); they are then inherited by all lexical signs which instantiate the type which bears the stipulation in question.

(306)
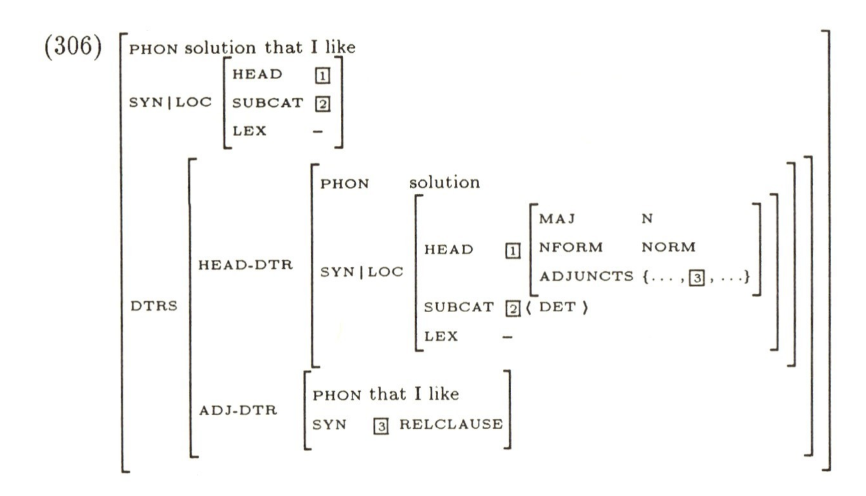

(307)
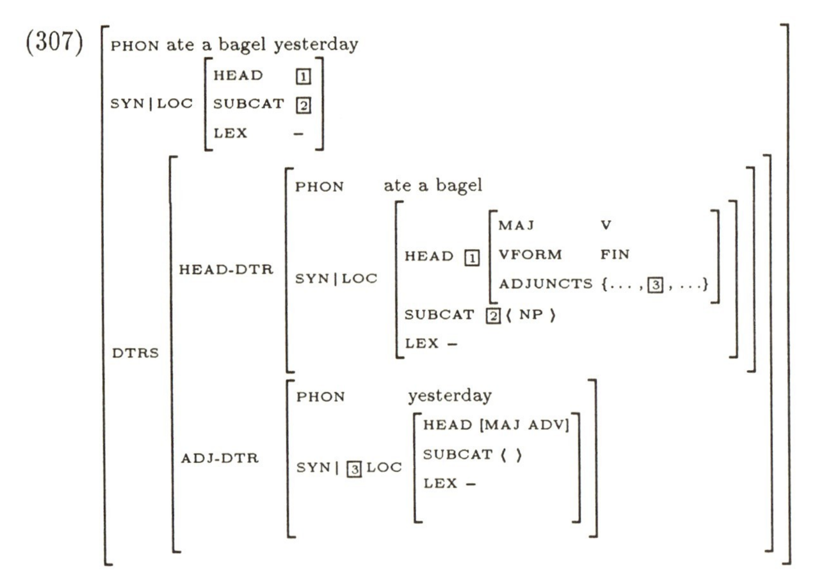

Note that, unlike the situation with complement daughters (which unify *qua* signs with members of the SUBCAT value-list on the head daughter), only the SYNTAX of the adjunct daughter unifies with a category in the ADJUNCTS value-set on the head daughter. This is because, unlike complements, adjuncts of the same kind can *iterate*; e.g. two or more relative clauses may modify the same head, as in (308) below (the label "A" on tree branches is mnemonic for ADJUNCT-DAUGHTER).

In such cases two distinct constituents have their SYNTAX values unified with the same category in the head's ADJUNCTS value-set. If we had insisted on unifying with a whole sign specification, then unification would generally fail in such cases, since the distinct adjunct constituents would differ in their phonology, semantics, and constituent structure.

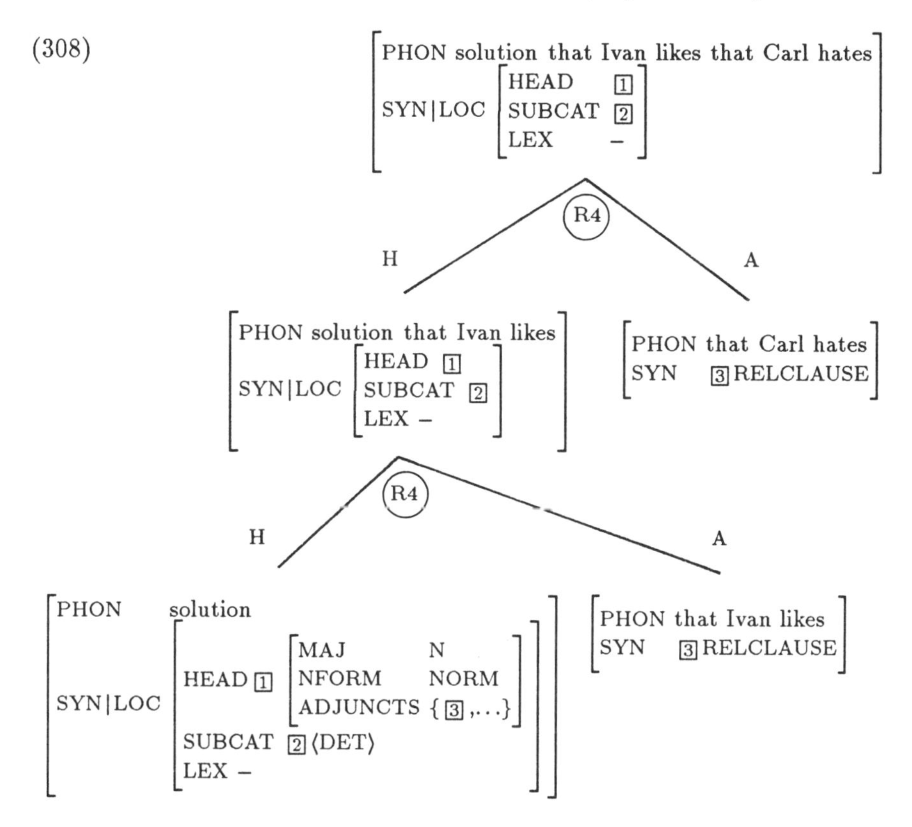

A major technical problem remains to be solved before the formulation of a rule such as (305) can be formalized within HPSG. This has to do with the notation {... , 1, ...} that appears in (305). Intuitively, the intention of the notation is clear: the value of the path DTRS|ADJUNCT-DTR must unify with one of the members of the value-set of the path DTRS |HEAD-DTR|SYN|LOC|HEAD|ADJUNCTS. Unfortunately constraints of this kind, which require that some *relational* dependency (in the present case, set membership) hold among the values of two or more paths in a feature structure, are beyond the expressive power of the HPSG formal apparatus; thus, a major augmentation of the formalism would be required whose mathematical and computational consequences are poorly understood.[7]

[7] As formulated in Chapter 2, our formal apparatus allows only *functional* dependencies, whereby the value of some path is constrained to be a function (usually some simple operation on finite lists or sets) of the values of certain other paths. The augmentation required seems similar in character to the *conditioned unification* proposed by Hasida (1985), wherein structures to be unified contain variables which are subject to side conditions.

As noted above, the foregoing analysis incorporates the assumptions that only a single adjunct daughter can be sister to a given head, that adjuncts modify only phrasal heads, and that adjuncts never have complement sisters. But these assumptions are by no means universally accepted, and alternative analyses can be expressed within the theory. For example, we might reformulate Rule 4 so as to permit one or more adjunct sisters to the same head. To do this, we first replace the attribute ADJUNCT-DAUGHTER in head-adjunct structures with a nonempty-set-valued attribute ADJUNCT-DAUGHTERS; in addition, the relational dependency in Rule 4 (requiring that the category of the adjunct daughter match one of the categories in the ADJUNCTS value-set on the head) must be replaced with a more complex relational dependency between the ADJUNCT-DAUGHTERS value-set and the head's ADJUNCTS value-set (requiring that the category of each member of the former unify with a member of the latter). Again, the formulation of such a dependency is beyond the expressive power of our formalism; for the time being we simply state it as an informal "side condition". The revised rule is given in (309):

(309) Rule 4′

[DTRS [HEAD-DTR|SYN|LOC|HEAD|ADJUNCTS [1]
ADJUNCTS-DTRS [2]]]

CONDITION: ∀X ∈ [2] ∃Y ∈ [1] such that SYNTAX(X) = Y

This revised rule gives rise to multiply-branching head-adjunct structures such as (310):

(310)

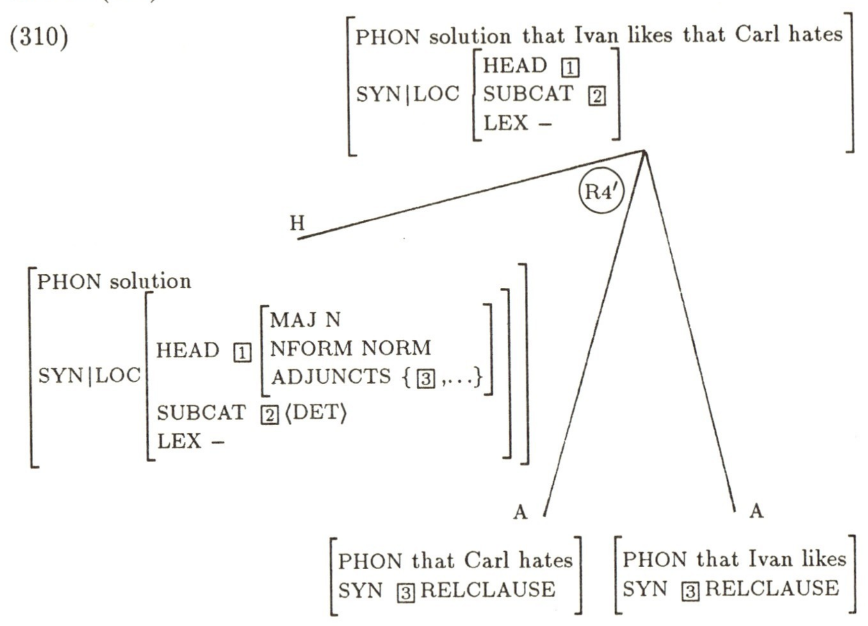

In fact, it is obvious that Rule 4′ produces the binary-branching analysis (308) as well as the ternary-branching analysis (310); therefore in choosing between the two formulations, one must consider the question of whether or not such purely structural ambiguities (which seem to lack any clear semantic motivation) are theoretically desirable. We withhold judgment on this question.

There are additional facts about adjuncts that are not treated by either of these proposals. In particular, adjuncts are sometimes interspersed among complements, as in example (311).

(311) Sandy proved to her class yesterday that the Axiom of Infinity is inconsistent.

The most natural approach to examples like this is to allow adjunct daughters to be introduced as sisters to complements in Rule 2 (or, more generally, in head-complement rules). This amounts to little more than saying that objects of the type *head-complement structure* bear the additional attribute ADJUNCT-DAUGHTERS. Because more than one adjunct may appear within such structures, ADJUNCT-DAUGHTERS takes a (possibly empty) set of signs as its value. Structures licensed by Rule 2 will then have the general shape of (312).

(312)

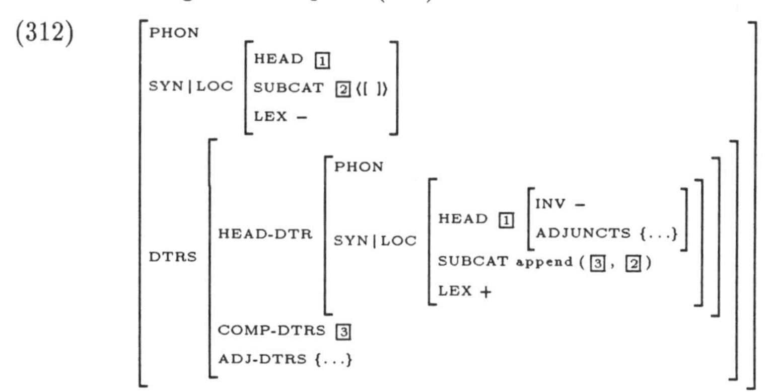

The surface ordering of adjuncts with respect to complements is then treated by LP rules which are presented in greater detail in Chapter 7. Allowing adjuncts within head-complement structures *in addition to* positing a rule like Rule 4, of course, will result in multiple analyses for unambiguous sentences like *Kim ate a bagel yesterday.* The consequences of this fact, which is also entailed by most other theories of adjuncts, remain unclear; perhaps Rule 4 should be eliminated, or its range of applicability substantially reduced.

Any analysis along these lines must, of course, provide some mechanism for ensuring that the adjuncts introduced within a given head-complement structure are of the appropriate kind. In the rule given in (309) above, the desired result was achieved via a certain rule-specific relational dependency. Evidently, precisely the same relational dependency must obtain in any structure where an adjunct daughter is introduced, no matter what rule subsumes that structure. This suggests that the relational dependency should be factored out of individual rules (including Rule 4) and stated as an independent, universal Adjuncts Principle. Thus, by eliminating the "side condition", we simplify Rule 4 to the form (313):

(313) Rule 4 (final version)

$$[\text{DTRS}\ _{\textit{head-adjunct-structure}}[\ ]]$$

This simply says that one option for a sign is that its constituent structure be a head-adjunct structure. We then add (314) to our inventory of universal principles.

(314) Adjuncts Principle (preliminary formulation)

$$_{\textit{constituent-structure}}[\ ] \Rightarrow \begin{bmatrix} \text{HEAD-DTR}|\text{SYN}|\text{LOC}|\text{HEAD}|\text{ADJUNCTS}\ \boxed{1} \\ \text{ADJ-DTRS}\ \boxed{2} \end{bmatrix}$$

CONDITION: $\forall X \in \boxed{2}\ \exists Y \in \boxed{1}$ such that SYNTAX(X) = Y

The effect of (314) is to guarantee that the category of *any* adjunct daughter must be unified with *some* member of the head daughter's SYNTAX|LOCAL|HEAD|ADJUNCTS value-set. In other words, each adjunct must be one of the kinds of adjuncts selected for by the head daughter.

The final issue related to adjuncts that we will address is the analysis of extraposed adjuncts of the sort illustrated in (315), which are not adjacent to the phrases which they are intuitively felt to modify:

(315) a. I met a Swede yesterday that I really liked.
b. A book arrived yesterday that I was expecting.

To accommodate such structures, we revise the Adjuncts Principle to allow adjuncts to be 'licensed' by *either* the head or by a NP complement:

(316) Adjuncts Principle (final formulation)

$$_{\textit{constituent-structure}}[\ ] \Rightarrow \begin{bmatrix} \text{HEAD-DTR}|\text{SYN}|\text{LOC}|\text{HEAD}|\text{ADJUNCTS}\ \boxed{1} \\ \text{COMP-DTRS}\ \boxed{3} \\ \text{ADJ-DTRS}\ \boxed{2} \end{bmatrix}$$

CONDITION: $\forall X \in \boxed{2}\ \exists Y \in \boxed{1}$ such that
SYNTAX(X) = Y or
$\exists Z \in \boxed{3}\ \exists Y \in$ SYN|LOC|HEAD|ADJUNCTS(Z) such that
SYNTAX(X) = Y and SYN|LOC|HEAD|MAJ (Z) = N

Principle (316) will allow VP signs like the one in (315), where each adjunct is licensed by either the verbal head or the NP complement.

(317)
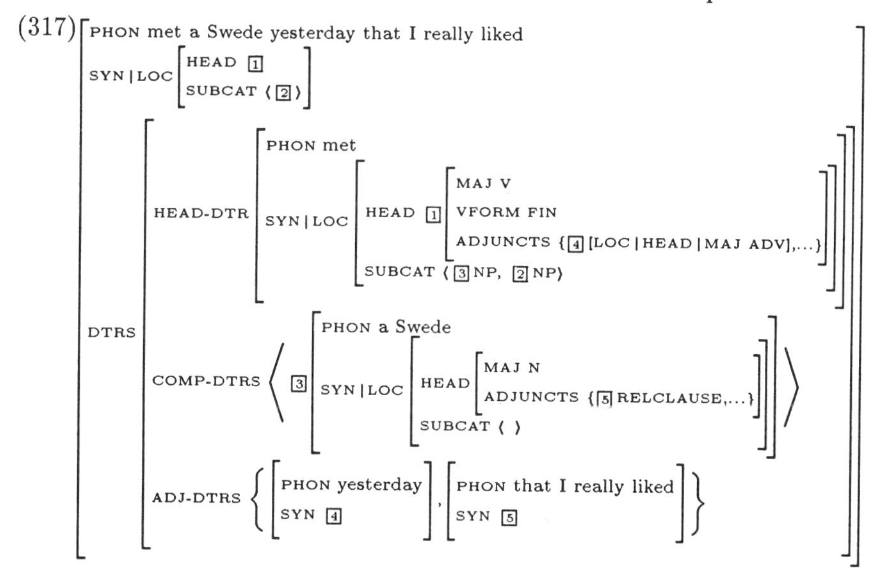

Again, the linear order of the sister constituents is fixed by LP rules described in Chapter 7. And the extraposed relative clause in (315b) is also grammatical, for it is licensed by the NP subject complement, as shown in (318).

(318)
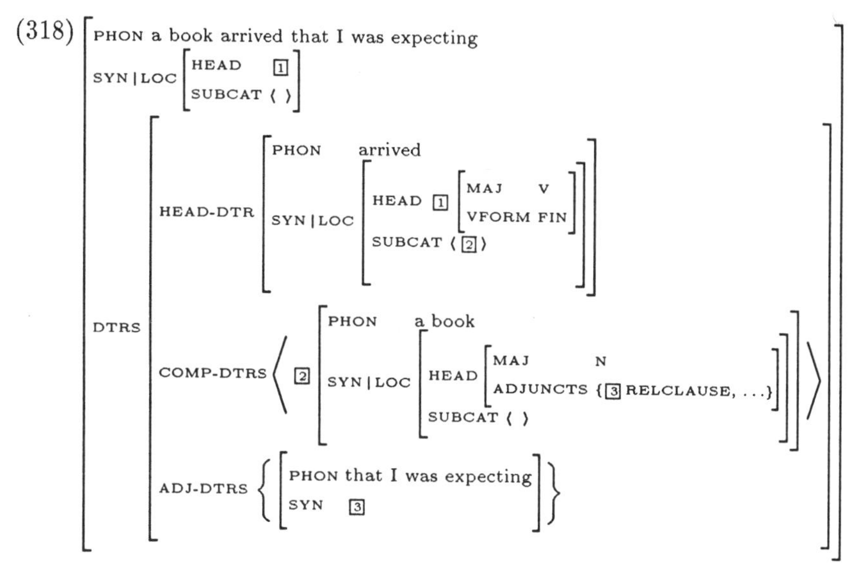

There are two important consequences of this analysis of extraposed adjunct phrases. First, an extraposed phrase associated with an object complement is necessarily contained within the VP, whereas if such a phrase is associated with a subject complement, then it must be 'outside' the VP, i.e. a daughter of S. This is so because ADJUNCTS is a head feature, and is therefore specified on the maximal phrase the licensing word projects (by the HFP), but on no superordinate phrase. Hence the Adjuncts Principle ensures that an NP complement can license an adjunct only if it is a sister to it. Baltin (1978) argues at length that this is exactly the right prediction for the constituent structure of extraposed phrases.

A second consequence, related to the first, is that the licensing NP cannot be located within an embedded clause. Thus examples like (319) are ill-formed.

(319) *[That a book arrived] was exciting that I was expecting.

Examples like this have caused considerable consternation for transformational theories of extraposition, which have been forced to posit *ad hoc* constraints on extraposition rules (e.g. the "Right Roof Constraint" investigated by Ross (1967) and Grosu (1972)). But the ill-formedness of examples like (319), as well as all others where the licensing NP complement is not a sister of the extraposed phrase, follows immediately from the Adjuncts Principle we have proposed.

6.4 Conclusion

In this chapter, we have sketched the basic syntax of headed structures in English. Three (or perhaps four) grammar rules interact with the principles of universal grammar that we have discussed and the English Constituent Ordering Principle (to be discussed in the following chapter) to characterize a wide range of syntactic phenomena, including (possibly extraposed) adjuncts. A striking property of the analyses we have presented here is the simplicity of the grammar rules themselves. This simplicity is achieved in virtue of the essential modularity of the overall theory, whereby information about signs which can be predicted from their lexical heads on the basis of general principles can be factored out of the rules themselves.

6.5 Suggestions for Further Reading

Rules 1–3 were first proposed in their present form (with constituent order information factored out) in Pollard (1985); the highly schematic phrase structure rules of Pollard (1984) are similar, except that they make direct reference to concatenation and head-wrapping operations which determine constituent order. The Head Feature Principle is a reformulation in terms of unification of the Head Feature Convention, first stated explicitly by Gazdar, Pullum, and Sag (1981). The Subcategorization Principle, first stated (in procedural terms) in Pollard (1985), is a generalization of the Subcategorization-Control Principle of Pollard (1984). The Adjuncts Principle was first proposed by Sag (1987).

7 Principles of Constituent Order

Grammar rules in HPSG, as we have seen, specify the syntactic nature of the daughters (immediate constituents) in phrasal signs. However, as we noted in the previous chapter, they do *not* constrain the temporal order in which the phonological realizations of constituents occur in utterances. Rule 1, for example, makes no reference to the fact that the phonological realization of the subject NP always precedes the phonological realization of the VP in utterances of English sentences. It has long been realized that constituent order is not an idiosyncratic property of individual grammar rules. In every human language, there are language-specific constraints upon the linear order of sister constituents which apply to all the signs of the language, and hence are to be factored out of grammar rules. In this chapter we explore some tentative formulations of constraints on constituent order which are valid for English.

The overall structure of the analysis proposed here is as follows. For each language, we assume that there is a Constituent Ordering Principle (COP) specific to that language. To be precise, we should refer not to *the* COP, but rather to COP_{French}, $\text{COP}_{Japanese}$, etc.; but since our discussion here will be limited primarily to English, we write simply "COP" for the English Constituent Ordering Principle. The essential content of the COP is simply that the phonology of a phrasal sign is functionally dependent upon the daughters. That is, the PHONOLOGY value of a phrasal sign is specified as a function, called *order-constituents*, of the sign's DAUGHTERS value, as indicated in (320):

(320) Constituent Order Principle

$$_{phrasal\text{-}sign}[\ ] \Rightarrow \begin{bmatrix} \text{PHON order-constituents}(\boxed{1}) \\ \text{DTRS } \boxed{1} \end{bmatrix}$$

Of course the precise identity of the function order-constituents varies from language to language. (In addition, as we shall see below, for languages which permit various forms of "scrambling" the COP may have to be defined in terms of a function which *interleaves* rather than orders the phonological realizations of constituents.) In general, however, we assume that order-constituents always gives as its value a permutation (or disjunction of permutations) of the PHONOLOGY values of the sign's daughters. A caveat:

considerable oversimplification is involved here, since we are focusing on the problem of getting the ordering right. We are ignoring more subtle prosodic effects; in many languages, account must also be taken of complex morphophonemic effects (e.g. external sandhi in Sanskrit, tone change rules in Chinese, etc.). The important point here is that the PHONOLOGY value of a phrasal sign in general depends not only on the PHONOLOGY values of the daughters, but on other things as well, including their syntactic category, their daughter type, and (in the case of complement daughters) their position in the obliqueness hierarchy given by the ordering of SUBCAT lists.

In principle, the precise statement of the COP requires an explicit definition of the function order-constituents. Since the analysis of English constituent order proposed here is still quite tentative, that course is not open to us. Instead, we will attempt to isolate a number of constraints of a particular kind which have been known in the literature as *linear precedence* (LP) constraints. Informally, an LP constraint is simply a statement that, for any phrase in language L, any daughter with property X necessarily linearly precedes any of its sisters with property Y, written "X < Y"; an example is the LP constraint, stated in (326) below, that a lexical head linearly precedes any of its sisters. We then define order-constituents to be that function whose value is the disjunction of all permutations (of the PHONOLOGY values of the daughters) which are consistent with all of the LP constraints.

7.1 Lexical Heads

We have seen two grammar rules (Rule 2 and Rule 3) that introduce lexical heads. Rule 2 characterizes numerous phrase types (VP's, common noun phrases, PP's and AP's), whereas Rule 3 characterizes inverted finite clauses. In all of these phrase types, the lexical head must be ordered before all of its sister constituents, as illustrated in (321)–(325).

(321)

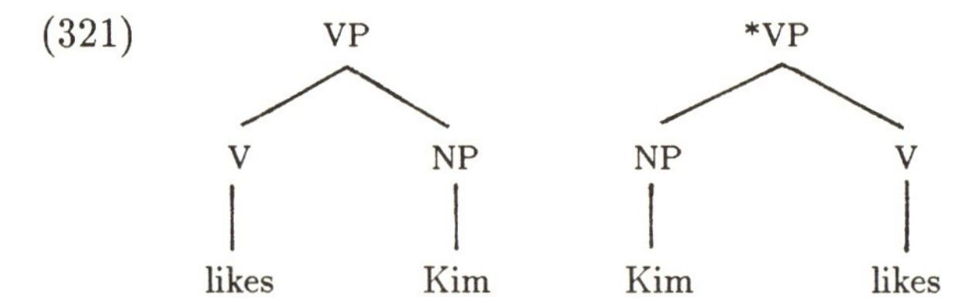

(322)

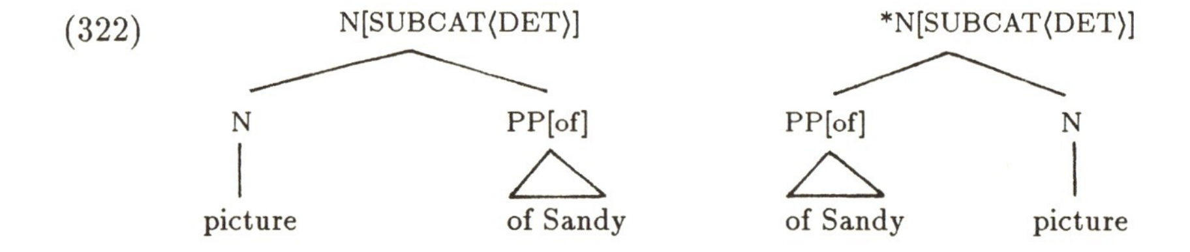

(323)

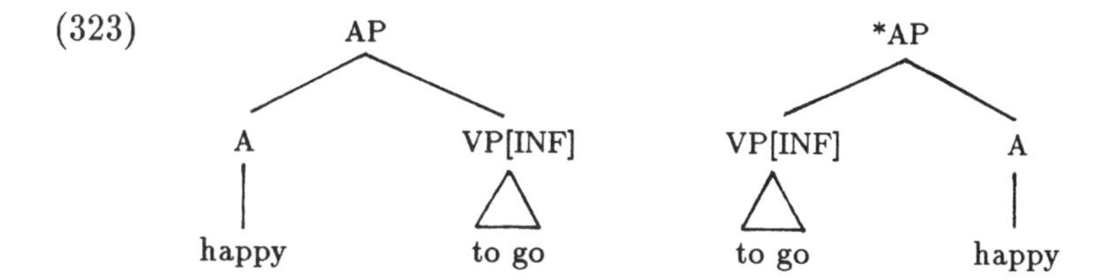

(324)

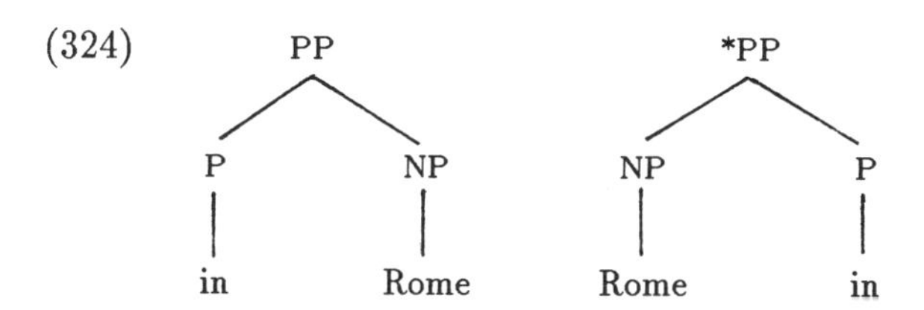

(325)

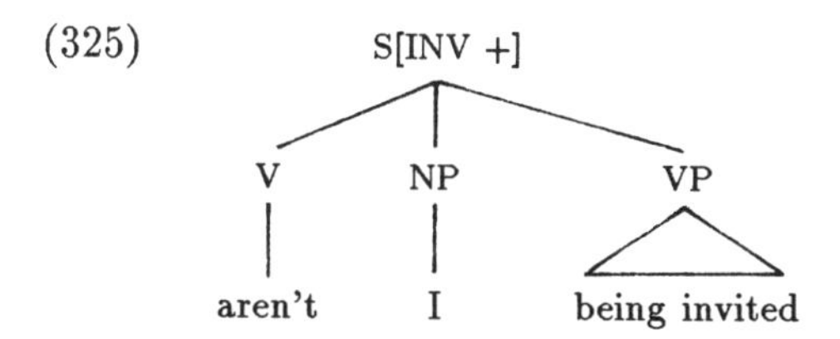

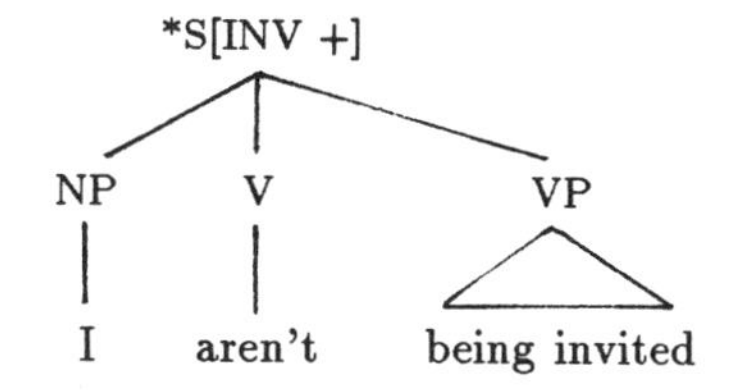

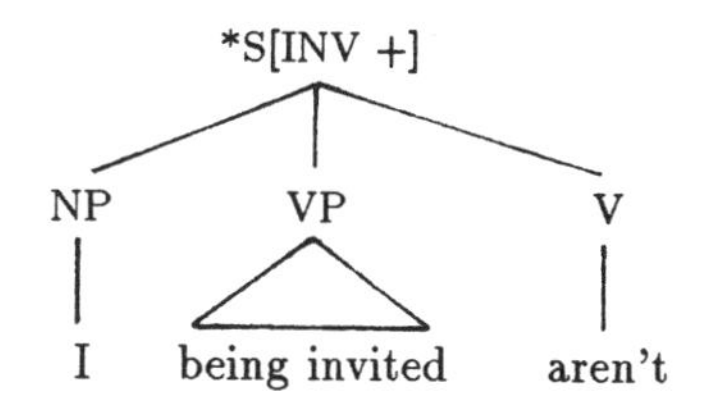

This simple generalization about headed constructions in English is expressed succinctly by the following LP constraint:

(326) Linear Precedence Constraint 1 (LP1)

HEAD[LEX +] < [ ]

LP1 says only that in any phrasal sign of English, (the phonological realization of) a daughter which is a lexical head is constrained to temporally precede (the phonological realization of) *any* of its sisters. In short, lexical heads in English are phrase-initial.

As we noted above, a different function order-constituents is involved in the statement of the COP (320) for each language. Correspondingly, LP constraints vary from from language to language. Thus for languages like Hindi or Japanese, where verbs are final within VP's, nouns are final within common noun phrases or NP's, and where we find postpositions rather than prepositions, the phrasal signs would all be consistent with the LP constraint in (327):

(327) Linear Precedence Constraint for Head-Final Languages:

[ ] < HEAD[LEX +]

Thus languages which are pure head-initial languages (like English) or pure head-final languages (like Japanese or Hindi) require but a single LP constraint to order lexical heads. Other languages of mixed type may require two or more distinct LP rules, each suitably restricted, but otherwise in the form of (326) or (327). For example, a language that was verb-final but otherwise head-initial, (i.e. a language that had prepositions and postnominal complements but exhibited basic Subject-Object-Verb order) would have LP constraints like those in (328):

(328) a. [ ] < HEAD[LEX +, MAJ V]
b. HEAD[LEX +, MAJ N $\vee$ A $\vee$ P] < [ ]

Thus if we take complexity of a system of LP rules seriously as an indication of language complexity (or markedness), then we have the beginning of an explanation for the observations made by Greenberg (1962, 78ff.) that the overwhelming majority of human languages are of one of the two non-intermediate types vis-à-vis ordering of their lexical heads.

7.2 Complement Order

From LP1 it follows that in any phrase with a lexical head and a single complement, the complement must be ordered after the head. But English phrases frequently contain more than one complement, and these often occur in a fixed order. If LP1 were the only LP constraint, of course, then it would follow that sister complements would be freely ordered with respect to each other (in general, absence of LP constraints corresponds to freedom of constituent order). Whereas it might appear that some languages, such as Japanese, work in roughly this fashion (i.e. with heads whose position is fixed and complements whose position is free), English is clearly not such a language. As examples like the following show, there are certain constructions where multiple complements must occur in a prescribed order.

(329)

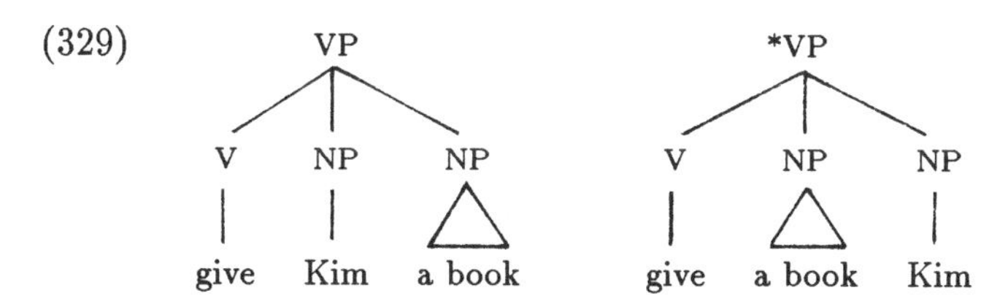

(330)

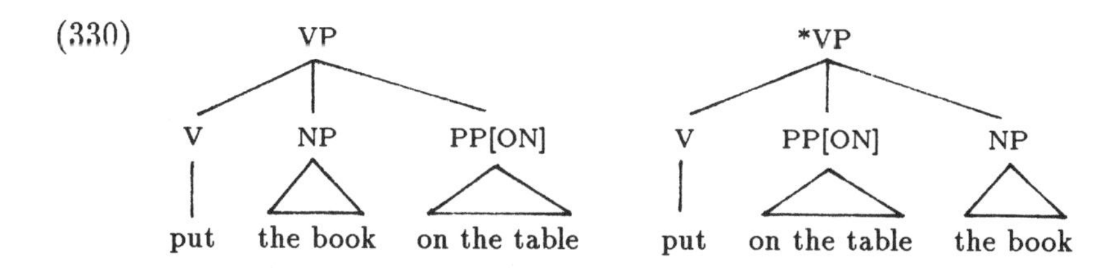

(331)

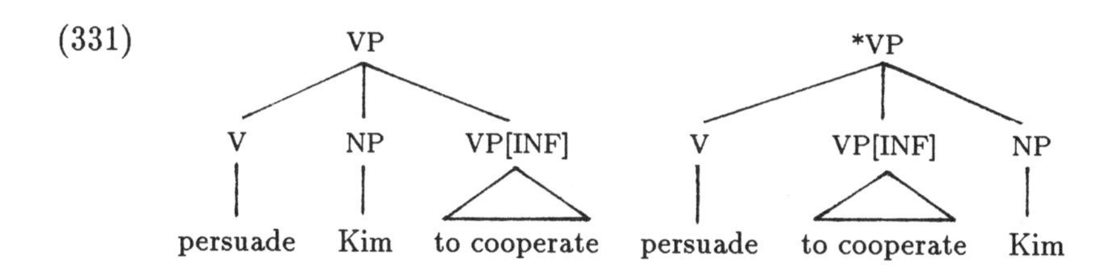

(332)

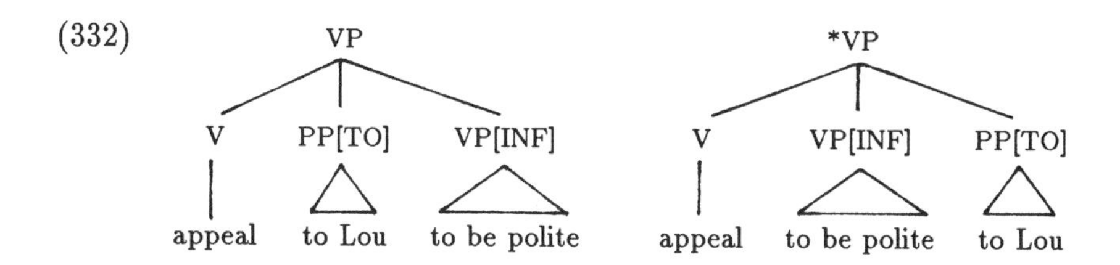

(333)

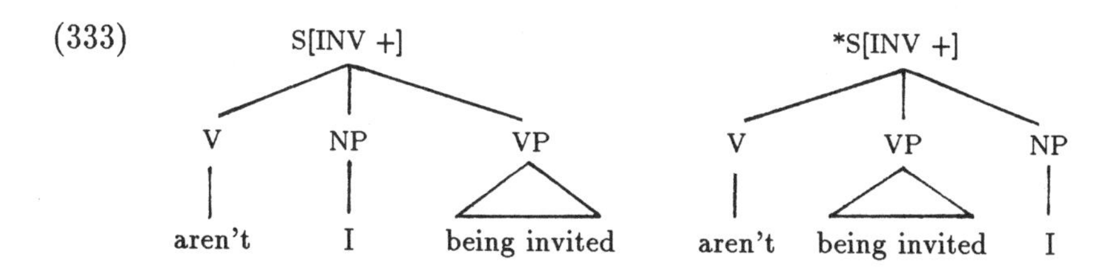

There is a generalization to be expressed about all of these examples: less oblique complements precede more oblique complements, i.e. a complement that corresponds to an element on the lexical head's SUBCAT list must linearly precede complements that correspond to earlier elements on that SUBCAT list. This generalization is expressed in (334):

(334) LP2 (first formulation):

COMPLEMENT ≪ COMPLEMENT

Here the symbol "≪" designates a special kind of restricted linear precedence constraint which has force only in case the left-hand element is less oblique than the right-hand element. The content of (334), then, is that (the phonological realization of) any complement daughter is constrained to temporally precede (the phonological realization of) any of its sisters which is a more oblique complement (in the sense that it occurs further to the left on the head daughter's SUBCAT list, or equivalently, on the mother's COMP-DTRS list). The effect of LP2 can be illustrated by reconsidering the previous examples in terms of the SUBCAT properties of their heads:

(329′)

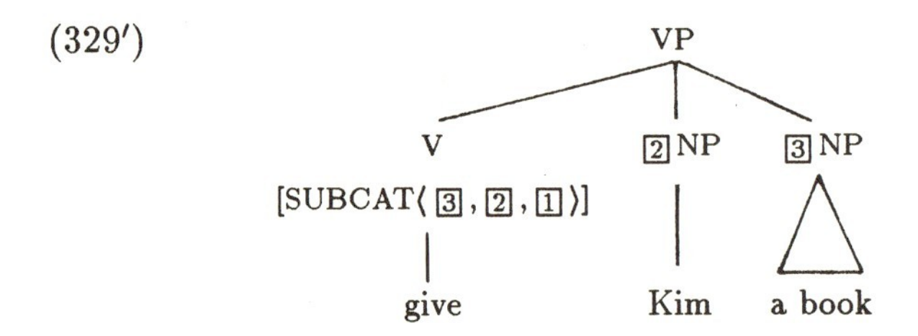

(330′)

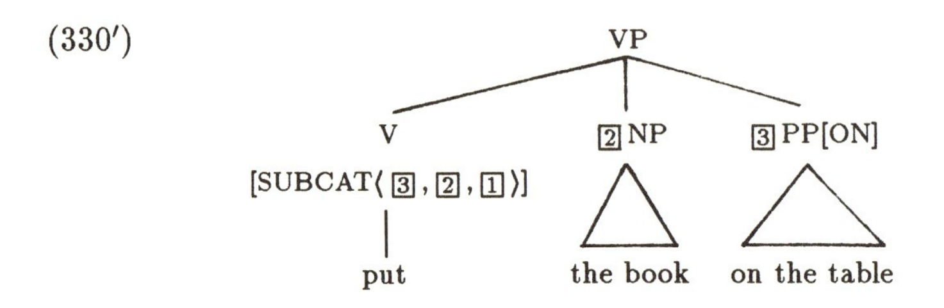

(331′)

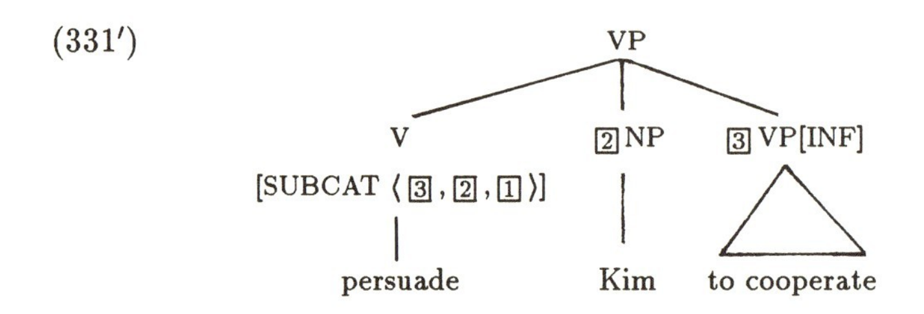

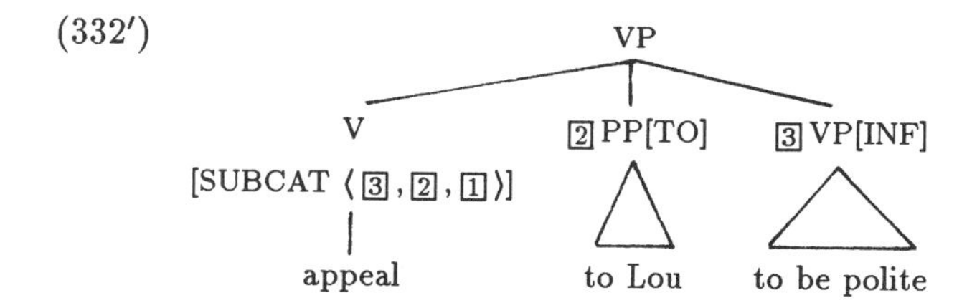

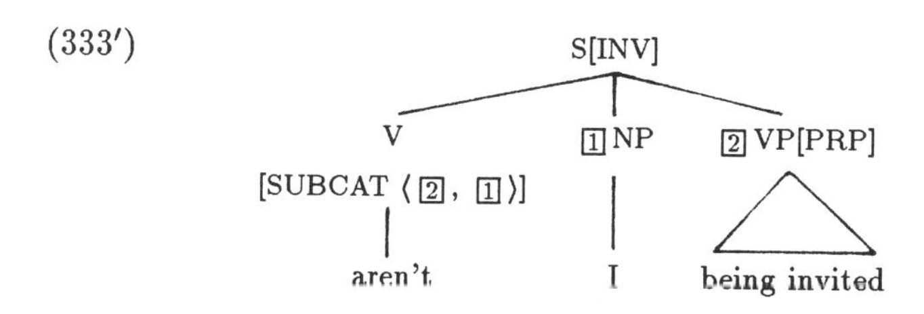

It is important to realize that the generalization we are isolating here has strong empirical consequences, for there is ample independent justification for the proposed order of elements on SUBCAT lists, apart from its rough correspondence with surface order. At least four distinct kinds of evidence should be mentioned in this connection: the applicability of lexical rules, control, binding, and agreement. In (329), for instance, we know independently that the first NP complement is the direct object (next-to-last NP on the head's SUBCAT list), because of the possibility of passivizing it in all varieties of English. The lexical rule for passivization sketched in Chapter 8 embodies the traditional assumption that only direct object NP's may be passivized. Exactly the same argument establishes that the NP complements in (330) and (331) are direct objects. The theory of control developed in Volume 2 requires that the unexpressed subject of a VP complement must be controlled by a less oblique complement, i.e. construed to be "identical" with it in a sense to be made precise. Since the VP complements in (331′) and (332′) are obviously controlled by the object NP and the PP[TO], respectively, the control theory implies that these elements are less oblique than their VP[INF] sisters. Similarly, the binding theory developed in Volume 2 explains familiar constraints on the distribution of reflexive and nonreflexive pronouns in terms of the same hierarchical obliqueness relations required for the theory of control. Finally, the NP in (333) must be the subject, i.e. the last NP on the verb's SUBCAT list, because *aren't* clearly agrees with this NP, and English verbs exhibit agreement only with subjects. Thus the LP constraint in (334) constitutes a generalization that relates the surface ordering of complements to a different, more abstract, and independently motivated ordering, namely the one imposed by the obliqueness hierarchy.

A minor modification of the generalization embodied in LP2 comes from the *verb-particle* construction, the hallmark of which is the word order variation illustrated in (335).

(335) I looked up the answer.

I looked the answer up.

We can account for this order variation by assuming that the relevant sense of *look* is expressed by the lexical sign (336):

(336)
$$\begin{bmatrix} \text{PHON} & \text{look} \\ \text{SYN|LOC|SUBCAT} & \langle \text{PART[UP]}, \text{NP}_{\boxed{1}}, \text{NP}_{\boxed{2}} \rangle \\ \text{SEM|CONT} & \begin{bmatrix} \text{RELN} & \text{LOOK-UP} \\ \text{SEARCHER} & \boxed{2} \\ \text{SOUGHT} & \boxed{1} \end{bmatrix} \end{bmatrix}$$

Here the specification PART[UP] is a stand-in for whatever analysis of the particle one chooses to adopt. The only property that will be relevant here is that it is unspecified with respect to the feature LEX; the significance of this assumption will emerge presently. We know that the NP complement occurring in the VP is a direct object (second-last on the SUBCAT list) because of the possibility of passivization. We have included the SEMANTICS|CONTENT value to make clear that this lexical form is associated semantically with the LOOKING-UP relation. The syntactic combination with the *up* phrase is according to general syntactic principles, but the *up* particle itself is making no direct contribution to the semantics; rather the entire lexical form, which is characterized by subcategorizing for such a particle, is itself associated with LOOKING-UP.

The modification required of LP2 is to restrict the more oblique complement to phrasal ([LEX −]) signs. That is, the modified generalization is that complements must precede more oblique *phrasal* complements, as illustrated in (337):

(337) LP2 (second formulation):

$$\text{COMPLEMENT} \ll \text{COMPLEMENT[LEX } -]$$

Thus if the first complement of the verbal form in (336) is realized as [LEX −], then LP2 will require that the direct object NP, which is higher on the obliqueness hierarchy, must linearly precede the PP. If that complement is realized as [LEX +], however, then LP2 imposes no ordering restriction on the direct object.

This may seem at first to be an unmotivated distinction to draw between the two occurrences of the particle *up* until one considers the fact that there are a few modifiers, e.g. *right*, which may modify particles (as well as prepositions, as discussed in Emonds (1976)). When such modifiers are present, the particle is necessarily phrasal, and must follow the direct object:[1]

(338) a.*I looked right up the answer.
b. I looked the answer right up.

Let us now turn to a problem which arises in connection with the interaction of the verb-particle construction with second objects. The problem here is to account for contrasts like the following:

(339) a. The chairman sent the members (right) out a report.
b.*The chairman sent the members a report (right) out.

In addition, as noted by Emonds (1976), some speakers also allow the particle to precede both NP complements:

(340) a. The chairman sent out the members a report.
b.*The chairman sent right out the members a report.

Under the LP analysis we are proposing, these data have a natural account if we assume the lexical sign partially specified in (341) is appropriate in those dialects which disallow (340).[2]

(341) [PHON sent
SYN|LOC|SUBCAT ⟨NP, PART[DIR,LEX –], NP, NP⟩]

By LP2, the direct object NP will be required to precede both the phrasal particle and the second object; the particle will be required to linearly precede the second object. Thus (339a) is the only permissible order. In the case of dialects permitting (340a), the only adjustment required is that the particle is unspecified for LEX:

(342) [SYN|LOC|SUBCAT ⟨NP, PART[DIR], NP, NP⟩]

When this complement is realized as [LEX +], LP2 will no longer require that the direct object precede it, thus allowing (340a) as well as (339a). (339b) remains blocked in such varieties, as desired. And (340b) is impossible because *right out* is phrasal.

It is important to be aware that the LP constraints we have considered thus far govern only "unmarked" constituent orders, i.e. those orders of

[1] Example (338a) is of course grammatical on an irrelevant and implausible reading where *right up the answer* is a directional phrase.

[2] Here "DIR" abbreviates 'directional'; presumably the distinction in question is semantic in nature.

elements not dictated by considerations of specialized discourse function. It remains to provide an account of the variations of order involving "focused" constituents such as those in (343), usually discussed under the somewhat inaccurate rubric of "Heavy NP Shift" (inaccurate because non-NP's may be affected as well):

(343) a. Kim [put [on the table] [the book he bought in Vienna]].

b. Sandy [gave [to Kim] [the book she bought in Vienna]].

Roughly speaking, the focused constituent is permitted to occur phrase-finally instead of in its expected position, provided it is sufficiently "heavy" (in some poorly understood sense). The constituent ordering within the VP's of these examples clearly contradict LP2.

A question arises here as to just how a certain constituent order is identified as unmarked. One heuristic we have found useful is the possibility of placement of contrastive pitch accent on prefinal major constituents, which seems impossible in the case of marked orders. This is illustrated by the deviance of such examples as: I put [on the TABLE] an autographed copy of Situations and Attitudes. (Capitalization is here used to indicate placement of contrastive pitch accent.)

In order to account for examples such as (343), we propose the new LP constraint given in (344):

(344) Focus Rule (LP3):

$$[\text{MAJ } \neg\text{N}] \quad < \quad [\text{FOCUS } +]$$

Here [FOCUS +] abbreviates whatever analysis one chooses to adopt of the notion of focus (possibly involving both phonological and discourse factors). The stipulation [MAJ ¬N] on the left-hand side is required to block the shifting of a focused element to the right of an NP sister, for (345) is ungrammatical:

(345) *Kim [gave [a book] [the fine young student who came to the reception.]]

Unfortunately, there is a problem with (344) as matters stand. For although the examples in (343) are consistent with (344), it is in violation of LP2! (Recall that LP constraints are assumed to apply to every phrasal sign in the language.) Of course the desired analysis is that (333) is just the *usual* order, while a focused complement which fails to precede some more oblique sister should not count as a violation.

A solution to problems of this kind, developed by Uszkoreit (1986), involves grouping LP constraints into disjunctive sets. On this proposal, in order for a permutation to be well-formed, it need only satisfy one LP rule in each disjunctive set. Adopting this approach, we would simply collapse LP2 and LP3 into single disjunctive LP constraint. This proposal, though somewhat speculative, suggests interesting further directions for studying the complex interaction between grammatical constraints and discourse-based constraints on constituent order.

7.3 Extending the Obliqueness Hierarchy

All the ordering restrictions discussed in the previous section involve subcategorized-for elements that occur as sisters in a given phrasal sign. In this section, we consider the ordering properties of certain modifiers that also appear as sisters to subcategorized-for complements.

Given that adverbs typically follow subcategorized-for complements, as in (346), it is tempting to conclude that they always attach higher in the constituent structure.

(346) a. Kim gave Sandy a book yesterday.
b.*Kim gave yesterday Sandy a book.
c.*Kim gave Sandy yesterday a book.

The relevant attachment might be either to S, as shown in (347), or to VP, as shown in (348):

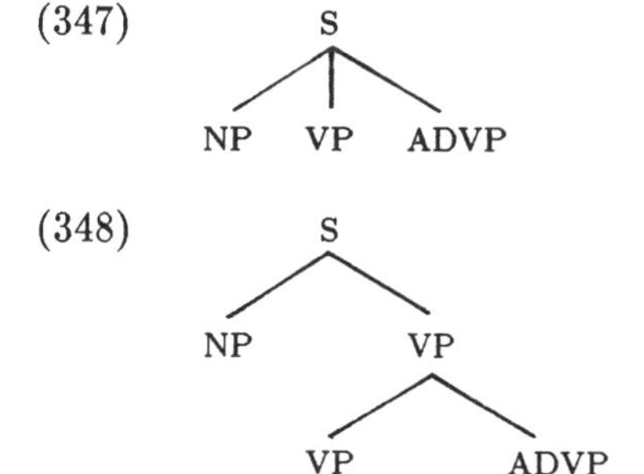

In addition, of course, certain classes of adverbial modifiers may appear preverbally, as in (349).

(349) a. Yesterday Kim gave Sandy a book.
b. Kim yesterday gave Sandy a book.

The structures for these sentences are presumably very much like those in (350).

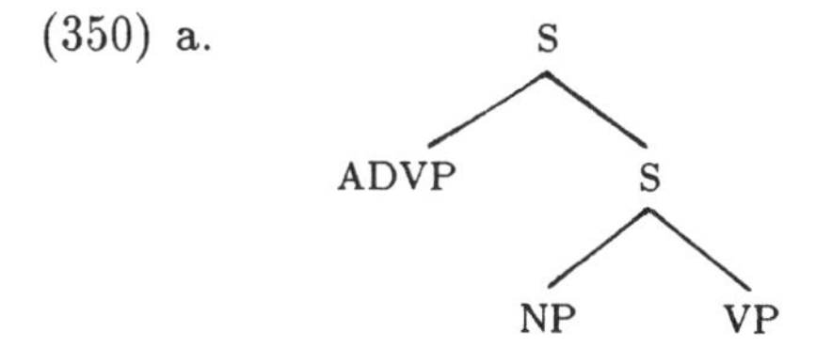

(350) b.

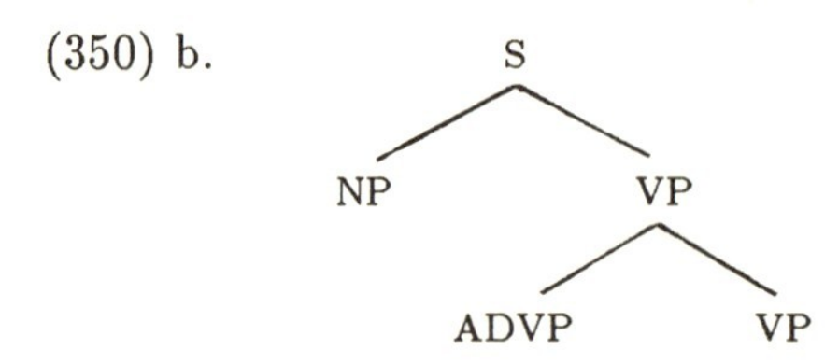

We will have very little more to say about structures like (350). Rather, we will here focus our attention on the analysis of post-verbal adverbial modifiers.

Certain complements may appear after adverbial modifiers:

(351) a. We persuaded Sandy last week to resign from the committee.

b. They argued convincingly that Lou should resign.

c. I want very much to participate.

d. They want very much for us to participate.

And unless we are willing to introduce what would seem to be otherwise unmotivated grammar rules, the existence of VP's like those in (351) leads directly to the conclusion that adjunct phrases of various sorts may be introduced as daughters of VP, interspersed with complement phrases, as shown in (352).

(352) a.

b.

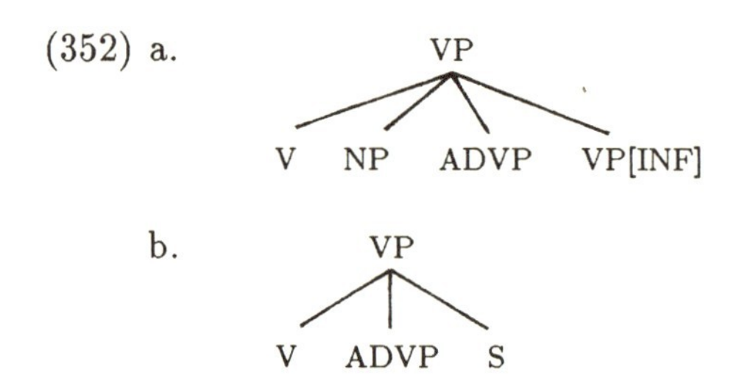

Structures like these, which are discussed in Chapter 6, are analyzed in terms of the attribute ADJUNCT-DAUGHTERS.

The introduction of adjunct daughters, of course, raises the question of what LP constraints govern the ordering of adjuncts relative to complements. As the examples in (351) show, VP and S complements may follow adjuncts, but the data in (346) above show clearly that (in the unmarked case) NP complements must precede adjuncts. Similarly, on the basis of the following contrasts, we may conclude that the unmarked position for complement PP's and AP's is before any adjuncts that might be introduced as their sisters.

(353) a. Lou handed a book to the kids last Sunday.

b.*Lou handed last SUNDAY a book to the kids.

c.*Lou handed a book last SUNDAY to the kids.

(354) a. Chris put the book on the table after lunch.

b.*Chris put after LUNCH a book on the table.

c.*Chris put a book after LUNCH on the table.

(355) a. Leslie turned red last Tuesday.

b.*Leslie turned last TUESDAY red.

As before, we indicate placement of a pitch accent on a pre-final constituent by capitalization. (It should be recalled that we regard the impossibility of pitch accent placement on a pre-final constituent as evidence that a given constituent ordering is marked, i.e. licensed by the overriding discourse-based LP rule in (344), rather than by the general principles determining unmarked constituent order patterns.)

A natural analysis of these data can be obtained by extending the obliqueness hierarchy discussed earlier to include adjuncts as well as complements. The idea is very simple: adjuncts are more oblique than complements. Thus LP2, which requires that complements precede more oblique complements, can be generalized to require that complements precede adjuncts as well. Since we have seen that VP and S complements are not affected by this requirement, we must exclude them from the domain of application of the generalization of LP2, which we now reformulate as (356):

(356) LP2 (final formulation):

$$\text{COMPLEMENT[MAJ} \neg\text{V]} \quad \ll \quad \text{[LEX} -\text{]}$$

This formulation guarantees that NP, PP and AP complements are ordered before more oblique sister phrases, whether these are complements or adjuncts. Because it does not require VP or S complements to come before more oblique sisters, it correctly allows for the examples in (351), as well as their reordered counterparts in (357).

(357) a. We persuaded Sandy to resign from the committee last week.

b. They argued that Lou should resign convincingly.

c. I want to participate very much.

d. They want (for) us to participate very much.

LP2 also now explains further data involving the verb-particle construction, namely the contrasts in (358).

(358) a. He looked up the number quickly.

b. He looked the number up quickly.

c.*He looked the number quickly up.

d.*He looked quickly up the number.

e.*He looked quickly the number up.

f.*He looked up quickly the number.

These facts follow directly from the lexical form in (336) above and the generalized form of LP2 just given. The adverb phrase is the most oblique sister of the post-verbal complements, and hence must follow them all.

In addition, it is interesting to observe that the strict ordering of the complements of the verb *appeal* (see (332) above), i.e. the obligatory ordering of the PP[TO] complement before the VP[INF] complement, does not hold for the superficially similar verb *appear*. Both (359a) and (359b) are well-formed.

(359) a. Kim appeared to Sandy to be unhappy.

b. Kim appeared to be unhappy to Sandy.

As noted earlier, the theory of control to be outlined in Volume 2 dictates that the PP[TO] complement of *appeal* be less oblique than the VP[INF] complement (because a complement's controller must always be less oblique). But there is no such motivation for saying that the PP[TO] complement of *appear* is less oblique than the VP[INF] complement. Moreover, once we assume the opposite complement obliqueness order, i.e. once we assume that *appear* is specified lexically as [SUBCAT ⟨PP[TO],VP[INF],NP⟩], then we have an immediate explanation for the facts in (359). Because LP2 does not require that VP complements precede more oblique phrases, both orderings in (359) are permitted.

Now consider the ordering properties of passive verb phrases. The PP[BY]'s that optionally appear in such phrases must follow NP complements, but are freely ordered with respect to VP complements:

(360) a. René was given a book by Dominique.

b.*René was given by DOMINIQUE a book.

(361) a. Lou was persuaded to go home by Terry.

b. Lou was persuaded by TERRY to go home.

This contrast follows under the assumption that PP[BY]'s are more oblique than their sister complements (which in turn is a consequence of the passive lexical rule formulated in Chapter 8). LP2 then requires that the less oblique NP complement in (360) precede the PP[BY], but freely permits either order with respect to the less oblique VP[INF] complement.

It is interesting to note that by applying our prosodic criterion for unmarked word order carefully, we can also ascertain that PP[TO] complements are less oblique than PP[BY]'s in passives:

(362) a. The book was given to a TEACHER by Sandy.

b.?*The book was given by a TEACHER to Sandy.

This contrast, though subtle, suggests that indeed PP[BY]'s are more oblique than any subcategorized-for sister element.

Matters are different when we consider the order of PP[BY]'s with respect to adverbial modifiers. The unmarked ordering, as suggested by the contrast in (363), is for the *by*-phrase to precede the adverbial.

(363) a. Sandy was killed by a TRUCK last night.

b.?*Sandy was killed last NIGHT by a truck.

Notice that we are not claiming that the orderings in (362b) and (363b) are completely unacceptable, but only that they are orderings licensed by specialized discourse considerations rather than by unmarked grammatical patterns. Of course, when such orderings do occur, we should expect the pitch accent, if any, to fall within the final (focused) major constituent, as in (363′):

(363′) Sandy was killed last night by a TRUCK.

If these observations are correct, then we have reason to conclude that PP[BY]'s are themselves complements, but the most oblique of the complements subcategorized for by any given passive verb form. This conclusion will lead to an account of all the data just considered, for it renders PP[BY]'s more oblique than other complements, but less oblique than adverbial modifiers.

The appropriate passive verb forms are produced by a lexical rule (see Chapter 8) that performs a *cyclic permutation* of the SUBCAT list of active verb inputs as it produces passive form outputs.[3] The passive lexical rule thus maps the active verbal forms in (364) into the passive forms in (365).

(364) a.
$$\begin{bmatrix} \text{PHON} & \text{kill} \\ \text{SYN}|\text{LOC} & \begin{bmatrix} \text{HEAD} & \begin{bmatrix} \text{MAJ} & \text{V} \\ \text{VFORM} & \text{BSE} \end{bmatrix} \\ \text{SUBCAT} & \langle \text{NP,NP} \rangle \end{bmatrix} \end{bmatrix}$$

b.
$$\begin{bmatrix} \text{PHON} & \text{give} \\ \text{SYN}|\text{LOC} & \begin{bmatrix} \text{HEAD} & \begin{bmatrix} \text{MAJ} & \text{V} \\ \text{VFORM} & \text{BSE} \end{bmatrix} \\ \text{SUBCAT} & \langle \text{NP,NP,NP} \rangle \end{bmatrix} \end{bmatrix}$$

c.
$$\begin{bmatrix} \text{PHON} & \text{give} \\ \text{SYN}|\text{LOC} & \begin{bmatrix} \text{HEAD} & \begin{bmatrix} \text{MAJ} & \text{V} \\ \text{VFORM} & \text{BSE} \end{bmatrix} \\ \text{SUBCAT} & \langle \text{PP[TO],NP,NP} \rangle \end{bmatrix} \end{bmatrix}$$

---

[3] The semantic role assignments are of course preserved under passivization, the PP[BY] in the output form being assigned the same semantic role as the subject in the active form input.

(364) d.
$$\begin{bmatrix} \text{PHON} & \text{persuade} \\ \text{SYN}\mid\text{LOC} & \begin{bmatrix} \text{HEAD} & \begin{bmatrix}\text{MAJ} & \text{V}\\ \text{VFORM} & \text{BSE}\end{bmatrix} \\ \text{SUBCAT} & \langle\text{VP[INF],NP,NP}\rangle \end{bmatrix}\end{bmatrix}$$

e.
$$\begin{bmatrix} \text{PHON} & \text{send} \\ \text{SYN}\mid\text{LOC} & \begin{bmatrix} \text{HEAD} & \begin{bmatrix}\text{MAJ} & \text{V}\\ \text{VFORM} & \text{BSE}\end{bmatrix} \\ \text{SUBCAT} & \langle\text{NP,PART,NP,NP}\rangle \end{bmatrix}\end{bmatrix}$$

(365) a.
$$\begin{bmatrix} \text{PHON} & \text{killed} \\ \text{SYN}\mid\text{LOC} & \begin{bmatrix} \text{HEAD} & \begin{bmatrix}\text{MAJ} & \text{V}\\ \text{VFORM} & \text{PAS}\end{bmatrix} \\ \text{SUBCAT} & \langle\text{(PP[BY]),NP}\rangle \end{bmatrix}\end{bmatrix}$$

b.
$$\begin{bmatrix} \text{PHON} & \text{given} \\ \text{SYN}\mid\text{LOC} & \begin{bmatrix} \text{HEAD} & \begin{bmatrix}\text{MAJ} & \text{V}\\ \text{VFORM} & \text{PAS}\end{bmatrix} \\ \text{SUBCAT} & \langle\text{(PP[BY]),NP,NP}\rangle \end{bmatrix}\end{bmatrix}$$

c.
$$\begin{bmatrix} \text{PHON} & \text{given} \\ \text{SYN}\mid\text{LOC} & \begin{bmatrix} \text{HEAD} & \begin{bmatrix}\text{MAJ} & \text{V}\\ \text{VFORM} & \text{PAS}\end{bmatrix} \\ \text{SUBCAT} & \langle\text{(PP[BY]),PP[TO],NP}\rangle \end{bmatrix}\end{bmatrix}$$

d.
$$\begin{bmatrix} \text{PHON} & \text{persuaded} \\ \text{SYN}\mid\text{LOC} & \begin{bmatrix} \text{HEAD} & \begin{bmatrix}\text{MAJ} & \text{V}\\ \text{VFORM} & \text{PAS}\end{bmatrix} \\ \text{SUBCAT} & \langle\text{(PP[BY]),VP[INF],NP}\rangle \end{bmatrix}\end{bmatrix}$$

e.
$$\begin{bmatrix} \text{PHON} & \text{sent} \\ \text{SYN}\mid\text{LOC} & \begin{bmatrix} \text{HEAD} & \begin{bmatrix}\text{MAJ} & \text{V}\\ \text{VFORM} & \text{PAS}\end{bmatrix} \\ \text{SUBCAT} & \langle\text{(PP[BY]),NP,PART,NP}\rangle \end{bmatrix}\end{bmatrix}$$

And the forms in (365) combine with complements and adjuncts in accordance with the very same grammar rules as active forms. LP1 and LP2 interact to predict the constraints on the ordering of complements of passive verbs, as illustrated in (366)–(368).

(366) a.

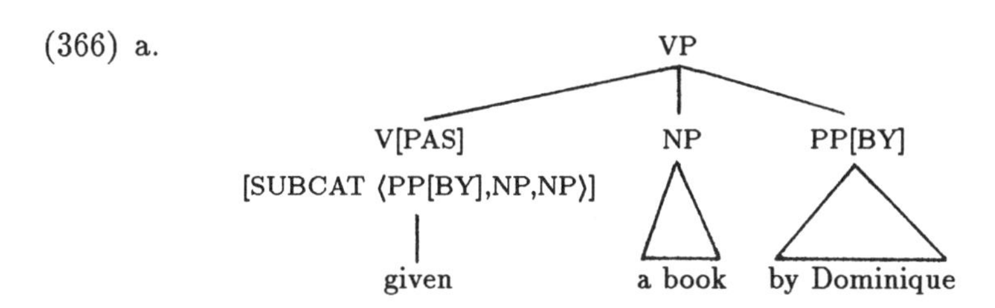

b.

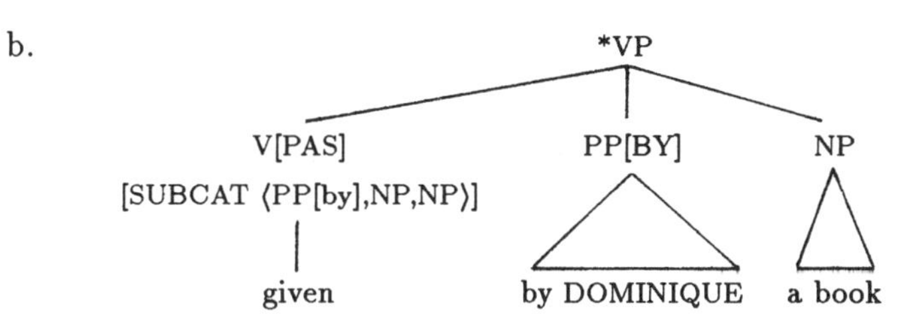

(367) a.

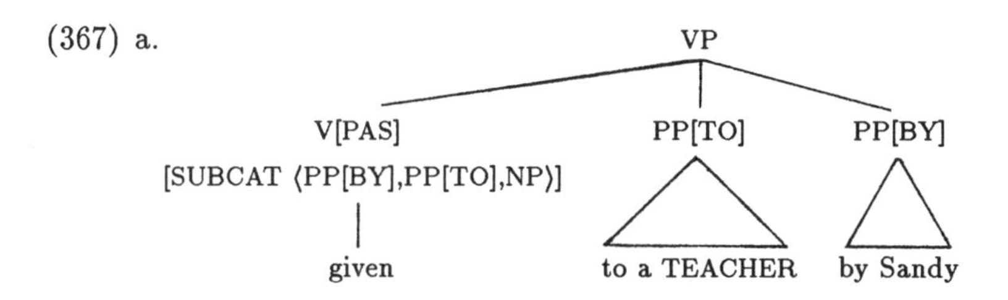

b.

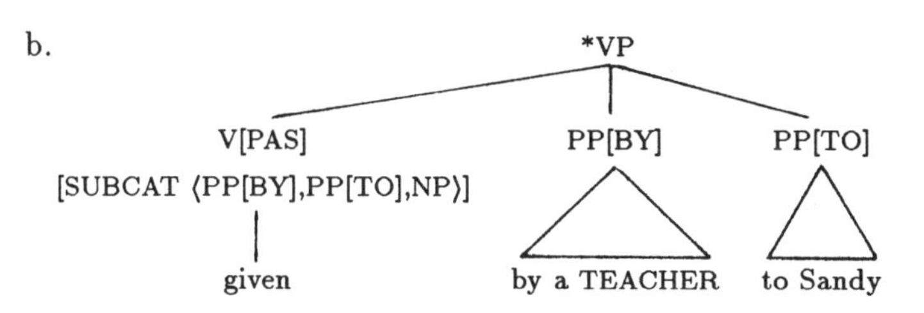

(368) a.

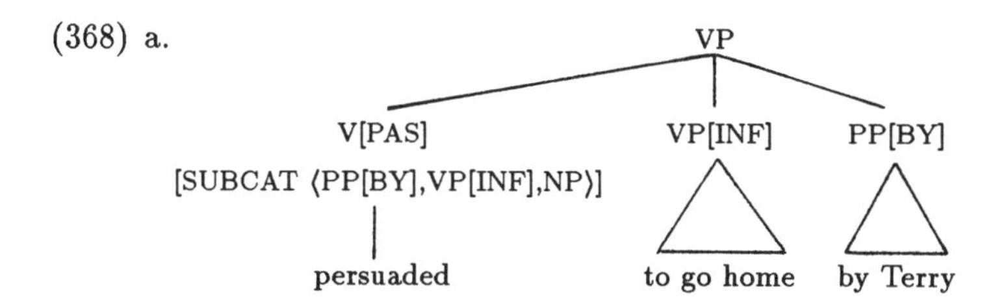

(368) b.

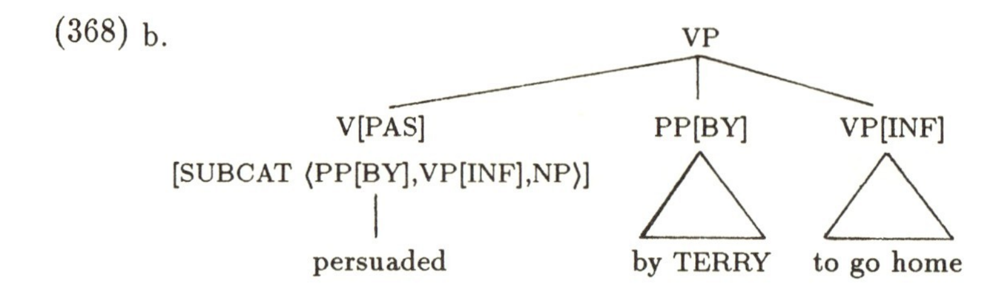

Moreover the following additional facts regarding the passivization of particle-taking verbs like *send* are also predicted to the letter.

(369) a.

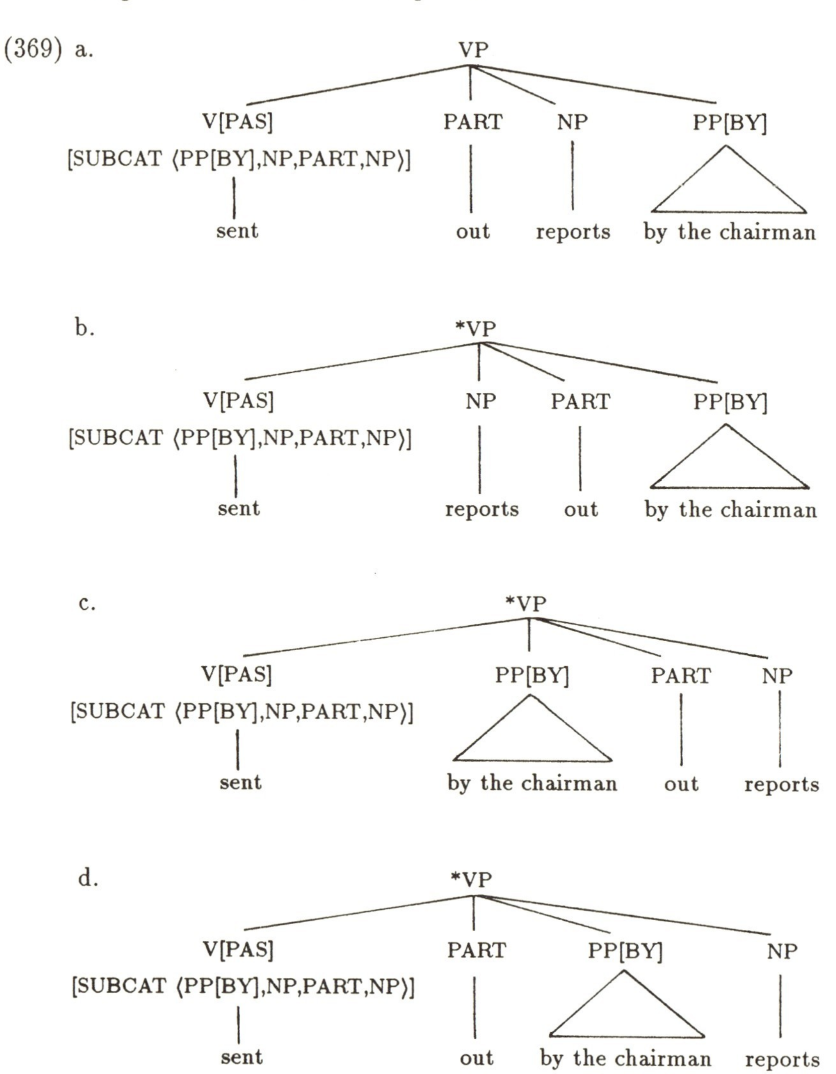

(369) e.

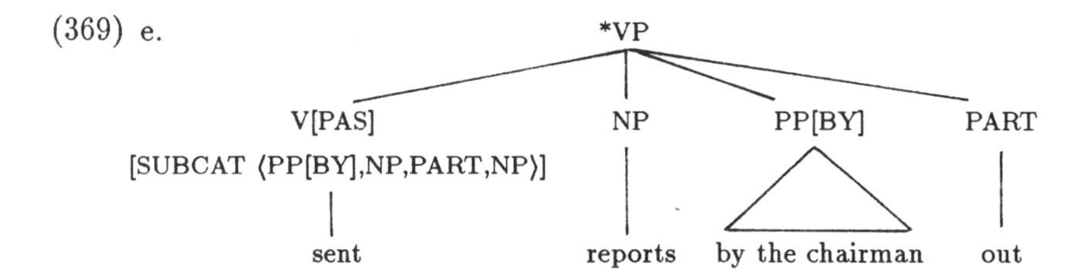

Of these examples, only (369a) contains no occurrence of a more oblique complement ordered before a less oblique complement, as guaranteed by our revision of LP2, taken together with the lexical form for passive *sent* in (365e).

Finally, let us point out that the range of data accounted for by LP2 may be extended further if we assume that heads of phrases also participate in the obliqueness hierarchy. If we assume that heads, like adjuncts, are more oblique than all complements, then LP2, as formulated, accounts for the ordering of subject complements in non-inverted clauses and saturated predicative phrases (small clauses), as well as for the ordering of determiners and possessive NP complements before the nominal phrasal head. These structures are illustrated in (370).

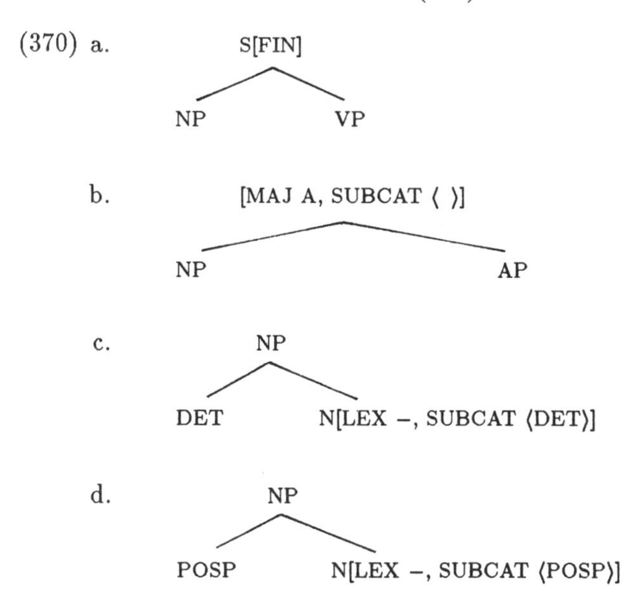

This is one of two available analyses for dealing with the position of subjects and prenominal complements. The alternative is to generalize the following LP rule, which apparently is required independently to ensure that filler daughters in filler-gap constructions are ordered before the clauses they combine with.

(371) Filler-Head Rule (LP4):

FILLER < HEAD[LEX –]

LP4 correctly ensures the ordering restriction illustrated in (372).

(372) a.

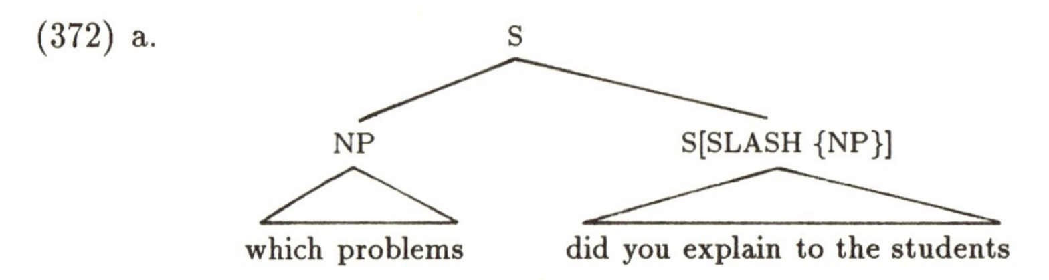

b.

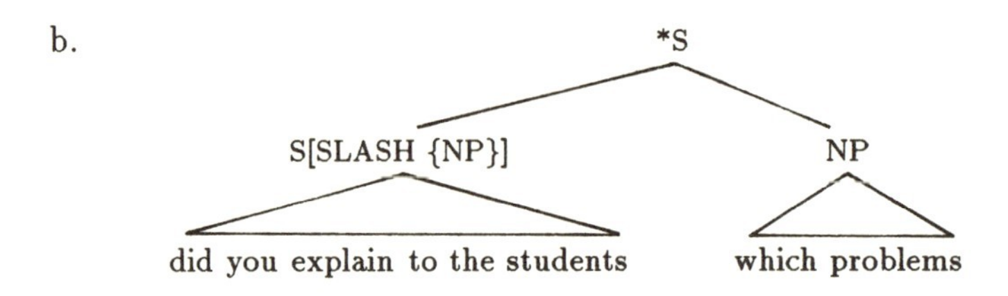

7.4 Conclusion

In this chapter, we have presented an informal and somewhat tentative sketch of a theory of constituent order for English. This theory assumes a function order-constituents, which constrains the PHONOLOGY value of a phrasal sign in such a way that it must be one of the permutations of the PHONOLOGY values of the sign's daughter constituents which are consistent with all of the LP constraints of English. The LP constraints that we have considered make reference to information of diverse sorts: syntactic category (LEX, MAJ), grammatical function (the obliqueness hierarchy) and discourse information (FOCUS). This approach incorporates the traditional wisdom that the ordering of constituents is a complex function of grammatical and functional information.

It is interesting to speculate about languages with greater word order freedom, though the claims that are often made with respect to such languages appear to be somewhat exaggerated, and the data upon which they are based seem often to be equivocal. It is a fundamental fact of human languages that they exhibit varying degrees of word order freedom, i.e. they do not pattern neatly into "configurational" languages and "free word order" languages, as is often assumed. Our approach to word order variation seeks to explain the "gray area" between these two ordering types, as well as to provide an account of the fact that certain types of constituents (often clauses) allow relatively free word order internally, but require that none of their internal elements "escape" to higher clauses.

A language that allows "scrambling" of certain constituents is a language where the PHONOLOGY value of phrasal signs is not always a permutation of the PHONOLOGY values of the daughter signs. Scrambled signs, in other words, are not constrained by the function order-constituents, however parameterized. Rather, they are constrained by a function we may call "interleave-constituents". This function allows the pieces of the PHONOLOGY strings of daughter signs to be interleaved with those of other daughters in the construction of larger signs. Interleave-constituents, like order-constituents, is subject to language- specific LP constraints (and "free" word order languages typically obey some LP constraints, e.g. the second position of auxiliary elements in Warlpiri, which is a standard example of such a language.). An interleaving of subject and VP PHONOLOGY values is illustrated in (373).

(373) 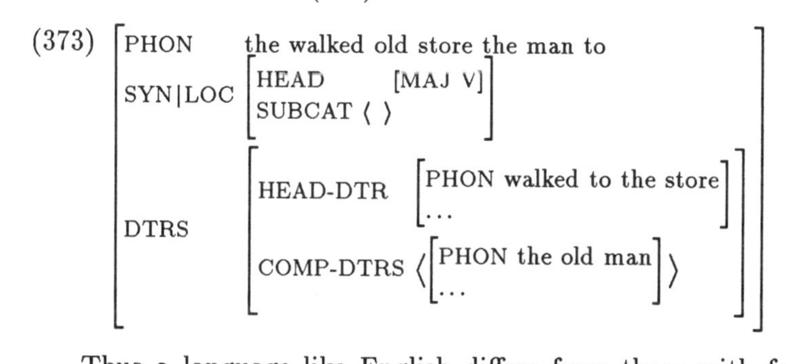

Thus a language like English differs from those with freer ordering possibilities in its utilization of the function ORDER-CONSTITUENTS, and of course its particular LP constraints. A true "free word order" language would be one that lacked LP constraints and whose phrasal signs all unified with the Scrambling Principle in (374).

(374) Scrambling Principle

$$\begin{bmatrix} \text{PHON interleave-constituents}(\boxed{1}) \\ \text{DTRS } \boxed{1} \end{bmatrix}$$

As we have stated, we are skeptical of the claim that any human languages are really of this type. The approach to the problem of word order variation we have outlined, however, provides ample room for the description of languages with varying degrees of scrambling, allowing a principled account of LP constraints, interleaving, and the interaction of discourse-based factors.

7.5 Suggestions for Further Reading

The theory of linear precedence presented in this chapter, first presented in Sag (1987), is an elaboration and refinement of the ID/LP theory of Gazdar and Pullum (1981), but owes much to the work of Hans Uszkoreit (1986b,c).

Similar ideas are proposed within the tradition of LFG by Falk (1983) who states linear precedence generalizations in terms of functional notions such as subject and direct object. For a comparison of Falk's approach with the theory presented here, see Sag (1987).

8 The Lexical Hierarchy and Lexical Rules

In HPSG, as in categorial grammar, the lexicalization of linguistic information leads to a drastic reduction in the number and complexity of phrase structure (ID) rules. For example, the presence of subcategorization information in lexical signs, in conjunction with the Subcategorization Principle, enables rules introducing lexical heads (e.g. the lexical ID rules of GPSG) to be replaced by a handful of combinatory schemata; and the explicit encoding of semantic content (including role assignment) in lexical signs, in conjunction with the Semantics Principle, obviates the necessity for pairing phrase structure rules with Montague-style interpretative rules. The other side of the coin, of course, is that lexical signs must be correspondingly richer in information content. The remarkable complexity of lexical signs is evident from the partial descriptions of a representative noun and verb given in (375):[1,2]

---

[1] As complex as these descriptions are, a good deal of information has been suppressed or simplified for expository purposes. For example, specifications for binding features, necessary in the account of unbounded dependencies, are omitted, and the specification of semantic indices disregards their classification by referential type which is crucial for the theory of anaphora. Both of these topics will be treated in detail in Volume 2.

[2] Agreement phenomena such as person, number, and gender are treated as part of the internal structure of NP variables (e.g. [1] in (375)), as discussed in detail in Volume 2. The two occurrences of the tag [1] within the SYN|LOC|SUBCAT list of (376) characterize *tried* as a subject-control verb; control too is treated in Volume 2. Except for inessential details, the treatment of verb tense in terms of a restricted (space-time) location parameter (e.g. [3] in (376)) is due to Fenstad et al. (1985). Here the notation "l_d" refers to another location parameter, the *discourse location*; the basic idea is that past-tense verbs refer to situations which temporally precede the utterance. In a more complete analysis which took contextual factors into account, the discourse location would be indicated by a tag, with another occurrence of the same tag within a substructure of the sign devoted to information about the circumstances of utterance (discourse location, speaker, audience, etc.).

(375) The common noun *dog*

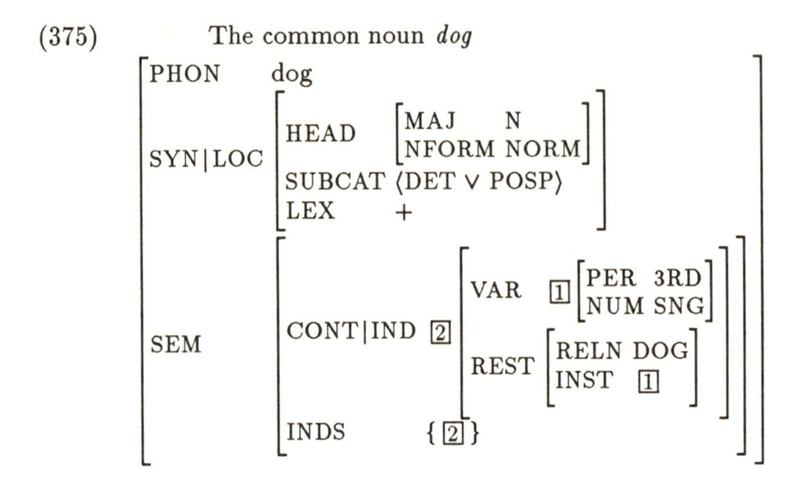

(376) The past-tense verb *tried*

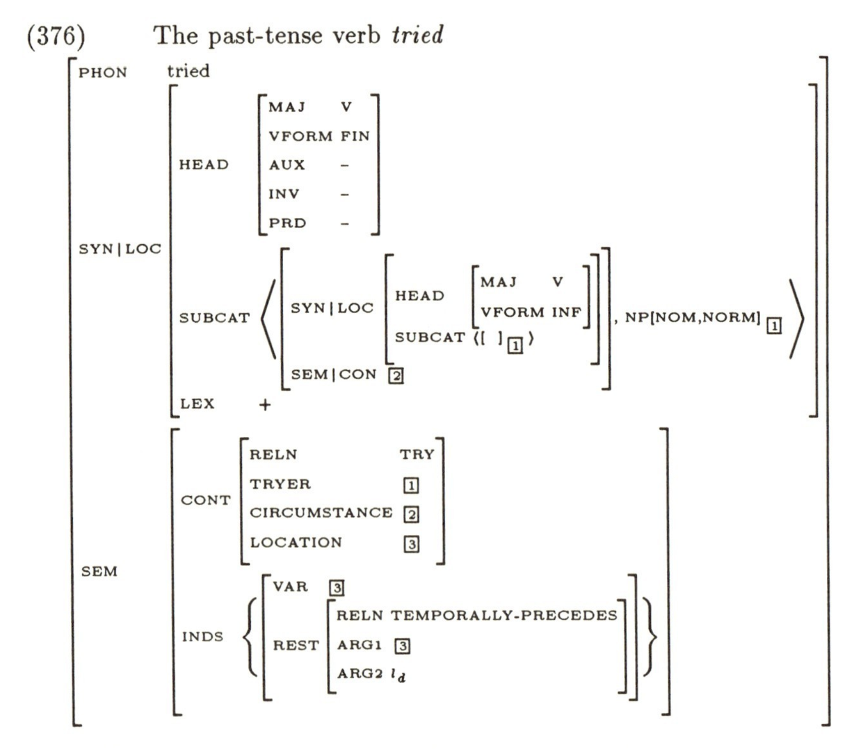

The following question then naturally presents itself: How can such complex lexical information be structured in such a way as to capture linguistic generalizations about classes of words with common behavior, while avoiding unnecessary redundant stipulation? The answer, we suggest here, is that language users have knowledge of a taxonomic system of lexical *types*. That is, lexical information is organized on the basis of relatively few—perhaps several dozen—word types arranged in cross-cutting hierarchies which serve to classify all words on the basis of shared syntactic, semantic, and morphological properties. By factoring out information about words which can be predicted from their membership in types (whose properties can be stated in a single place once and for all), the amount of idiosyncratic information that needs to be stipulated in individual lexical signs is dramatically reduced.

Of course, this principle is familiar to anyone who has ever studied a highly inflected language. One does not memorize the entire inflectional paradigm of every noun, adjective, or verb; instead, one remembers the inflectional class and part of speech (e.g. second-conjugation verb, fourth declension neuter noun) and a set of *schematic* paradigms on whose basis the paradigms of each instance can be determined. (Of course, there are usually exceptions that have to be remembered separately; we return to this point in due course.) The system of lexical types that we sketch here is essentially similar, except that in addition to such traditional morphosyntactic distinctions such as part of speech, case, verb form, person, number, and gender, we propose that words are also cross-classifed on the basis of their *valence*, i.e. their potential for combining with other signs as reflected in their SUBCAT lists.

In the first section of this chapter, we set forth a partial and tentative classificatory scheme for the English lexicon in terms of shared syntactic and semantic properties, employing the notion of type subsumption for feature structures introduced in Chapter 2. In the second section, we show how the notion of *lexical rules*, familiar in the linguistic analysis of word formation, can be introduced into such a scheme, thereby providing an elegant and completely lexicon-internal account of a wide range of phenomena that apply to whole classes of lexical signs, including inflectional and derivational processes, polyvalency patterns, and numerous other phenomena (such as *tough*-"movement" and *it*-"extraposition") standardly treated within other theories by syntactic mechanisms.[3]

8.1 The Hierarchy of Lexical Types

By way of illustration, let us begin by considering the English *dog* sign (375). How much of the information that it contains is specific to that sign, in the sense that it cannot be determined on the basis of well-defined word classes to which it belongs? The answer is: very little indeed. For example, the information (377a) (that the sign is lexical rather than phrasal) is

---

[3] For a closely related and much more detailed account of the lexical hierarchy and lexical rules, see Flickinger (1987). His account and the one sketched here both arise from work on the lexicon of an HPSG-based natural language processing system described in Flickinger, et al. (1985).

shared with every word.[4] (377b) (that the sign is a noun) is shared with all nouns. (377c) is shared with all nouns that are additionally third-singular as opposed to any other combination of person and number values. And (377d) (that the sign can combine with a determiner or possessive phrase) is shared with all nouns that are additionally common as opposed to proper; note that this last bundle of information is essentially concerned with valence rather than with traditional inflectional distinctions.

(377) a. Shared by all words

$$[\text{SYN}|\text{LOC}|\text{LEX} \ +]$$

b. Shared by all nouns (in addition to a)

$$\begin{bmatrix}\text{SYN}|\text{LOC}|\text{HEAD}|\text{MAJ} & \text{N}\\ \text{SEM}|\text{CONT} & {}_{\textit{indexed-object}}[\ ]\end{bmatrix}$$

c. Shared by all third-singular nouns (in addition to a, b)

$$\begin{bmatrix}\text{SEM}|\text{CONT}|\text{IND}|\text{VAR} & \begin{bmatrix}\text{PER} & \text{3RD}\\ \text{NUM} & \text{SNG}\end{bmatrix}\end{bmatrix}$$

d. Shared by all common nouns (in addition to a, b)

$$\begin{bmatrix}\text{SYN}|\text{LOC} & \begin{bmatrix}\text{HEAD}|\text{NFORM} & \text{NORM}\\ \text{SUBCAT} & \langle \text{DET} \vee \text{POSP}\rangle\end{bmatrix}\\ \text{SEM} & \begin{bmatrix}\text{CONT}|\text{IND} & \boxed{2}\begin{bmatrix}\text{VAR} & \boxed{1}\\ \text{REST}|\text{INST} & \boxed{1}\end{bmatrix}\\ \text{INDS} \ \{\boxed{2}\} & \end{bmatrix}\end{bmatrix}$$

If all this information is factored out of the lexical sign, all that remains is (378):

---

[4] This is a slight simplification, for we assume that *saturated* words (see the discussion of subcategorization types below), i.e. proper nouns and pronouns, are unspecified for LEX. One way to handle this is to add a rule (it is unclear whether to call it a grammar rule or a lexical rule) that creates [LEX −] NP's from lexical NP's. Alternatively, the specification [LEX + ∨ −] might be stipulated on the subcategorization type *saturated* as *overriding* the specification [LEX +] inherited from the supertype *lexical-sign*. Such an overriding mechanism, a standard feature of computer-based knowledge representation systems, introduces limited nonmonotonicity by allowing "default" information specified on types to be overruled on certain subtypes or instances. It has frequently been suggested (e.g. Flickinger et al. (1985), Flickinger (1987)) that such a mechanism might be appropriate for dealing with lexical exceptions and subregularities in general.

(378) Information specific to *dog*

$$\begin{bmatrix} \text{PHON dog} \\ \text{SEM|CONT|IND|REST|RELN DOG} \end{bmatrix}$$

Thus we can totally characterize *dog* as a lexical third-singular common noun whose phonology is /dɔg/ and which "means dog" (i.e. which restricts the parameter that it introduces to dogs).

Similarly, the verb *tried* contains information shared with all words (379a); information shared with all verbs (379b); further information shared with all verbs that are main verbs (as opposed to auxiliaries) (379c) and with all verbs that are finite (379d); and information shared with all finite verbs that are additionally past-tense. Moreover, *tried* shares with many other verbs, but also with ceratin adjectives (e.g. *eager*) the information (379f) which characterizes it as a member of a certain valence class called *intransitive-equi control*.[5]

(379) a. Shared by all words

[SYN|LOC|LEX +]

b. Shared by all verbs (in addition to a)

$$\begin{bmatrix} \text{SYN|LOC|HEAD|MAJ V} \\ \text{SEM|CONT } {}_{\textit{basic-circumstance}}[\ ] \end{bmatrix}$$

c. Shared by all main verbs (in addition to a, b)

$$\begin{bmatrix} \text{SYN|LOC|HEAD} \begin{bmatrix} \text{AUX} & - \\ \text{INV} & - \end{bmatrix} \end{bmatrix}$$

d. Shared by all finite verbs (in addition to a, b)

$$\begin{bmatrix} \text{SYN|LOC} & \begin{bmatrix} \text{HEAD} & \begin{bmatrix} \text{VFORM} & \text{FIN} \\ \text{PRD} & - \end{bmatrix} \\ \text{SUBCAT } \langle \ldots, \text{NP[NOM]} \rangle & \end{bmatrix} \\ \text{SEM} & \begin{bmatrix} \text{CONT|LOCATION } \boxed{3} \\ \text{INDS } \{[\text{VAR } \boxed{3}]\} \end{bmatrix} \end{bmatrix}$$

---

[5] Intransitive-equi words are intransitive verbs and adjectives that subcategorize for an unsaturated VP[INF] complement whose "understood subject" (i.e. subject SUBCAT element) is controlled by (i.e. has its variable unified with the variable of) the subject of the word itself. Control is discussed at length in Volume 2.

(379) e. Shared by all past tense verbs (in addition to a, b, c)

$$\left[\text{SEM}\left[\begin{array}{ll}\text{CONT}\,|\,\text{LOCATION } \boxed{3} & \\ \text{INDS} & \left\{\left[\begin{array}{ll}\text{VAR} & \boxed{3}\\ \text{REST} & \left[\begin{array}{l}\text{RELN TEMPORALLY-PRECEDES}\\ \text{ARG1 } \boxed{3}\\ \text{ARG2 } l_d\end{array}\right]\end{array}\right]\right\}\end{array}\right]\right]$$

f. Shared by all intransitive-equi control words

$$\left[\text{SYN}\,|\,\text{LOC}\,|\,\text{SUBCAT}\left\langle\left[\text{SYN}\,|\,\text{LOC}\left[\begin{array}{l}\text{HEAD}\left[\begin{array}{ll}\text{MAJ} & \text{V}\\ \text{VFORM} & \text{INF}\end{array}\right]\\ \text{SUBCAT } \langle [\ ]_{\boxed{1}} \rangle\end{array}\right]\right], \text{NP[NOM,NORM]}_{\boxed{1}}\right\rangle\right]$$

Factoring out of the lexical sign (376) the information that it is a lexical, past-tense (and therefore finite), main verb of the intransitive-equi valence type, all that remains is the idiosyncratic information about phonology, kind of situation described, and semantic role assignments, as indicated in (380):

(380) Information specific to *tried*

$$\left[\begin{array}{ll}\text{PHON} & \text{tried}\\ \text{SYN}\,|\,\text{LOC}\,|\,\text{SUBCAT} & \langle[\text{SEM}\,|\,\text{CON}\ \boxed{2}],[\ ]_{\boxed{1}}\rangle\\ \text{SEM}\,|\,\text{CONT} & \left[\begin{array}{l}\text{RELN TRY}\\ \text{TRYER } \boxed{1}\\ \text{CIRCUMSTANCE } \boxed{2}\end{array}\right]\end{array}\right]$$

Now let us formalize the intuitive content of the foregoing examples. We begin by recalling some relevant properties of feature structures. First, feature structures are *typed*; different types of feature structures (e.g., *sign*, *constituent-structure*, *syntactic-category*, etc.) are used to model different kinds of linguistic objects. Each feature structure type comes equipped with a set of attributes appropriate to that type. Thus *sign* has the attributes PHONOLOGY, SYNTAX, and SEMANTICS; *syntactic-category* has the attributes LOCAL and BINDING; etc.

In addition, a given feature structure type prescribes certain types for the values of its attributes. For example, *sign* requires that its SYNTAX value be of type *syntactic-category*; more colloquially, we say that SYNTAX is *typed* to *syntactic-category*. *Syntactic-category* in turn requires that its LOCAL value be of another type—let us call it *local*—whose attributes are HEAD, SUBCAT, and LEX.[6] Descending one level further, within *local*, HEAD is typed to yet another type *head*, whose attributes we will discuss presently; SUBCAT is typed to a list of *sign*; and LEX is typed to the *atomic* type *boolean*, which ranges over the values + and −. Atomic types are just types which have no attributes.

The set of feature structure types is assumed to be partially ordered by subsumption. That is, we have a notion of one type being a subtype of another type; then we say the latter *subsumes* the former, and the subsumption relation is transitive, symmetric, and antireflexive. Each type can be identified, or associated, with a feature structure in a natural way, e.g. we associate the type *sign* with the feature structure ${}_{sign}[\;]$ which simply describes an object about which nothing is known except that it is a sign. Thus type subsumption corresponds to ordinary subsumption for feature structures. For example, *sign* subsumes *lexical-sign* and *phrasal-sign*. In fact, this is a rather special case, for *lexical-sign* and *phrasal-sign* are mutually inconsistent types which between them exhaust the possibilities for *sign*; that is, they *partition* the type *sign*. Formally, we write this as follows:

(381) $${}_{sign}[\;] = {}_{lexical\text{-}sign}[\;] \vee {}_{phrasal\text{-}sign}[\;]$$

(382) $${}_{lexical\text{-}sign}[\;] \wedge {}_{phrasal\text{-}sign}[\;] = \bot$$

Informally, we can express this information by the *type subsumption graph* (383):

(383)

sign

lexical-sign *phrasal-sign*

In such a graph, each node represents a type, and its daughters represent a partition of that type. Such graphs can descend to arbitrary depth; for example, the graph (384) represents some subsumption relations among types of constituent structures:

(384)

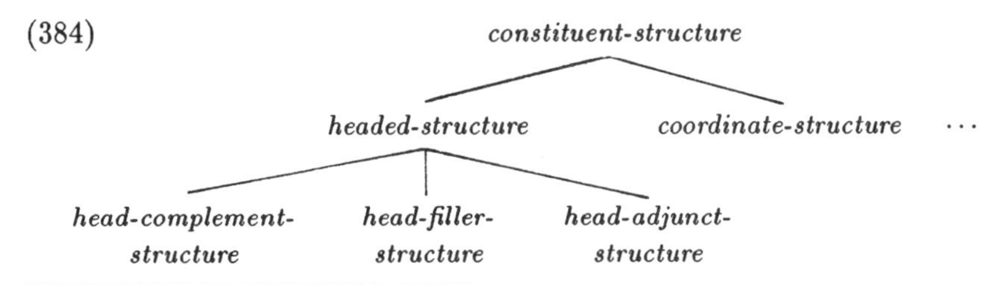

[6] For mnemonic purposes, we will often follow the convention of naming the type prescribed for a certain attribute after the attribute itself; in such cases the intended interpretation is disambiguated by the typeface (upper-case for attributes, lower-case italics for types).

It is obvious that a feature structure type *inherits* all the attributes and corresponding type restrictions on their values from all of its supertypes. For example PHONOLOGY, SYNTAX, and SEMANTICS are appropriate attributes for *phrasal-sign* because they are appropriate for *sign*, and the SYNTAX value in a feature structure of type *phrasal-sign* is required to be of type *syntactic-category* because that same restriction holds for feature structures of type *sign*. But a subtype may introduce attributes and type restrictions of its own, in addition to those that it inherits from its supertypes. For example, in addition to PHONOLOGY, SYNTAX, and SEMANTICS, *phrasal-sign* introduces the attribute DAUGHTERS, which is typed to *constituent-structure*. Another example: *phrasal-sign* and *lexical-sign* require that the path SYNTAX|LOCAL|LEXICAL have the values − and + respectively.

Subsumption also makes sense for atomic types. Consider, for example, the type *head*, whose attributes include MAJOR, which is typed to the atomic type *major*. Speaking informally, we say *major* "ranges over the atomic values" N, A, V, P, D, ...; technically, this means that N, A, V, P, D, ... are subtypes which partition the type *major*. An atomic value is nothing more than an atomic type which has no further subtypes. Another example: the atomic values + and − partition the type *boolean*. The corresponding graphs appear in (385):

(385)

The type subsumption graphs we have presented thus far are of a particularly simple kind. Like the "family tree" diagrams familiar from biological taxonomy and historical linguistics, each type is partitioned in at most one way. But for our analysis of the lexicon, something a little more elaborate is required, for we shall often need to cross-classify a single lexical type along several different dimensions at once. In such cases, it is convenient to attach labels to each of the cross-cutting partitions for easy reference, as indicated in the graph (386), which might be used to cross-classify literary works by genre and national origin. In reading such graphs, it is important to keep in mind that the partition labels do *not* correspond to subtypes themselves.

In type subsumption graphs, we use dotted lines to connect "instances" to the types they belong to. In terms of our formalism, of course, instances are just minimal types, i.e. types for which no finer distinctions exist. (Thus, for example, diagram (386) might just as well have been drawn with dotted lines, since atomic values are minimal atomic types.) In our system of lexical subtypes the instances will just be individual lexical signs.

With these preliminaries out of the way, we are now in a position to analyze the overall structure of the English lexicon, i.e. the system of subtypes of *lexical-sign*. We begin by making a top-level distinction between

(386)

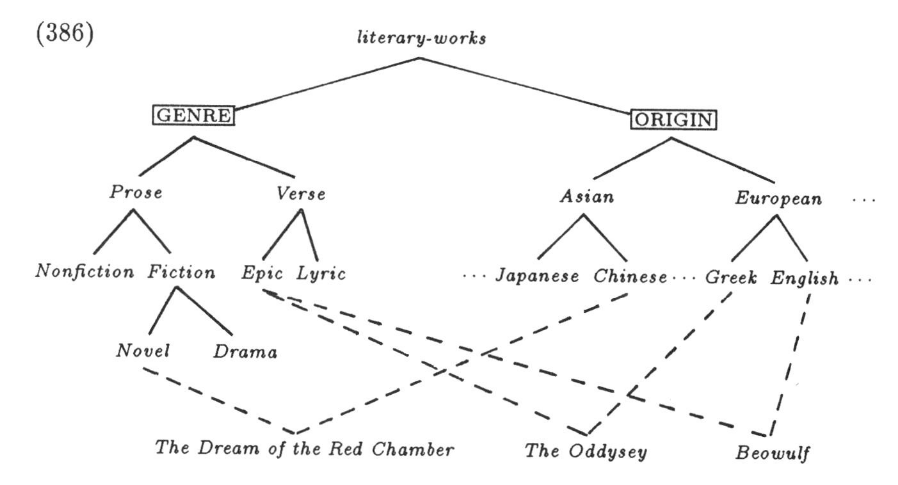

major and minor lexical signs. Major lexical signs are the "substantive" words that can serve as heads of phrases and for which the notion of subcategorization makes sense; minor lexical signs are "little" words such as determiners, complementizers, and conjunctions, about which we will have no more to say. Major lexical signs, in turn, are cross-classified on the basis of their head features and their subcategorization. The first few levels of the lexical hierarchy are shown in (387):

(387)

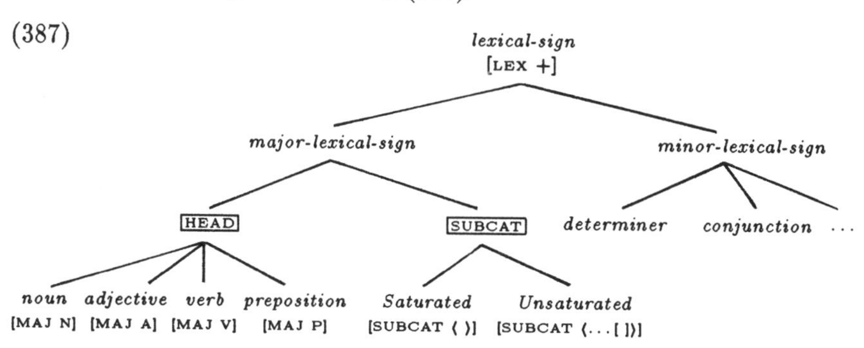

Note that some of the subtypes are annotated with some of the syntactic attributes or type restrictions which they introduce; of course these attributes and type restrictions are inherited by all the subtypes of the types which bear them. In the partition of major lexical signs according to subcategorization, the top-level distinction is between words which are saturated (proper nouns and pronouns) and those which subcategorize for at least one sign (everything else); in the partition according to head features, the top-level distinction is among different values of the MAJOR feature. In short, we assume that the fundamental linguistically significant dimensions for classifying substantive words are valence and part of speech. We will descend to finer distinctions in a moment, but first some remarks are in order concerning head features.

As we noted above, the path LOCAL|HEAD within syntactic categories is typed to *head.* But what does a feature structure of type head look like? What are its attributes? Thus far, we have contented ourselves with an inventory of the atomic-valued head features MAJOR, CASE, VFORM, NFORM, PFORM, AUX, INV, and PRD. (We postpone till the end of this section discussion of the head feature ADJUNCTS, which is typed to a set of *syntactic-category.*) But this is overly simple, and allows distinctions to be introduced that are not reflected in the linguistic facts. For of the head features listed, only MAJOR and PRD are appropriate for all HEAD values. Of the others, NFORM and CASE make sense only for HEAD values of nouns; PFORM applies only to prepositions; and VFORM and AUX are suitable only for verbs. (We will deal with the INV feature presently.) These facts suggest that the type *head* itself be partitioned as indicated in (388).

(388)

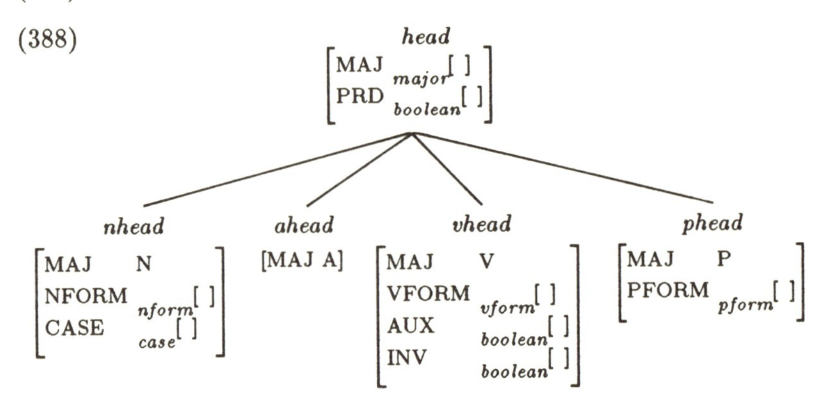

Suitably modified to reflect this improvement, the partition by head of the type *major-lexical-sign* ((387) above) is as follows:

(389)

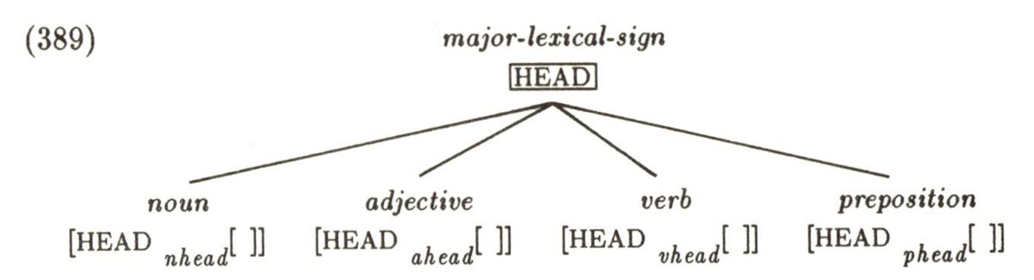

Of course, (389) indicates only the syntactic information associated with the types in question. As we noted earlier (see (377)b and (379)b above), lexical types also constrain the types of their semantic contents. Thus, for example, we can define the type *noun* as a subtype of *major-lexical-sign* whose SYNTAX|LOCAL|HEAD is typed to *nhead* and whose SEMANTICS |CONTENT is typed to *indexed-object.* In terms of feature structures, this can be expresed as (390):

(390)
$$ {}_{noun}[\ ] = {}_{major\text{-}lexical\text{-}sign}\begin{bmatrix} \text{SYN}\,|\,\text{LOC}\,|\,\text{HEAD} & {}_{nhead}[\ ] \\ \text{SEM}\,|\,\text{CONT} & {}_{indexed\text{-}object}[\ ] \end{bmatrix} $$

Likewise, we can define *verb* as in (391):

(391)
$$ {}_{verb}[\ ] = {}_{major\text{-}lexical\text{-}sign}\begin{bmatrix} \text{SYN}\,|\,\text{LOC}\,|\,\text{HEAD} & {}_{vhead}[\ ] \\ \text{SEM}\,|\,\text{CONT} & {}_{basic\text{-}circumstance}[\ ] \end{bmatrix} $$

Descending further in the partition according to head features, we turn next to the classification of verbs.[7] Here again, we cross-classify along two dimensions, as shown in (392).

As expected, one of these dimensions corresponds to the traditional notion of verbal inflectional form; the other involves the important syntactic distinction between auxiliary and main verbs. (For an overview of these two distinctions, see Section 3.1.) The type *auxiliary* is where the feature INV is introduced, typed to *boolean*; this specification has the effect of permitting auxiliaries in general to occur both inverted and noninverted.[8]

Let us focus now on the partition according to verb form. This system of subtypes constitutes the inflectional paradigm in which nearly all English verbs participate (with numerous subregularities and exceptions, of course). As before, we have indicated in the graph only some of the syntactic information introduced by the subtypes. Some of them introduce valence and semantic information as well. For example, *finite* introduces a location parameter and the requirement that the subject be in nominative case (as in (380)d above). *Past* additionally restricts the location parameter to precede the discourse location (as in (380)e above) while *nonpast* restricts it to temporally overlap the discourse location. *Modal*, which is also a subtype of *auxiliary*, is not part of the inflectional paradigm; we do not attempt to characterize this subtype semantically. *3rdsng* and *non3rdsng* additionally constrain the PERSON and NUMBER values of the (variable introduced by) the subject. These properties serve to differentiate the non-third-singular finite form from the homophonous (except for the verb *be*) base form, and

---

[7] We pass over the subclassification of adjectives, prepositions, and nouns. For nouns, the fundamental cross-cutting partitions are between common nouns and saturated nouns (lexical NP's), and between singular and plural; saturated nouns divide in turn into proper nouns and pronouns. Pronouns are cross-classified according to traditional distinctions of case and agreement, as well as *referential type* (e.g. regular, reflexive, reciprocal, expletive, etc.); this last notion is addressed at length in volume 2.

[8] Restricting the applicability of the INV feature to just auxiliaries requires a slight modification to one of the grammar rules in Chapter 6. In particular, the INV specification in Rule 2 must be changed from [INV $-$] to $\neg$[INV $+$].

(392) Classification of Verbs
According to Head Features

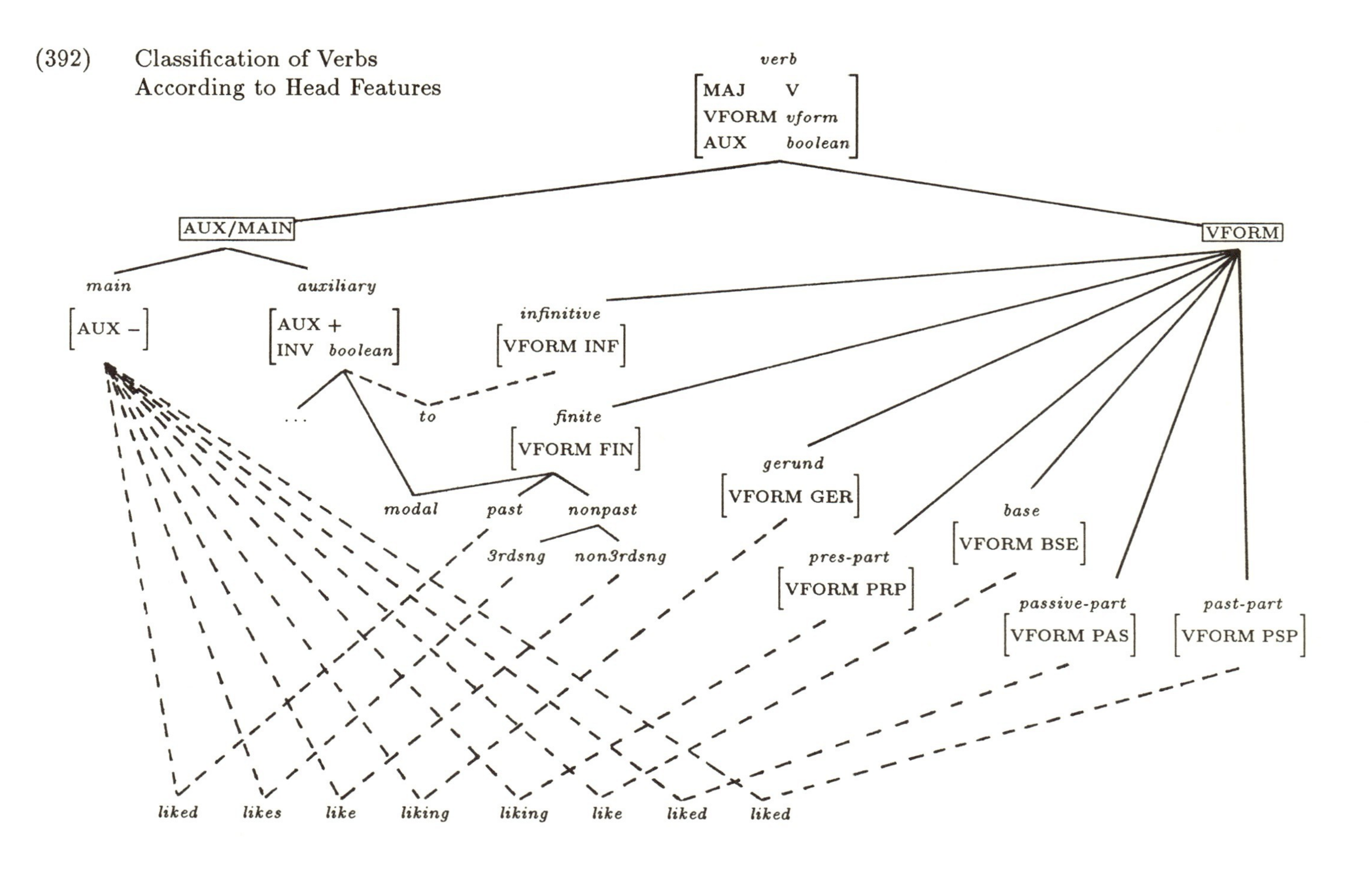

the past form from the often homophonous past-participle (and passive-participle) form. We also suppose that *gerund* introduces some semantic information that gives these forms nounlike properties, though we leave the precise analysis to further study; this differentiates gerunds from the homophonous present participles.

The fact that this paradigm is repeated over and over, with minor variations, for nearly all English verbs, is a massive redundancy which remains unaccounted for thus far. We tackle this problem in the following section where we consider the interaction of "horizontal" lexical rules (including inflectional rules) with the kind of "vertical" inheritance of information which characterizes the lexical type hierarchy. Likewise, we postpone to the following section the discussion of "relation-changing" lexical rules, such as the passive rule, which systematically alters the valence of the base form, while ensuring that the passive form is always homophonous with the past participle. Of course, *infinitive* is not part of the inflectional paradigm; following work in GPSG, we assume that the only lexical infinitive is the infinitive auxiliary *to*. Thus, for example, in the phrase *to see John*, *to see* is not a constituent; rather, *to* heads the phrase and subcategorizes for for the VP[BSE] *see John*.

Descending further still into our verb hierarchy, we next consider the subtypes of *auxiliary*, which are indicated in (393).

The basis for the classification is inflectional behavior, which we discuss in detail in the following section; the facts to be accounted for are the following: modals (such as *must* and *will*) are finite and do not inflect; *to* is infinitive and does not inflect; *perfective* (forms of auxiliary *have*) has the full range of inflections; *copula* (forms of *be*) makes more distinctions than the standard inflectional paradigm; and *auxiliary-do* has finite inflected forms only. In addition, each subtype specifies a characteristic subcategorization for the unsaturated complement.[9] It should be noted that few auxiliaries are exceptional with respect to invertibility; for example, *aren't* (the contracted negative form of *am*) and *better* are further specified as [INV +] and [INV −] respectively.

In (394) we return to the top of our lexical hierarchy and examine the partition of *major-lexical-sign* according to valence (i.e. subcategorization), which crosscuts the partition by head features.

Here the top-level distinction is between *saturated* (major lexical signs which do not subcategorize for anything, i.e. proper nouns and pronouns) and unsaturated; *unsaturated* in turn divides naturally into *common* (common nouns), which seek a determiner or possessive phrase, and all others,

---

[9] In (393), the notation "XP[PRD]" in the subcategorization of the copula abbreviates

$$\left[\text{SYN}|\text{LOC}\begin{bmatrix}\text{HEAD}|\text{PRD} + \\ \text{SUBCAT} \langle[\ ]\rangle\end{bmatrix}\right]$$

(393) Classification of Auxiliary Verbs

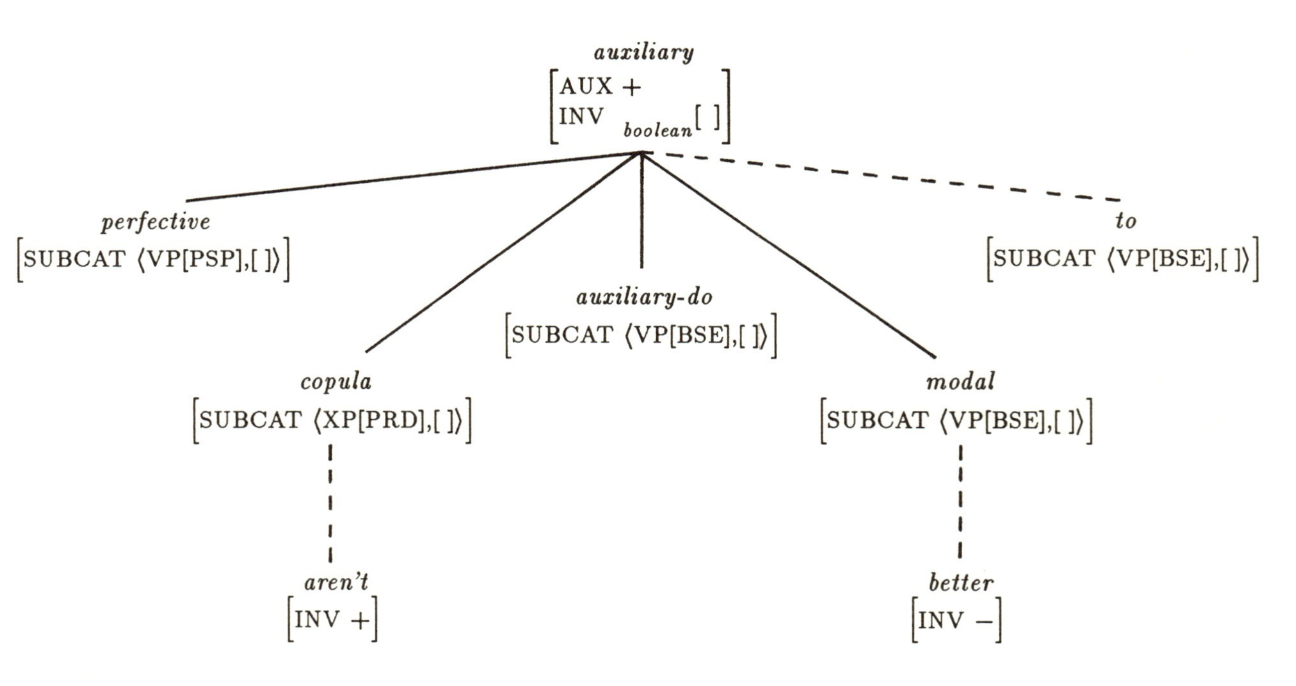

(394) Subcategorization Types

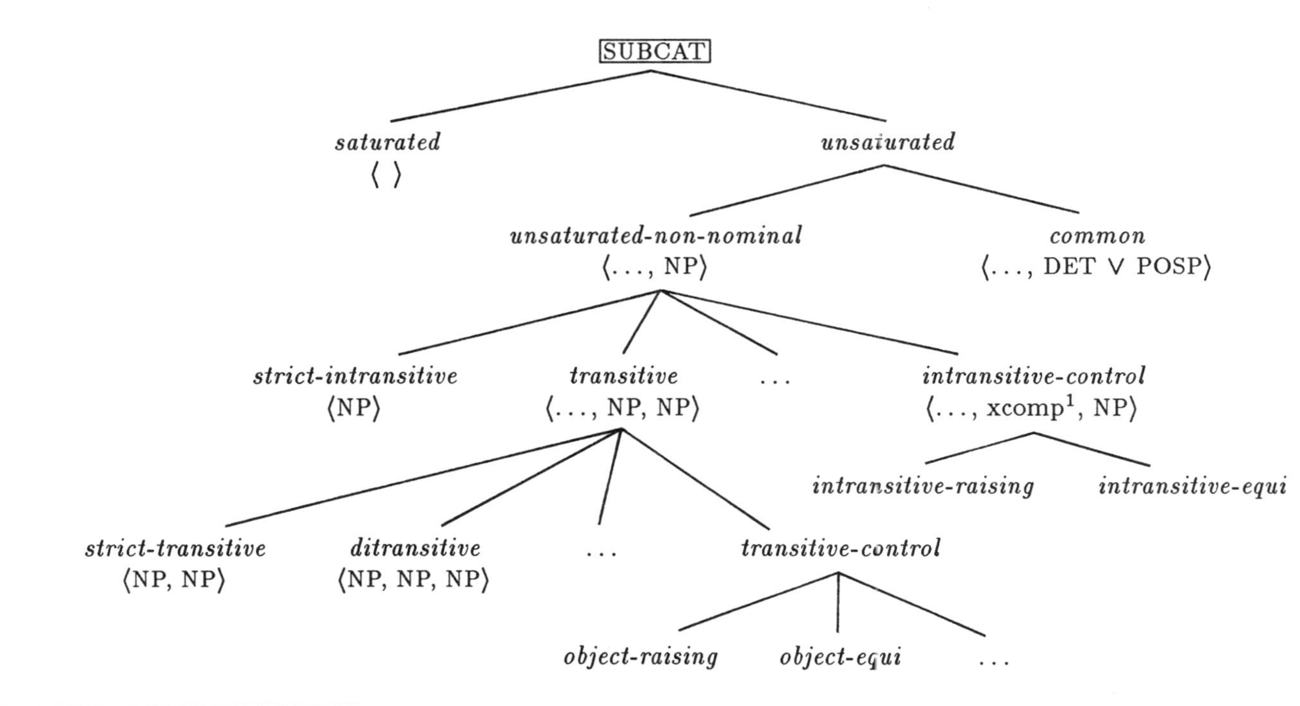

[1] The notation "xcomp" abbreviates [SYN|LOC|SUBCAT ⟨[ ]⟩].

(395) Cross-Classification of Major Lexical Signs by Head Features and Subcategorization

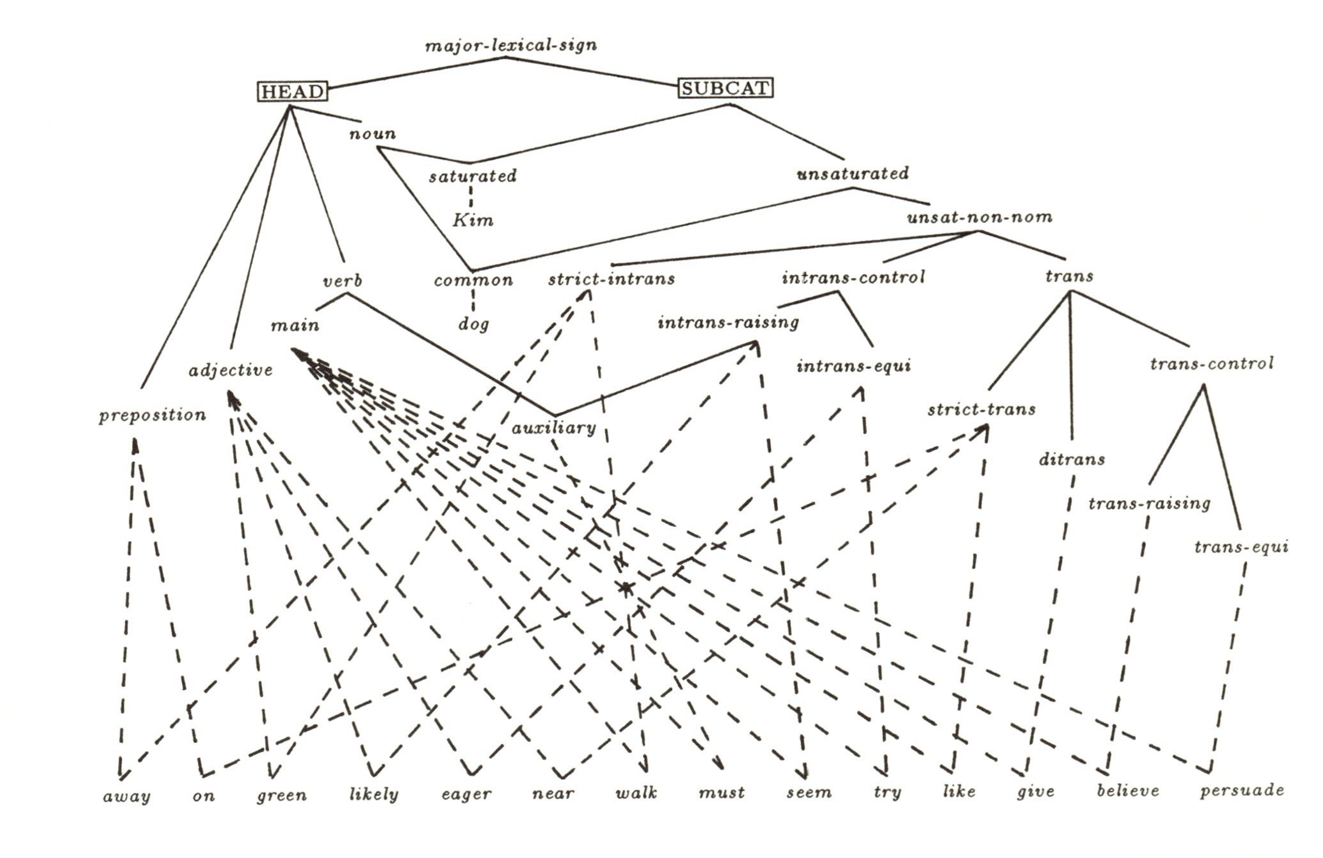

which seek an NP. Among unsaturated non-nominals, further distinctions are made according to the number of additional complements and whether or not one of the additional complements is controlled (unsaturated).

The additional subtypes of *intransitive-control* and *transitive* control have to do with the much-studied distinction between raising (e.g. *seem, believe*) and equi (e.g. *try, persuade, promise*), which we discuss at great length in Volume 2. The overall effect of the two main cross-cutting partitions is illustrated in (396); for simplicity the finer distinctions among verbs are omitted.

Note that the subcategorization types *saturated* and *common* are relevant only for nouns (in fact they partition *noun*); the ternary subcategorization types are relevant only for verbs. Also, *auxiliary* is a subtype of *intransitive-raising*.

Further elaboration of the lexical type system is possible, of course, but the distinctions already mentioned will suffice for present purposes. The key point is that much of the redundancy of lexical information can be eliminated by factoring out of individual lexical signs those properties which are shared with a class of similar signs. The total number of types about which the language user must have explicit information is relatively small; but by organizing information about words in terms of cross-cutting type hierarchies, a very large number of fine distinctions can be articulated. Thus, for example, the place of the verb *likes* in the lexical hierarchy is roughly as shown in (396):

(396)

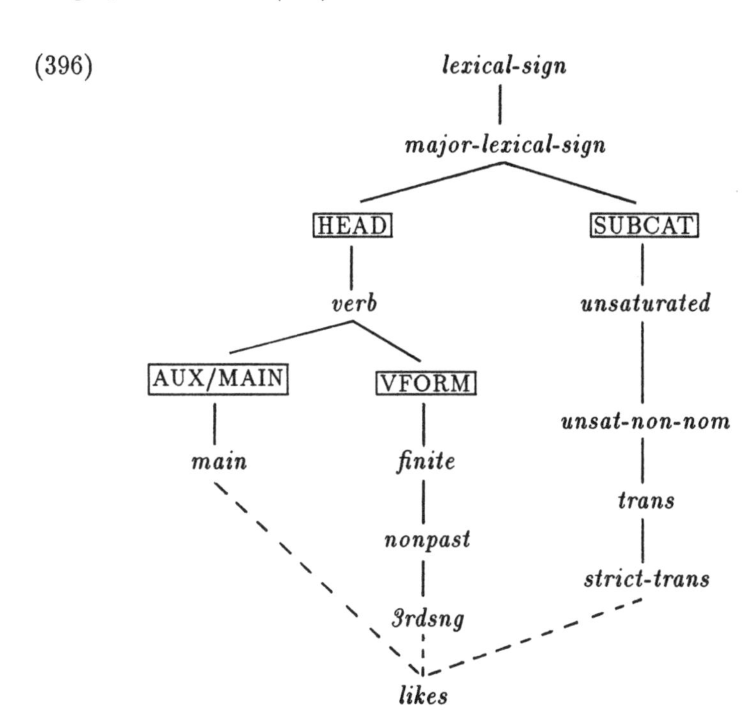

Since the total information content of *likes*, shown in (397), is just the result of unifying the idiosyncratic information particular to *likes* with the information inherited from the types to which it belongs, and since every type inherits all the information of its supertypes, it follows that (397) is equivalent to (398).

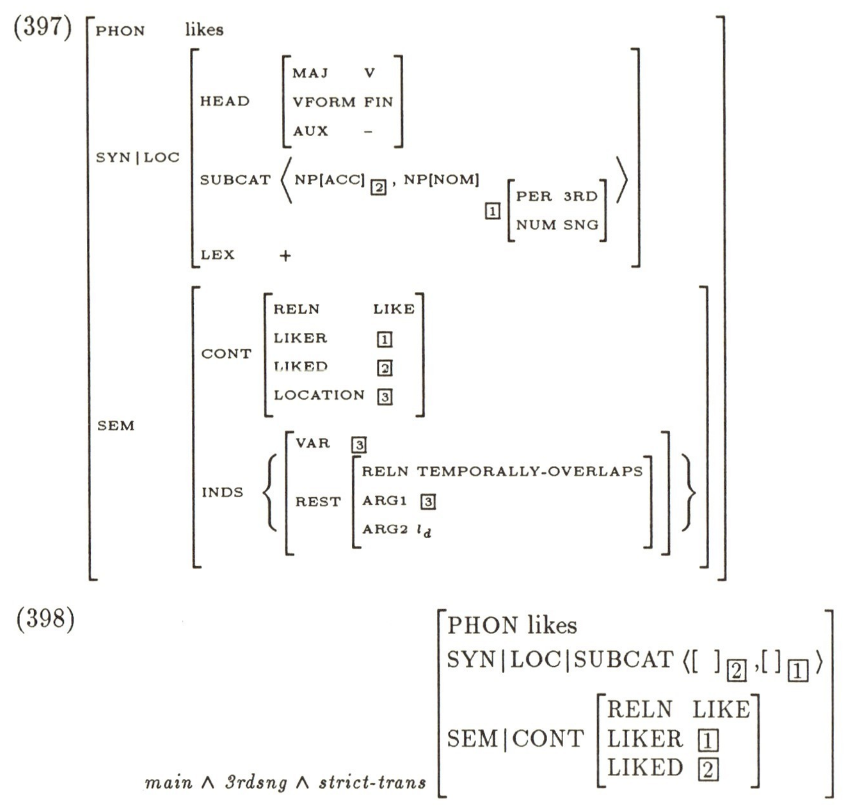

As we shall see in the next section, further reduction of lexical redundancy can be achieved by making use of the type hierarchy to define the domain of application of word formation processes (lexical rules). We speculate that organizational principles of the general nature sketched here would lend themselves well to being embedded into a sensible model of linguistic processing, in which efficient representation of information enables much of the work in lexical access to be accomplished by simple and highly constrained deductive mechanisms.

To conclude this section, we comment briefly on the role of the lexical hierarchy in accounting for selection of adjuncts. In Chapter 6 we argued that heads select for the adjuncts that modify them, rather than the other way around. An apparent difficulty with this approach is that it introduces massive redundancy: for example, every lexical common noun has to specify that its value set for the head feature ADJUNCTS contains the specification RELCLAUSE (where this symbol abbreviates whatever official analysis we adopt for relative clauses). But if the lexicon is organized along the lines that we have suggested here, this problem drops away. All that is needed is to state the specification [SYN|LOC|HEAD|ADJUNCTS {RELCLAUSE, ...}] once and for all for the lexical type *noun*; the specification will then be inherited by all instances of that type. Since this same mechanism is available in all cases where a particular lexical type (and the corresponding phrasal projections) select a particular kind of adjunct, we can eliminate specialized phrase structure rules whose only purpose is to combine a certain kind of head with a certain kind of adjunct, in favor of a single schematic rule, as noted in Chapter 6.

8.2 Lexical Rules

In the preceding section, we saw that the organization of the lexicon into a multiple hierarchy of types enables us to drastically simplify our descriptions of lexical signs by factoring out information of a *general* nature that is shared with with whole word classes (e.g. parts of speech, valence classes, etc.). This move can be viewed as a kind of elimination of "vertical" redundancy. But as it stands, our lexicon still contains massive "horizontal" redundancy: we have not accounted for groups of words whose *specific* information content (e.g. phonology, the relation within semantic content, semantic role assignment) are related according to recurrent patterns. These patterns include inflectional paradigms such as English verb conjugation and Latin noun declensions; derivational relationships such as nominalization and *un*-prefixation; and polyvalency patterns, wherein homophonous or morphologically related versions of the "same" word differ in the assignment of semantic roles to grammatical functions, such as active versus passive forms and the "dative-shift" alternation (*give Kim Felix* vs. *give Felix to Kim*). Among linguists there is a well-established tradition of treating relationships of this kind in terms of *lexical (redundancy) rules*, functions which map one class of words to another.[10] Given the lexical rule, the "output" (inflected, derived, or "shifted") form can be predicted from the "input" (base, stem, or "unshifted") form. Lexical rules can be viewed from either a declarative or a procedural perspective: on the former view, they capture generalizations about static relationships between members of two or more word classes; on the latter view, they describe processes which produce the output form from the input form.[11] Evidently, the procedural

---

[10] See, e.g., Stanley (1967), Jackendoff (1975); Bresnan (1982).

[11] Mathematically, we think of the base forms and lexical rules as a signature from which the full lexicon is generated as a free algebra. In fact, given the hierarchy of lexical types, this algebra is *order-sorted* in the sense of Meseguer, Goguen, and Smolka (1987); the lexical rules can then be re-

view of lexical rules is well-suited to playing a role in a model of language use. For example, it is unlikely in the extreme that the language user explicitly represents the full inflectional paradigm of each verb; it seems more reasonable to assume that regular inflected forms are computed (deduced) from a single base form (or set of "principal parts" in highly inflected languages where multiple stems are needed to generate the full inflectional paradigm) on an as-needed basis.

The organization of the lexicon into hierarchies of types allows us to specify the domain and effect of lexical rules in a strikingly simple fashion. For example, the inflectional rule which produces the third-singular (nonpast finite) form of a verb from the base form can be stated as in (399):

(399) Third-Singular Inflectional Rule (preliminary version)

3RDSNG:

$$\begin{bmatrix} \text{PHON } \boxed{1} \\ \text{SYN|LOC|SUBCAT } \boxed{2} \\ \text{SEM|CONT } \boxed{3} \end{bmatrix}_{base} \mapsto \begin{bmatrix} \text{PHON } f_{3RDSNG}\,(\boxed{1}) \\ \text{SYN|LOC|SUBCAT } \boxed{2} \\ \text{SEM|CONT } \boxed{3} \end{bmatrix}_{3rdsng}$$

The intended interpretation is that the function 3RDSNG takes as input a lexical sign of type *base* with phonology $\boxed{1}$, subcategorization $\boxed{2}$, and semantics $\boxed{3}$, and produces as output the result of *unifying* specific information obtained or computed from the input form with the general information inherited from the type *3rdsng*. In particular, the phonology of the output form is obtained from the phonology of the input form (the stem) by application of the morphological operation f_{3RDSNG}, which adds *-s* to the stem,[12] while the semantic content and subcategorization are brought over intact; further information unified in from the output type *3rdsng* include the head features and the nonpast location index, as well as the nominative case and third-singular agreement information on the subcategorized subject. The effect of this lexical rule on the base verb *like* is illustrated in (400).

---

garded as free record-type constructors (Smolka and Ait-Kaci (1987)). This algebraic perspective, which is neutral between the declarative and procedural interpretations, lends much conceptual clarity to the analysis of word formation; e.g. inflection, derivation, and compounding correspond to unary sort-preserving, unary sort-changing, and binary algebra operations respectively. The murkiness of the distinction between inflection and derivation is then seen to arise from the hierarchiality of the system of lexical types: the input and ouput forms may be of the same type and of distinct types simultaneously if they belong to different subtypes of the same type (e.g. positive and comparative forms of degree adjectives).

[12] Of course a more adequate characterization of this and other morphological operations would have to take account of more subtle morphophonemic effects.

(400) a. Input:

$$\textit{main} \wedge \textit{base} \wedge \textit{strict-trans}\begin{bmatrix} \text{PHON like} & \\ \text{SYN}|\text{LOC}|\text{SUBCAT } \langle [\ ]_{\boxed{2}}, [\ ]_{\boxed{1}} \rangle & \\ \text{SEM}|\text{CONT} & \begin{bmatrix} \text{RELN} & \text{LIKE} \\ \text{LIKER} & \boxed{1} \\ \text{LIKED} & \boxed{2} \end{bmatrix} \end{bmatrix}$$

b. Specific output information (computed from input):

$$\begin{bmatrix} \text{PHON likes} & \\ \text{SYN}|\text{LOC}|\text{SUBCAT } \langle \text{NP[ACC]}_{\boxed{2}}, \text{NP}_{\boxed{1}} \rangle & \\ \text{SEM}|\text{CONT} & \begin{bmatrix} \text{RELN} & \text{LIKE} \\ \text{LIKER} & \boxed{1} \\ \text{LIKED} & \boxed{2} \end{bmatrix} \end{bmatrix}$$

c. General output information (inherited from *3rdsng* and its supertypes):

$$\begin{bmatrix} \text{SYN}|\text{LOC} & \begin{bmatrix} \text{HEAD} & \begin{bmatrix} \text{MAJ} & \text{V} \\ \text{VFORM} & \text{FIN} \end{bmatrix} \\ \text{SUBCAT} & \left\langle \ldots, \text{NP[NOM]}_{\boxed{2}\begin{bmatrix} \text{PER} & \text{3RD} \\ \text{NUM} & \text{SNG} \end{bmatrix}} \right\rangle \\ \text{LEX} & + \end{bmatrix} \\ \text{SEM} & \begin{bmatrix} \text{CONT}|\text{LOCATION } \boxed{3} & \\ \text{INDS} & \left\{ \begin{bmatrix} \text{VAR} & \boxed{3} \\ \text{REST} & \begin{bmatrix} \text{RELN} & \text{NOT-PRECEDES} \\ \text{ARG1} & \boxed{3} \\ \text{ARG2} & l_d \end{bmatrix} \end{bmatrix} \right\} \end{bmatrix} \end{bmatrix}$$

d. Final result obtained by unifying (b) and (c).

There are a number of points to make here in connection with the rule (399). First, successful application of the rule does not depend upon the availability of *all* the information about the input form; it is enough to know which types it inherits from and to have access to the specific pieces of information about the input form which are required in the determination of the output form. Thus, rules of the general kind described here could be incorporated into a highly modular processing model of language use in which lexical information consists of (i) general knowledge about the type hierarchy, including knowledge of which lexical rules apply to which types; and (ii) a collection of lexical entries for the base forms, where each entry specifies the idiosyncratic information about the word in question together with pointers to the minimal lexical types from which it inherits. Thus, for example, the lexical entry for *like* would essentially be a pair of the form (401):

(401) Specific: $\begin{bmatrix} \text{PHON like} \\ \text{SYN|LOC|SUBCAT } \langle [\ ]_{\boxed{2}}, [\ ]_{\boxed{1}} \rangle \\ \text{SEM|CONT} \begin{bmatrix} \text{RELN} & \text{LIKE} \\ \text{LIKER} & \boxed{1} \\ \text{LIKED} & \boxed{2} \end{bmatrix} \end{bmatrix}$

Types: {*base, main, strict-transitive*}

On such a model, information of a general nature about words, even base forms, need not be stored explicitly in the lexical entries, but can be obtained on demand from the appropriate types as needed during interpretation or lexical rule application.

Second, it is necessary to take into account the fact that lexical rules characteristically have systematic or idiosyncratic *exceptions* which fail to undergo the rule at all. Such exceptions can be dealt with in a number of ways. For example, the English verb inflectional rules systematically do not apply to the modal auxiliaries, which occur in a single (finite) form. Thus we assume that the modals are simply explicitly listed in the finite form; the absence of the other forms then follows from the fact that they have no base forms to which the inflectional rules can apply. A somewhat different example of systematic non-application is provided by the derivational rule of nominalization which produces a common noun (in many cases homophonous with the verbal gerund); nominalization does not apply to auxiliaries. We can account for this fact by simply taking care to specifying the input type as *base* ∧ *main*. An example of idiosyncratic non-application is provided by the English copula, which does not have the usual past form; instead it has the distinct past-singular and past-plural forms *was* and *were*. Of course these forms must be listed separately, but that does not quite solve the problem: we still have to account for the absence of a normal past (singular and plural) form *beed*. In such cases, there is evidently no recourse but to record the exception explicitly, e.g. by specifying the domain of the past inflectional rule as *base* ∧ ¬*cop*. Similarly, idiosyncratic exceptions to the valence-changing rule of passivization (see below), such as *cost* and *resemble*, must be recorded explicitly. There are also idiosyncratic "anti-exceptions", i.e. forms such as passive *rumored* for which no base "source" exists; in this case, the form passive must be explicitly listed in the lexicon as an instance of the type *passive*, even though it is not produced by the lexical rule.

Third, lexical rules often apply *irregularly* to certain forms. For example, the third-singular form of *have* is *has* rather than **haves* as predicted by (399) above. To account for irregularities of this kind, we assume that base lexical entries contain information about irregular morphology as well as the stems (this is a variant of the idea that in highly inflected languages, the base entries list all the principal parts from which the inflectional paradigm is determined). For example, we might suppose that the lexical entry for *have* has roughly the form given in (402):

(402)
$$\begin{bmatrix} \text{PHONOLOGY} & \text{have} \\ \text{3RDSNG} & \text{has} \\ \text{PAST} & \text{had} \\ \text{PAST-PART} & \text{had} \\ \text{SYNTAX} & \ldots \\ \text{SEMANTICS} & \ldots \end{bmatrix}$$

Concomitantly, we revise the third-singular rule to the form indicated in (403):

(403) Third-Singular Lexical Rule (revised version)

3RDSNG:

$$_{base}\begin{bmatrix} \text{PHON } \boxed{1} \\ \text{3RDSNG } \boxed{2} \\ \text{SYN|LOC|SUBCAT } \boxed{3} \\ \text{SEM|CONT } \boxed{4} \end{bmatrix} \mapsto {}_{3rdsng}\begin{bmatrix} \text{PHON } f_{3RDSNG}(\boxed{1}, \boxed{2}) \\ \text{SYN|LOC|SUBCAT } \boxed{3} \\ \text{SEM|CONT } \boxed{4} \end{bmatrix}$$

Here, we assume that the morphological operator f_{3RDSNG} is redefined to return the (irregular) 3RDSNG value of the input if one is provided, and add *-s* to the input's PHONOLOGY otherwise. Note that this general approach automatically accounts for the phenomenon of *blocking*, in which the existence of an irregular form precludes the coexistence of a regular form. That is, (403) produces the irregular form *has*; at the same time there is no mechanism in the grammar to produce the nonexistent "regular" form **haves*.

Fourth, patterns of homophony persist across inflectional paradigms. For example, in English, the base form of the verb is always homophonous (except for the verb *be*) with the non-third-singular finite form (though we leave the precise analysis to further study); likewise the verbal gerund is homophonous with the present participle (and also with the deverbative nominal, if regular), and the past participle is homophonous with with the passive participle. To account for such patterns, we assume that distinct lexical rules may utilize the same morphological operations. Thus we posit additional lexical rules in (404) (only the phonological effects are indicated). Note here that the non-third-singular rule duplicates the base phonology. The passive rule uses the same morphological operation as the passive-participle rule, and therefore the two forms are homophonous whenever both exist, even when they are irregular. Likewise, the gerund rule uses the same morphological operation as the present-participle rule; it should be

(404)

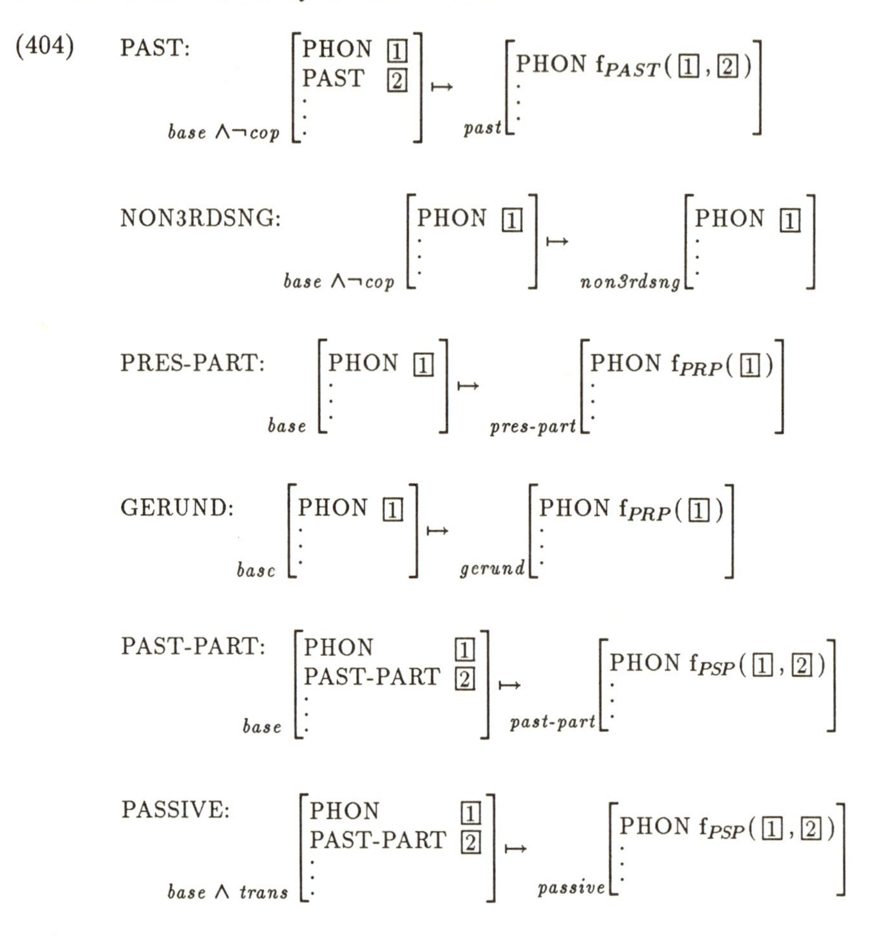

observed that this operation, unlike the others mentioned above, depends only on the PHONOLOGY of the input since it is always regular.

Fifth, two different verbs can be homophonous throughout their paradigms; for example, the main verb *have* and the auxiliary verb *have* are homophonous in all their inflected forms, although their subcategorization and semantics are totally dissimilar. Patterns of this kind are easily accounted for within our approach by positing "generic words", i.e. lexical types with just a few instances. In the present case, for example, we assume there is a "generic-*have*" type containing the morphological information given in (402) above, from which (the base forms of) main *have* and auxiliary *have* inherit. This situation is illustrated in (405).

Note that the *base* node in this diagram is annotated with the name of the lexical rules that apply to its instances. Since both forms of *have* are subject to the inflectional rules, and since both inherit the morphological information utilized by those rules from the same place, it follows that their inflected forms, even the irregular ones, are all pairwise homophonous.

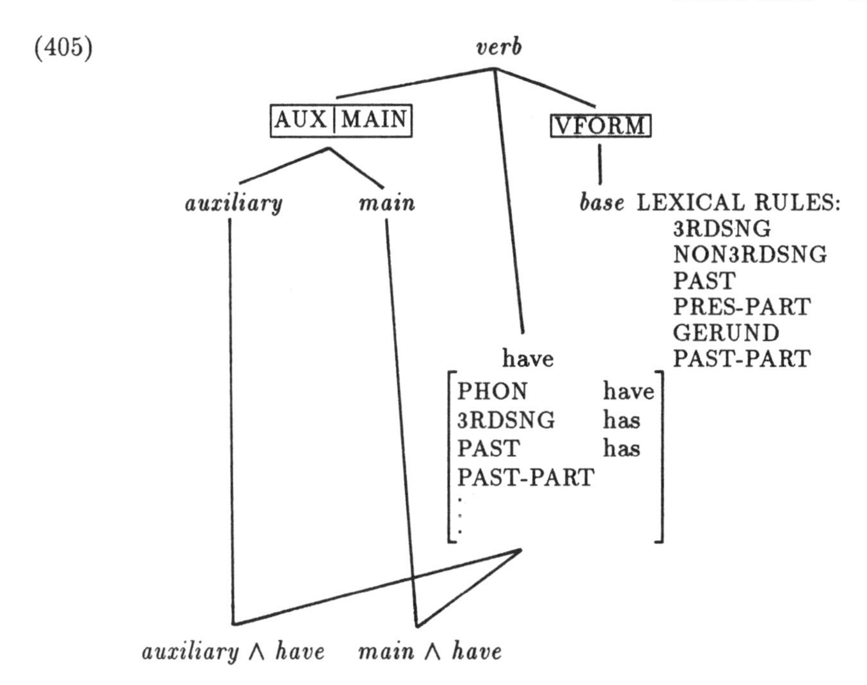

Every theory of English grammar is obliged to deal with passivization. Our version, which is broadly similar to those provided by other current nontransformational theories, is given in (406):

(406) Passive Lexical Rule

PASSIVE:

[PHON [1]
PAST-PART [2]
SYN|LOC|SUBCAT ⟨...,[ ]$_{[3]}$,[ ]$_{[4]}$⟩
SEM|CONT [5]]$_{base \wedge trans}$ ↦

[PHON f_{PSP} ([1], [2])
SEM|LOC|SUBCAT ⟨(PP[BY]$_{[4]}$),...,[ ]$_{[3]}$⟩
SEM|CONT [5]]$_{passive}$

The semantic content is simply carried over from the input form without change; as noted earlier, the phonology of the passive form is determined from the input form by the same morphological operation as the past participle, thereby ensuring the homophony of the two forms even when irregular. The heart of the action, of course, is in the subcategorization: the input form's subject is simply dropped off the SUBCAT list and its index reasigned to an optional PP[BY]. The overall effect is illustrated in (407):

(407)

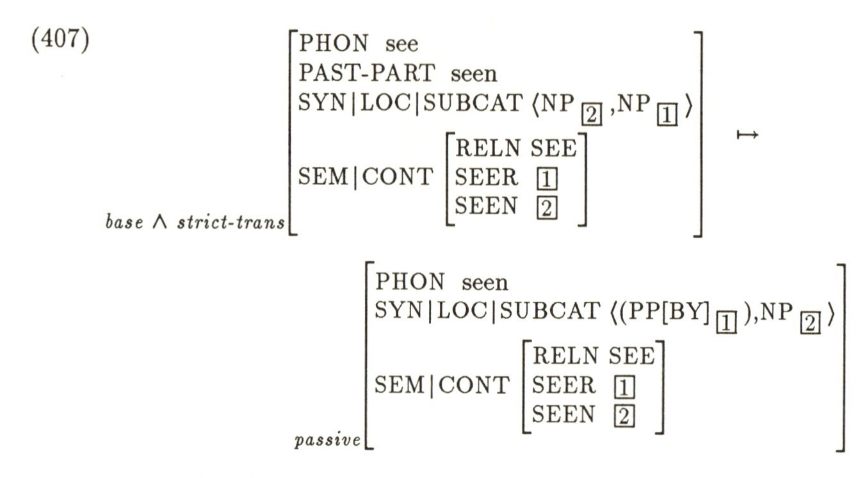

Note that the domain of application of the passive rule is the class of base transitive verbs. In this connection, it should be recalled (Figure 395) that the type *transitive* subsumes not only strictly transitive verbs (which subcategorize only for subject and object NP's), but other subtypes which subcategorize for additional complements (e.g. second object or xcomp), including ditransitives and transitive control verbs. The effect of passive on the subcategorization of such verbs is illustrated in (408)–(410):

(408) a. *introduce*: V[BSE, SUBCAT ⟨PP[TO], NP, NP⟩]
b. *introduced*: V[PAS, SUBCAT ⟨(PP[BY]), PP[TO], NP⟩]

(409) a. *blame*: V[BSE, SUBCAT ⟨PP[ON], NP, NP⟩]
b. *blamed*: V[PAS, SUBCAT ⟨(PP[BY]), PP[ON], NP⟩]

(410) a. *persuade*: V[BSE, SUBCAT ⟨VP[INF], NP, NP⟩]
b. *persuaded*: V[PAS, SUBCAT ⟨(PP[BY]), VP[INF], NP⟩]

Like any other unsaturated lexical head, passive forms such as these are free to combine with their nonsubject complements by Rule 2, thereby forming a VP[PAS]; VP[PAS] in turn is subcategorized for by the copula. Thus passive sentences such as *Kim was introduced to Sandy by Chris* are produced in the usual fashion, as indicated in (412). The reassignment of semantic roles to grammatical functions guarantees that (412) has the same semantic content as *Chris introduced Kim to Sandy.*

More generally, we employ lexical rules, much as in LFG, to account for polyvalency patterns which apply across a whole word class. For example, the alternation between causative transitive verbs and corresponding intransitives (*Kim broke the vase* versus *The vase broke*) can be accounted for by a lexical rule of detransitivization whose effect on subcategorization is essentially the same as the passive rule (except that no optional PP[BY]

(411) Summary of Lexical Rules Referred to in Chapter 8

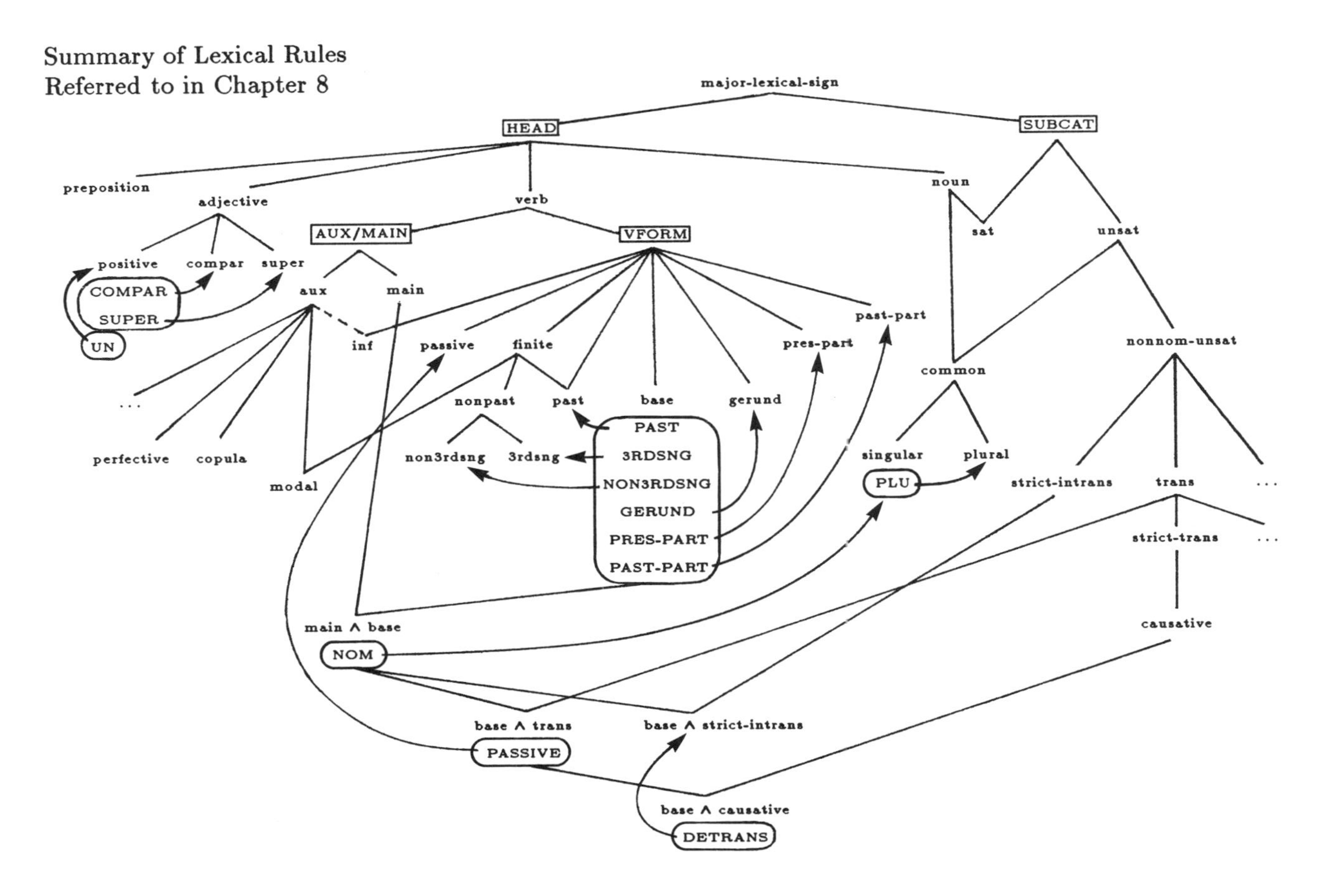

(412)

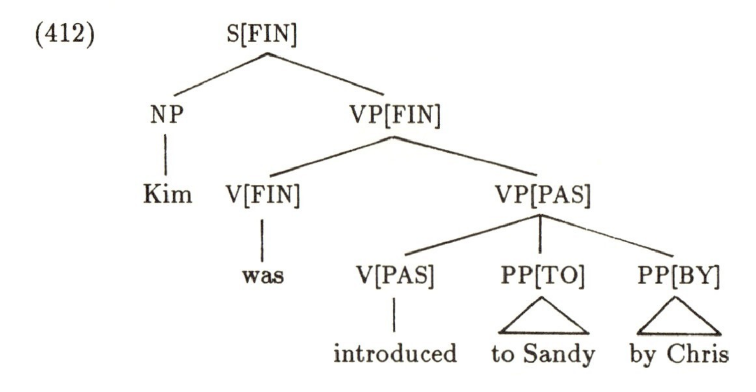

is introduced). Unlike the passive rule, however, the domain of application (input type) of the detransitivization rule must be characterized as semantically causative, and the rule itself operates in a nontrivial way upon the semantic content. In Volume 2, we will see that numerous other phenomena conventionally handled by syntactic mechanisms (e.g. GB's transformational rule Move-α or GPSG's metarules), including *tough*-"movement", "extraposition" with expletive *it*, and even subject "extractions" from sentential complements, can also be analyzed in wholly lexical terms, using lexical rules that operate upon SUBCAT lists.

8.3 Suggestions for Further Reading

The key ideas in this chapter arise not from previous linguistic studies, but rather from algebraic approaches to datatype theory and the semantics of programming, such as Ait-Kaci (1984) and Goguen and Meseguer (to appear); similar ideas are widely employed in frame-based knowledge representation systems (see, e.g. Goldstein and Roberts (1977)).

References

Ades, A. and M. Steedman 1982. On the Order of Words. *Linguistics and Philosophy* 4:517–558.

Ait-Kaci, H. 1984. *A Lattice-Theoretic Approach to Computation Based on a Calculus of Partially Ordered Types.* PhD Dissertation, Department of Computer Science, Moore School, University of Pennsylvania.

Andrews, A. 1982. The Representation of Case in Modern Icelandic. In Bresnan (Ed.), *The Mental Representation of Grammatical Relations.* Cambridge, Mass.: MIT Press, 427–503.

Asher, N. 1986. Belief in Discourse Representation Theory. *Journal of Philosophical Logic* 15:127–189.

Bach E. 1983. Generalized Categorial Grammars and the English Auxiliary. In F. Heny and B. Richards (Eds.), *Linguistic Categories, Auxiliaries, and Related Puzzles II.* Dordrecht: Reidel.

Bach, E. and B. Partee 1980. Anaphora and Semantic Structure. In *Papers From the Parasession on Pronouns and Anaphora* (CLS 10). Chicago: Chicago Linguistic Society.

Baltin, M. 1978. *Toward a Theory of Movement Rules.* PhD Dissertation, Massachusetts Institute of Technology.

Barwise, J. 1986a. Information and Circumstance. *Notre Dame Journal of Formal Logic* 27.3:324–338.

Barwise, J. 1986b. Noun Phrases, Generalized Quantifiers, and Anaphora. Report No. CSLI-86-52, Stanford: CSLI. Also to appear in P. Gaerdenfors (Ed.), *Generalized Quantifiers: Studies in Linguistics and Philosophy.* Dordrecht: Reidel.

Barwise, J. 1987. Unburdening the Language of Thought. In Two Replies, Report No. CSLI-87-74. Stanford: CSLI. Also to appear in *Language and Mind.*

Barwise, J., and R. Cooper 1981. Generalized Quantifiers and Natural Languages. *Linguistics and Philosophy* 4.2:159–219.

Barwise, J. and J. Perry 1983. *Situations and Attitudes.* Cambridge, Mass.: MIT Press.

Barwise, J. and J. Perry 1985. Shifting Situations and Shaken Attitudes: An Interview with Barwise and Perry. *Linguistics and Philosophy* 8.1: 105–161. Also appeared as Report No. CSLI-84-13, Stanford: CSLI.

Bloomfield, L. 1933. *Language*. New York: Holt, Rinehart, and Winston.

Borsley, R. 1987. A Note on HPSG. *Bangor Research Papers in Linguistics I*. Bangor: University College of North Wales.

Borsley, R. In press. Subjects and Complements in HPSG. Report No. CSLI-87-107, Stanford: CSLI.

Bresnan, J. (Ed.) 1982. *The Mental Representation of Grammatical Relations*. Cambridge, Mass.: MIT Press.

Carlson, G. Manuscript. Thematic Roles and their Role in Semantic Interpretation. Unpublished manuscript, University of Iowa.

Chomsky, N. 1957. *Syntactic Structures*. The Hague: Mouton.

Chomsky, N. 1981. *Lectures on Government and Binding*. Dordrecht: Foris.

Chomsky, N. 1982. *Some Concepts and Consequences of the Theory of Government and Binding*. Cambridge, Mass.: MIT Press.

Chomsky, N. 1986. *Knowledge of Language: Its Nature, Origin and Use*. New York: Praeger.

Cooper, R. 1975. *Montague's Semantic Theory and Transformational Syntax*. PhD Dissertation, University of Massachusetts, Amherst.

Cooper, R. 1983. *Quantification and Syntactic Theory*. Dordrecht: Reidel.

Cooper, R. Manuscript. Introduction to Situation Semantics. 1987 Linguistic Institute, Stanford University.

Creary, L. and C. Pollard 1985. A Computational Semantics for Natural Language. In *Proceedings of the 23rd Annual Meeting of the Association for Computational Linguistics*.

Dalrymple, M. and S. Joshi 1986. Relative Clauses and Relative Clause Linking in Marathi. Unpublished manuscript, Stanford University.

Dowty, D. 1982a. Grammatical Relations and Montague Grammar. In P. Jacobson and G. K. Pullum (Eds.), *The Nature of Syntactic Representation*. Dordrecht: Reidel.

Dowty, D. 1982b. More on the Categorial Analysis of Grammatical Relations. In A. Zaenen (Ed.), *Subjects and Other Subjects: Proceedings of the Harvard Conference on Grammatical Relations*. Bloomington: Indiana University Linguistics Club.

Emonds, J. 1976. *A Transformational Approach to English Syntax.* New York: Academic Press.

Falk, Y. 1983. Constituency, Word Order, and Phrase Structure Rules. *Linguistic Analysis* 11:331–360.

Fenstad, J. E., P.-K. Halvorsen, T. Langholm and J. v. Benthem 1985. Equations, Schemata, and Situations: A Framework for Linguistic Semantics. Report No. CSLI-85-29. Stanford: CSLI.

Fillmore, C. 1968. The Case for Case. In E. Bach and R. Harms (Eds.), *Universals in Linguistic Theory.* New York: Holt, Rinehart, and Winston.

Flickinger, D. 1983. Lexical Heads and Phrasal Gaps. In M. Barlow, D. Flickinger, and M. Wescoat (Eds.), *Proceedings of the Second West Coast Conference on Formal Linguistics.* Stanford: Stanford Linguistics Department.

Flickinger, D. 1987. *Lexical Rules in the Hierarchical Lexicon.* PhD Dissertation, Stanford University.

Flickinger, D., C. Pollard and T. Wasow 1985. Structure-Sharing in Lexical Representation. In *Proceedings of the 23rd Annual Meeting of the Association for Computational Linguistics.*

Fodor, J. A. 1986a. Information and Association. *Notre Dame Journal of Formal Logic* 27.3:307–323.

Fodor, J. A. 1986b. A Situated Grandmother? Unpublished manuscript, The Graduate Center, City University of New York.

Gawron, J. M. Manuscript. Lexical Representations and Lexical Rules. Unpublished manuscript, Stanford: CSLI.

Gawron, J. M., and P. S. Peters. Manuscript. Anaphora and Quantification in Situation Semantics. Unpublished manuscript, Stanford: CSLI.

Gazdar, G., E. Klein, G. K. Pullum, and I. A. Sag 1985. *Generalized Phrase Structure Grammar.* Cambridge: Blackwell, and Cambridge, Mass.: Harvard University Press.

Gazdar, G., and G. K. Pullum 1981. Subcategorization, Constituent Order and the Notion 'Head'. In M. Moortgat, H. v. Hulst, and T. Hoekstra (Eds.), *The Scope of Lexical Rules.* Dordrecht: Foris.

Gazdar, G., and G. K. Pullum 1982. *Generalized Phrase Structure Grammar: A Theoretical Synopsis.* Bloomington, Ind.: Indiana University Linguistics Club.

Gazdar, G., G. K. Pullum, and and I. A. Sag 1981. Auxiliaries and Related Phenomena in a Restricted Theory of Grammar. *Language* 58:591–638.

Gazdar, G., G. K. Pullum, R. Carpenter, E. Klein, T. Hukari, and R. Levine 1987. Category Structures. Report No. CSLI-87-102. Stanford: CSLI.

Goldstein, I., and B. Roberts 1977. The FRL Manual. MIT-AI Memo 409. Cambridge, Mass.: MIT Press.

Goguen, J. and J. Meseguer. In press. Order-Sorted Algebra I: Partial and Overloaded Operators, Errors and Inheritance. Computer Science Lab, SRI International.

Greenberg, J. 1962. Some Universals of Grammar With Particular Reference to the Order of Meaningful Elements. In Greenberg, J. (Ed.), *Universals of Language.* Cambridge, Mass.: MIT Press.

Grimshaw, J. 1982. Subcategorization and Grammatical Relations. In A. Zaenen (Ed.), *Subjects and Other Subjects: Proceedings of the Harvard Conference on Grammatical Relations.* Bloomington, Ind.: Indiana University Linguistics Club.

Grosu, A. 1972. The Strategic Nature of Island Constraints. *Ohio State Univerisity Working Papers in Linguistics* 13:1–225.

Gruber, J. 1965. *Studies in Lexical Relations.* PhD Dissertation, Massachusetts Institute of Technology.

Gunji, Takao 1986. *Japanese Phrase Structure Grammar.* Dordrecht: Reidel.

Haddock, N., E. Klein, and G. Morrill (Eds.) 1987. *Categorial Grammar, Unification Grammar, and Parsing.* Edinburgh Working Papers in Cognitive Science, Vol. 1. Edinburgh: Centre for Cognitive Science, University of Edinburgh.

Halvorsen, P.-K. 1983. Semantics for Lexical-Functional Grammar. *Linguistic Inquiry* 14.4:567–616.

Hasida, K. 1985. *Bounded Parallelism: A Theory of Linguistic Performance.* PhD Dissertation, Department of Information Science, University of Tokyo.

Heim, I. 1982. *The Semantics of Definite and Indefinite Noun Phrases.* PhD Dissertation, University of Massachusetts, Amherst.

Heny, F. 1979. Review of Noam Chomsky, The Logical Structure of Linguistic Theory. *Synthese* 40:317–352.

Higgins, R. 1973. *The Pseudo-Cleft Construction in English.* PhD Dissertation, Massachusetts Institute of Technology.

Jackendoff, R. 1972. *Semantic Interpretation in Generative Grammar.* Cambridge, Mass.: MIT Press.

Jackendoff, R. 1975. Morphological and Semantic Regularities in the Lexicon. *Language* 51:639–671.

Jackendoff, R. 1985. *Semantics and Cognition.* Cambridge, Mass.: MIT Press.

Jackendoff, R. 1987. The Status of Thematic Relations in Linguistic Theory. *Linguistic Inquiry* 18.3:369–411.

Johnson, M. Manuscript. Computing with Regular Path Formulae. Unpublished manuscript, Stanford: CSLI.

Johnson, M. and E. Klein 1986. Discourse, Anaphora, and Parsing. Report No. CSLI-86-63. Stanford: CSLI.

Kajita, M. 1967. *A Generative-Transformational Study of Semi-Auxiliaries in Present-Day American English.* Tokyo: Sanseido Company *LTD.*

Kamp, J. A. W. 1981. A Theory of Truth and Semantic Representation. In J. Groenendijk, T. Janssen, and M. Stokhof (Eds.), *Formal Methods in the Study of Language.* Amsterdam: Mathematical Center Tracts.

Kaplan, R. and J. Bresnan 1982. Lexical-Functional Grammar: A Formal System for Grammatical Representation. In Bresnan (Ed.), *The Mental Representation of Grammatical Relations.* Cambridge, Mass.: MIT Press.

Kaplan, R., J. Maxwell, and A. Zaenen 1987. Functional Uncertainty. CSLI Monthly, January 1987.

Karttunen, L. 1984. Features and Values. In *Proceedings of Coling* 1984: 28–33.

Karttunen, L. 1986a. D-PATR: A Development Environment for Unification-Based Grammars. Report No. CSLI-86-68. Stanford: CSLI.

Karttunen, L. 1986b. Radical Lexicalism. Report No. CSLI-86-68. Stanford: CSLI.

Kasper, R. and W. Rounds 1986. A Logical Semantics for Feature Structures. In *Proceedings of the 24th Annual Meeting of the Association for Computational Linguistics.*

Kay, M. 1979. Functional Grammar. In C. Chiarello et al. (Eds.), *Proceedings of the Fifth Annual Meeting of the Berkeley Linguistics Society.*

Kay, M. 1984. Functional Unification Grammar: A Formalism for Machine Translation. In *Proceedings of Coling* 1984:75–78.

Kay, M. 1985. Parsing in Functional Unification Grammar. In D. Dowty, L. Karttunen, and A. Zwicky (Eds.), *Natural Language Parsing.* Cambridge: Cambridge University Press.

Keenan, E. L. 1974. The Functional Princple: Generalizing the Notion of 'Subject of'. In M. La Galy, R. Fox, and A. Bruck (Eds.), *Papers From the Tenth Regional Meeting of the Chicago Linguistics Society.*

Keenan, E. L., and B. Comrie 1977. Noun Phrase Accessibility and Universal Grammar. *Linguistic Inquiry* 8:63–99.

Keenan, E. and J. Stavi. Forthcoming. A Semantic Characterization of Natural Language Determiners. *Linguistics and Philosophy.*

Kiparsky, P. Forthcoming. Morphology and Grammatical Relations. Stanford: Department of Linguistics and CSLI.

Ladusaw, W. and D. Dowty. Manuscript. Toward a Non-Grammatical Account of Thematic Roles. Unpublished manuscript, University of California at Santa Cruz and Ohio State University.

Meseguer, J., J. Goguen, and G. Smolka 1987. Order-Sorted Unification. Report No. CSLI-87-86. Stanford: CSLI.

Montague, R. 1974. *Formal Philosophy.* New Haven and London: Yale University Press.

Moshier, D. and W. Rounds 1987. A Logic for Partially Specified Data Structures. In *Proceedings of the 14th Annual Conference on Principles of Programming Languages.*

Mukai, K. 1985. Unification over Complex Indeterminates in Prolog. ICOT Technical Report No. TR-113. Tokyo: ICOT Research Center, Institute for New Generation Computer Technology.

Mukai, K. Manuscript. Anadic Tuples in Prolog. Unpublished manuscript, Institute for New Generation Computer Technology, Tokyo.

Pereira, F., and S. Shieber 1984. The Semantics of Grammar Formalisms Seen as Computer Languages. In *Proceedings of Coling* 1984:23–129.

Pollard, C. Manuscript 1. Generalized Grammar. Unpublished manuscript, Stanford University, March 1982.

Pollard, C. Manuscript 2. Lectures on HPSG. Unpublished manuscript, Stanford University, Febuary 1985.

Pollard, C. Manuscript 3. A Semantic Approach to Extraction in a Monostratal Theory. Unpublished manuscript, Stanford University.

Pollard, C. 1984. Generalized Context-Free Grammars, Head Grammars, and Natural Language. PhD Dissertation, Stanford University.

Pollard, C. 1985. Phrase Structure Grammar Without Metarules. In *Proceedings of the Fourth West Coast Conference on Formal Linguistics.* Stanford: Stanford Linguistics Department.

Pollard , C. In press. Categorial Grammar and Phrase Structure Grammar: An Excursion on the Syntax-Semantics Frontier. In R. Oehrle, E. Bach, and D. Wheeler (Eds.), *Categorial Grammars and Natural Language Structures.* Dordrecht: Reidel.

Proudian, D. and C. Pollard 1985. Parsing Head-Driven Phrase Structure Grammar. In *Proceedings of the 23rd Annual Meeting of the Association for Computational Linguistics.*

Rappaport, M. and B. Levin 1986. What to do with Theta-Roles. Lexicon Project Working Papers No. 11, Center for Cognitive Science, MIT.

Rooth, M. 1986. Noun Phrase Interpretation in Montague Grammar, File Change Semantics, and Situation Semantics. CSLI Report No. CSLI-86-51.

Ross, J. 1967. *Constraints on Variables in Syntax.* PhD Dissertation, Massachusetts Institute of Technology. Available from Indiana University Linguistics Club.

Rounds, W. and R. Kasper 1986. A Complete Logical Calculus for Record Structures Representing Linguistic Information. In *Proceedings of the IEEE Symposium on Logic in Computer Science*, June 1986.

Sag, I. A. 1987. Grammatical Hierarchy and Linear Precedence. In G. Huck and A. Ojeda (Eds.), *Syntax and Semantics (Vol. 20): Discontinuous Constituency.* New York: Academic Press. Also appeared as Report No. CSLI-86-60, Stanford: CSLI

Sag, I. A. and C. Pollard 1987. Head-Driven Phrase Structure Grammar: An Informal Synopsis. Report No. CSLI-87-79. Stanford: CSLI.

Sag, I. A. and C. Pollard. Manuscript. A Semantic Theory of Obligatory Control. Unpublished manuscript, Stanford University.

Sag, I. A., R. Kaplan, L. Karttunen, M. Kay, C. Pollard, S. Shieber, and A. Zaenen 1986. Unification and Grammatical Theory. In *Proceedings of the Fifth West Coast Conference on Formal Linguistics.* Stanford: Department of Linguistics.

Saussure, F. d. 1915. *Course in General Linguistics.* Published in 1959 by McGraw Hill, New York.

Sells, P. 1985a. *Lectures on Contemporary Syntactic Theories.* CSLI Lecture Notes Series No. 3. Stanford: CSLI.

Sells, P. 1985b. Restrictive and Non-Restrictive Modification. Report No. CSLI-85-28. Stanford: CSLI.

Shieber, S. 1984. The Design of a Computer Language for Linguistic Information. In S. Shieber, L. Karttunen and F. Pereira (Eds.), *Notes from the Unification Underground: A Compilation of Papers on Unification-Based Grammar Formalisms*. SRI Technical Note 327, Menlo Park, Cal.: SRI International.

Shieber, S. 1986. *An Introduction to Unification-Based Approaches to Grammar*. CSLI Lecture Notes 4. Stanford: CSLI.

Shieber, S., H. Uszkoreit, J. Robinson, and M. Tyson 1983. The Formalism and Implementation of PATR-II. In *Research on Interactive Acquisition and Use of Knowledge*. Menlo Park, Cal.: Artificial Intelligence Center, SRI International.

Smolka, G. and H. Ait-Kaci. Manuscript. Inheritance Hierarchies: Semantics and Unification. Draft for MCC Report No. AI-057-87. Austin, Texas: Microelectronics and Computer Technology Corporation.

Stanley, R. 1967. Redundancy Rules in Phonology. *Language* 43.2:393–436.

Steedman, M. 1985. Dependency and Coordination in the Grammar of Dutch and English. *Language* 61.3:523–568.

Steedman, M. In press. Combinators and Grammars. In R. Oehrle, E. Bach, and D. Wheeler (Eds.), *Categorial Grammars and Natural Language Structures*. Dordrecht: Reidel.

Steedman, M. 1987. Combinatory Grammars and Parasitic Gaps. In Haddock, Klein, and Morrill (Eds.), *Categorial Grammar, Unification Grammar, and Parsing*. Edinburgh Working Papers in Cognitive Science, Vol. 1. Edinburgh: Centre for Cognitive Science, University of Edinburgh.

Stump, G. 1981. *The Formal Semantics and Pragmatics of Adjuncts and Absolutes in English*. PhD Dissertation. Columbus, Ohio: The Ohio State University.

Thomason, R. Forthcoming. Remarks on Linguistic Semantics. In A. Manaster-Ramer (Ed.), *Mathematics of Language*. Amsterdam: John Benjamins.

Thrainsson, H. 1979. *On Complementation in Icelandic*. PhD Dissertation, Harvard University. Published by Garland Press, 1980.

Uszkoreit, H. 1986a. Categorial Unification Grammars. In *Proceedings of Coling* 1986. Bonn: University of Bonn. Also appeared as Report No. CSLI-86-66, Stanford: CSLI

Uszkoreit, H. 1986b. Constraints on Order. Report No. CSLI-86-46. Stanford: CSLI.

Uszkoreit, H. 1986c. Linear Precedence in Discontinuous Constituents: Complex Fronting in German. Report No. CSLI-86-47. Stanford: CSLI.

Zaenen, A., J. Maling and H. Thrainsson 1985. Case and Grammatical Functions: The Icelandic Passive. *Natural Language and Linguistic Theory* 3:441–483.

Zeevat, H., E. Klein, and J. Calder 1987. Unification Categorial Grammar. In Haddock, Klein, and Morrill (Eds.), *Categorial Grammar, Unification Grammar, and Parsing.* Edinburgh Working Papers in Cognitive Science, Vol. 1. Edinburgh: Centre for Cognitive Science, University of Edinburgh.

CSLI Publications

Reports

The following titles have been published in the CSLI Reports series. These reports may be obtained from CSLI Publications, Ventura Hall, Stanford University, Stanford, CA 94305.

The Situation in Logic–I. Jon Barwise. CSLI–84–2. ($*2.00*)

Coordination and How to Distinguish Categories. Ivan Sag, Gerald Gazdar, Thomas Wasow, and Steven Weisler. CSLI–84–3. ($*3.50*)

Belief and Incompleteness. Kurt Konolige. CSLI–84–4. ($*4.50*)

Equality, Types, Modules and Generics for Logic Programming. Joseph Goguen and José Meseguer. CSLI–84–5. ($*2.50*)

Lessons from Bolzano. Johan van Benthem. CSLI–84–6. ($*1.50*)

Self-propagating Search: A Unified Theory of Memory. Pentti Kanerva. CSLI–84–7. ($*9.00*)

Reflection and Semantics in LISP. Brian Cantwell Smith. CSLI–84–8. ($*2.50*)

The Implementation of Procedurally Reflective Languages. Jim des Rivières and Brian Cantwell Smith. CSLI–84–9. ($*3.00*)

Parameterized Programming. Joseph Goguen. CSLI–84–10. ($*3.50*)

Morphological Constraints on Scandinavian Tone Accent. Meg Withgott and Per-Kristian Halvorsen. CSLI–84–11. ($*2.50*)

Partiality and Nonmonotonicity in Classical Logic. Johan van Benthem. CSLI–84–12. ($*2.00*)

Shifting Situations and Shaken Attitudes. Jon Barwise and John Perry. CSLI–84–13. ($*4.50*)

Aspectual Classes in Situation Semantics. Robin Cooper. CSLI–85–14-C. ($*4.00*)

Completeness of Many-Sorted Equational Logic. Joseph Goguen and José Meseguer. CSLI–84–15. ($*2.50*)

Moving the Semantic Fulcrum. Terry Winograd. CSLI–84–17. ($*1.50*)

On the Mathematical Properties of Linguistic Theories. C. Raymond Perrault. CSLI–84–18. ($*3.00*)

A Simple and Efficient Implementation of Higher-order Functions in LISP. Michael P. Georgeff and Stephen F.Bodnar. CSLI–84–19. ($*4.50*)

On the Axiomatization of "if-then-else". Irène Guessarian and José Meseguer. CSLI–85–20. ($*3.00*)

The Situation in Logic–II: Conditionals and Conditional Information. Jon Barwise. CSLI–84–21. ($*3.00*)

Principles of OBJ2. Kokichi Futatsugi, Joseph A. Goguen, Jean-Pierre Jouannaud, and José Meseguer. CSLI–85–22. ($*2.00*)

Querying Logical Databases. Moshe Vardi. CSLI–85–23. ($*1.50*)

Computationally Relevant Properties of Natural Languages and Their Grammar. Gerald Gazdar and Geoff Pullum. CSLI–85–24. ($*3.50*)

An Internal Semantics for Modal Logic: Preliminary Report. Ronald Fagin and Moshe Vardi. CSLI–85–25. ($*2.00*)

The Situation in Logic–III: Situations, Sets and the Axiom of Foundation. Jon Barwise. CSLI–85–26. ($*2.50*)

Semantic Automata. Johan van Benthem. CSLI–85–27. ($*2.50*)

Restrictive and Non-Restrictive Modification. Peter Sells. CSLI–85–28. ($*3.00*)

Institutions: Abstract Model Theory for Computer Science. J. A. Goguen and R. M. Burstall. CSLI–85–30. (*$4.50*)

A Formal Theory of Knowledge and Action. Robert C. Moore. CSLI–85–31. (*$5.50*)

Finite State Morphology: A Review of Koskenniemi (1983). Gerald Gazdar. CSLI–85–32. (*$1.50*)

The Role of Logic in Artificial Intelligence. Robert C. Moore. CSLI–85–33. (*$2.00*)

Applicability of Indexed Grammars to Natural Languages. Gerald Gazdar. CSLI–85–34. (*$2.00*)

Commonsense Summer: Final Report. Jerry R. Hobbs, et al.. CSLI–85–35. (*$12.00*)

Limits of Correctness in Computers. Brian Cantwell Smith. CSLI–85–36. (*$2.50*)

On the Coherence and Structure of Discourse. Jerry R. Hobbs. CSLI–85–37. (*$3.00*)

The Coherence of Incoherent Discourse. Jerry R. Hobbs and Michael H. Agar. CSLI–85–38. (*$2.50*)

The Structures of Discourse Structure. Barbara Grosz and Candace L. Sidner. CSLI–85–39. (*$4.50*)

A Complete Type-free, Second-order Logic and its Philosophical Foundations. Christopher Menzel. CSLI–86–40. (*$4.50*)

Possible-world Semantics for Autoepistemic Logic. Robert C. Moore. CSLI–85–41. (*$2.00*)

Deduction with Many-Sorted Rewrite. José Meseguer and Joseph A. Goguen. CSLI–85–42. (*$1.50*)

On Some Formal Properties of Metarules. Hans Uszkoreit and Stanley Peters. CSLI–85–43. (*$1.50*)

Language, Mind, and Information. John Perry. CSLI–85–44. (*$2.00*)

Constraints on Order. Hans Uszkoreit. CSLI–86–46. (*$3.00*)

Linear Precedence in Discontinuous Constituents: Complex Fronting in German. Hans Uszkoreit. CSLI–86–47. (*$2.50*)

A Compilation of Papers on Unification-Based Grammar Formalisms, Parts I and II. Stuart M. Shieber, Fernando C.N. Pereira, Lauri Karttunen, and Martin Kay. CSLI–86–48. (*$4.00*)

An Algorithm for Generating Quantifier Scopings. Jerry R. Hobbs and Stuart M. Shieber. CSLI–86–49. (*$2.50*)

Verbs of Change, Causation, and Time. Dorit Abusch. CSLI–86–50. (*$2.00*)

Noun-Phrase Interpretation. Mats Rooth. CSLI–86–51. (*$2.50*)

Noun Phrases, Generalized Quantifiers and Anaphora. Jon Barwise. CSLI–86–52. (*$2.50*)

Circumstantial Attitudes and Benevolent Cognition. John Perry. CSLI–86–53. (*$1.50*)

A Study in the Foundations of Programming Methodology: Specifications, Institutions, Charters and Parchments. Joseph A. Goguen and R. M. Burstall. CSLI–86–54. (*$2.50*)

Quantifiers in Formal and Natural Languages. Dag Westerståhl. CSLI–86–55. (*$7.50*)

Intentionality, Information, and Matter. Ivan Blair. CSLI–86–56. (*$3.00*)

Graphs and Grammars. William Marsh. CSLI–86–57. (*$2.00*)

Computer Aids for Comparative Dictionaries. Mark Johnson. CSLI–86–58. (*$2.00*)

The Relevance of Computational Linguistics. Lauri Karttunen. CSLI–86–59. (*$2.50*)

Grammatical Hierarchy and Linear Precedence. Ivan A. Sag. CSLI–86–60. (*$3.50*)

D-PATR: A Development Environment for Unification-Based Grammars. Lauri Karttunen. CSLI–86–61. (*$4.00*)

A Sheaf-Theoretic Model of Concurrency. Luís F. Monteiro and Fernando C. N. Pereira. CSLI–86–62. (*$3.00*)

Discourse, Anaphora and Parsing. Mark Johnson. CSLI–86–63. (*$2.00*)

Tarski on Truth and Logical Consequence. John Etchemendy. CSLI–86–64. (*$3.50*)

The LFG Treatment of Discontinuity and The Double Infinitive Construction in Dutch. Mark Johnson. CSLI–86–65. (*$2.50*)

Categorial Unification Grammars. Hans Uszkoreit. CSLI–86–66. (*$2.50*)

Generalized Quantifiers and Plurals. Godehard Link. CSLI–86–67. (*$2.00*)

Radical Lexicalism. Lauri Karttunen. CSLI–86–68. (*$2.50*)

Understanding Computers and Cognition: Four Reviews and a Response. Mark Stefik, Editor. CSLI–87–70. (*$3.50*)

The Correspondence Continuum. Brian Cantwell Smith. CSLI–87–71. (*$4.00*)

The Role of Propositional Objects of Belief in Action. David J. Israel. CSLI–87–72. (*$2.50*)

From Worlds to Situations. John Perry. CSLI–87–73. (*$2.00*)

Two Replies. Jon Barwise. CSLI–87–74. (*$3.00*)

Semantics of Clocks. Brian Cantwell Smith. CSLI–87–75. (*$3.50*)

Varieties of Self-Reference. Brian Cantwell Smith. CSLI–87–76. (*Forthcoming*)

The Parts of Perception. Alexander Pentland. CSLI–87–77. (*$4.00*)

Topic, Pronoun, and Agreement in Chicheŵa. Joan Bresnan and S. A. Mchombo. CSLI–87–78. (*$5.00*)

HPSG: An Informal Synopsis. Carl Pollard and Ivan A. Sag. CSLI–87–79. (*$4.50*)

The Situated Processing of Situated Languages. Susan Stucky. CSLI–87–80. (*$1.50*)

Muir: A Tool for Language Design. Terry Winograd. CSLI–87–81. (*$2.50*)

Final Algebras, Cosemicomputable Algebras, and Degrees of Unsolvability. Lawrence S. Moss, José Meseguer, and Joseph A. Goguen. CSLI–87–82. (*$3.00*)

The Synthesis of Digital Machines with Provable Epistemic Properties. Stanley J. Rosenschein and Leslie Pack Kaelbling. CSLI–87–83. (*$3.50*)

Formal Theories of Knowledge in AI and Robotics. Stanley J. Rosenschein. CSLI–87–84. (*$1.50*)

An Architecture for Intelligent Reactive Systems. Leslie Pack Kaelbling. CSLI–87–85. (*$2.00*)

Order-Sorted Unification. José Meseguer, Joseph A. Goguen, and Gert Smolka. CSLI–87–86. (*$2.50*)

Modular Algebraic Specification of Some Basic Geometrical Constructions. Joseph A. Goguen. CSLI–87–87. (*$2.50*)

Persistence, Intention and Commitment. Phil Cohen and Hector Levesque. CSLI–87–88. (*$3.50*)

Rational Interaction as the Basis for Communication. Phil Cohen and Hector Levesque. CSLI–87–89. (*$3.50*)

An Application of Default Logic to Speech Act Theory. C. Raymond Perrault. CSLI–87–90. (*$2.50*)

Models and Equality for Logical Programming. Joseph A. Goguen and José Meseguer. CSLI–87–91. (*$3.00*)

Order-Sorted Algebra Solves the Constructor-Selector, Multiple Representation and Coercion Problems. Joseph A. Goguen and José Meseguer. CSLI–87–92. (*$2.00*)

Extensions and Foundations for Object-Oriented Programming. Joseph A. Goguen and José Meseguer. CSLI–87–93. (*$3.50*)

L3 Reference Manual: Version 2.19. William Poser. CSLI–87–94. (*$2.50*)

Change, Process and Events. Carol E. Cleland. CSLI–87–95. (*Forthcoming*)

One, None, a Hundred Thousand Specification Languages. Joseph A. Goguen CSLI–87–96. (*$2.00*)

Constituent Coordination in HPSG Derek Proudian and David Goddeau CSLI–87–97. (*$2.00*)

A Language/Action Perspective on the Design of Cooperative Work Terry Winograd CSLI–87–98. ($*3.00*)

Implicature and Definite Reference Jerry R. Hobbs CSLI–87–99. ($*1.50*)

Thinking Machines: Can There be? Are we? Terry Winograd CSLI–87–100. ($*2.50*)

Situation Semantics and Semantic Interpretation in Constraint-Based Grammars Per-Kristian Halvorsen CSLI–87–101. ($*1.50*)

Category Structures Gerald Gazdar, Geoffrey K. Pullum, Robert Carpenter, Ewan Klein, Thomas E. Hukari, Robert D. Levine CSLI–87–102. ($*3.00*)

Cognitive Theories of Emotion Ronald Alan Nash CSLI–87–103. ($*2.50*)

Toward an Architecture for Resource-Bounded Agents Martha E. Pollack, David J. Israel, and Michael E. Bratman CSLI–87–104. ($*2.00*)

On the Relation Between Default and Autoepistemic Logic Kurt Konolige CSLI–87–105. ($*3.00*)

Three Responses to Situation Theory Terry Winograd CSLI–87–106. ($*2.50*)

Subjects and Complements in HPSG Robert Borsley CSLI–87–107. ($*2.50*)

Tools for Morphological Analysis Mary Dalrymple, Ronald M. Kaplan, Lauri Karttunen, Kimmo Koskenniemi, Sami Shaio, Michael Wescoat CSLI–87–108. ($*10.00*)

Cognitive Significance and New Theories of Reference John Perry CSLI–87–109 (*Forthcoming*)

Aleph: A System Specification Language Terry Winograd CSLI–110. (*Forthcoming*)

Fourth Year Report of the Situated Language Research Program CSLI–87–111. (*Forthcoming*)

Bare Plurals, Naked Relatives, and Their Kin Dietmar Zaefferer CSLI–87–112. (*Forthcoming*)

Background Anaphora and Discourse Structure: Some Considerations Peter Sells CSLI–87–114. (*Forthcoming*)

Towards a Linking Theory of Relation Changing Rules in LFG Lori Levin CSLI–87–115. (*Forthcoming*)

Lecture Notes

The titles in this series are distributed by the University of Chicago Press and may be purchased in academic or university bookstores or ordered directly from the distributor at 5801 Ellis Avenue, Chicago, Illinois 60637.

A Manual of Intensional Logic. Johan van Benthem. Lecture Notes No. 1.

Emotion and Focus. Helen Fay Nissenbaum. Lecture Notes No. 2.

Lectures on Contemporary Syntactic Theories. Peter Sells with a Postscript by Thomas Wasow. Lecture Notes No. 3.

An Introduction to Unification-Based Approaches to Grammar. Stuart M. Shieber. Lecture Notes No. 4.

The Semantics of Destructive LISP. Ian A. Mason. Lecture Notes No. 5.

An Essay on Facts. Kenneth Russell Olson. Lecture Notes No. 6.

Logics of Time and Computation. Robert Goldblatt. Lecture Notes No. 7.

Word Order and Constituent Structure in German. Hans Uszkoreit. Lecture Notes No. 8.

Color and Color Perception: A Study in Anthropocentric Realism. David R. Hilbert. Lecture Notes No. 9.

Prolog and Natural-Language Analysis. Fernando C.N. Pereira and Stuart M. Shieber. Lecture Notes No. 10.

Working Papers in Grammatical Theory and Discourse: Interactions of Morphology, Syntax, and Discourse. M. Iida, S. Wechsler, and D. Zec (eds.), with an Introduction by Joan Bresnan. Lecture Notes No. 11.

Natural Language Processing in the 1980s: A Bibliography Gerald Gazdar, Alex Franz, Karen Osborne, and Roger Evans. Lecture Notes No. 12.

An Information-Based Syntax and Semantics Carl Pollard and Ivan Sag. Lecture Notes No. 13.

Non-Well-Founded Sets. Peter Aczel. Lecture Notes No. 14.

Outlines of Probabilism Richard Jeffrey. Lecture Notes No. 15.